The Need to Rename Tech

Crystal Chokshi • Robin Mansell
Editors

The Need to Rename Tech

palgrave
macmillan

Editors
Crystal Chokshi
School of Communication Studies
Mount Royal University
Calgary, AB, Canada

Robin Mansell
Department of Media and Communications
London School of Economics and Political Science
London, UK

ISBN 978-3-032-05154-7 ISBN 978-3-032-05155-4 (eBook)
https://doi.org/10.1007/978-3-032-05155-4

This Palgrave Macmillan imprint is published by the registered company Springer Nature Switzerland AG.
The registered company address is: Gewerbestrasse 11, 6330 Cham, Switzerland

Acknowledgements

Crystal and Robin thank the contributors to this book, whose dedication to the project shone from beginning to end and, not least of all, through the editing process. Emily Goodwin helped us with editing, and for that we are grateful.

We are also grateful to Doan Truong for creating and permitting us to print her evocative illustrations.

We were able to bring Emily on board and to commission Doan's work thanks to funds provided by Mount Royal University and an Explore Grant from Canada's Social Sciences and Humanities Research Council. Thank you to both institutions for supporting our vision.

During the summer of 2024, peer reviewers located around the world offered insightful and constructive comments, helping this volume to be sharper than it otherwise would have been. We appreciate you very much. We are also grateful for the comments of an anonymous manuscript reviewer.

Crystal would additionally like to thank Milena Radzikowska for confabbing throughout the editing journey; Nicolette Little for sharing advice (always solicited); John Moss for inspiring an enduring fascination with language; Catherine Chipuer and Terry Chipuer for supporting; and Jaya Chokshi and Priya Chokshi for listening and for understanding, always.

Crystal is deeply grateful to Robin for saying yes to this project and for providing unwavering mentorship throughout. Robin would like to thank Crystal for carrying the largest share of the work and for a lovely and productive collaboration. Robin also thanks all our writers for their commitment to this project.

Finally, we note that effort has been made to trace copyright holders and obtain permissions to reproduce figures that appear in this book.

Contents

List of Contributors

Melanie Baljko Department of Electrical Engineering and Computer Science, York University, Toronto, ON, Canada

Christina Boyles Department of Library and Information Science, Indiana University Bloomington, Bloomington, IN, USA

Crystal Chokshi School of Communication Studies, Mount Royal University, Calgary, AB, Canada

Luã Cruz Brazilian Institute for Consumer Protection (IDEC), São Paulo, Brazil

Brooks DeCillia School of Communication Studies, Mount Royal University, Calgary, AB, Canada

Olivier Driessens Department of Communication, University of Copenhagen, Copenhagen, Denmark

Gordon A. Gow Media and Technology Studies, University of Alberta, Edmonton, AB, Canada

Evangeline Holtz-Schramek Communication Studies & Media Arts, McMaster University, Hamilton, ON, Canada

Arun Jacob Faculty of Information, University of Toronto, Toronto, ON, Canada

Harriett Jernigan Program in Writing and Rhetoric, Stanford University, Stanford, CA, USA

Nathaniel Laywine Department of Communication & Media Studies, York University, Toronto, ON, Canada

Frédérik Lesage School of Communication, Simon Fraser University, Burnaby, BC, Canada

Kate Maddalena Institute of Communication, Culture, Information and Technology, University of Toronto Mississauga, Mississauga, ON, Canada

Robin Mansell Department of Media and Communications, London School of Economics and Political Science, London, UK

Gemma Milne Adam Smith Business School, University of Glasgow, Glasgow, Scotland

Zach Pearl School of the Arts, Media, Performance & Design, York University, Toronto, ON, Canada

Gabriela Perdomo School of Communication Studies, Mount Royal University, Calgary, AB, Canada

Jess Reia School of Data Science, University of Virginia, Charlottesville, VA, USA

Gillian Russell School of Interactive Arts & Technology, Simon Fraser University, Burnaby, BC, Canada

Eryk Salvaggio Cambridge Digital Humanities, University of Cambridge, Cambridge, UK

Victoria Simon School of Arts and Sciences, Felician University, Rutherford, NJ, USA

Anran Wang Department of Media and Communications, London School of Economics and Political Science, London, UK

List of Figures

List of Tables

CHAPTER 1

Introduction

Crystal Chokshi and Robin Mansell

> If we dwell differently among words, then we know different worlds. (Moss, 2000, p. 27)

1 Reductive Nouns and Misleading Metaphors

Wherever you are, push the 'rewind' button in your mind, and find yourself once more at the beginning of your day. Recall the technologies to which you have turned since then: a sleep app, a smart thermostat, a social media platform to check in on distant friends. A smartphone, a laptop, a browser, a chatbot. Think, too, of the technologies you did not use but read about, perhaps, in the morning news: artificial intelligence (AI) in development and apps in which you might invest.

C. Chokshi (✉)
School of Communication Studies, Mount Royal University, Calgary, AB, Canada
e-mail: cchokshi@mtroyal.ca

R. Mansell
Department of Media and Communications, London School of Economics and Political Science, London, UK
e-mail: r.e.mansell@lse.ac.uk

C. Chokshi, R. Mansell (eds.), *The Need to Rename Tech*,
https://doi.org/10.1007/978-3-032-05155-4_1

We wager there will be many. But rather than tally them up, notice their names. *Apple*. *Bluesky*. *Gemini* and *Google Nest*. *Llama*, *iCloud*, and *Amazon*. In the language surrounding technologies we use every day, there are echoes of planetary marvels, places we love, and journeys charted by the stars. These echoes are metaphors, asking us to understand one thing in terms of another. They render technology as intuitive and safe, as creating spaces where we were always intended to be, and as forging journeys we were always intended to take.

This book is about the plethora of words such as *Apple* and *Amazon*, language coined by Big Tech that fools us into thinking the technology industry and its products fit naturally, easily, and inconsequentially into our lives.[1] They do not. As the writers in this collection show, the technologies that seem to facilitate our daily lives have dangerous social and political consequences. These consequences are concealed by the use of reductive nouns and misleading metaphors, brilliantly conceived by the industry to sustain the status quo—or to bring about change in the industry's interest.

2 Deceptive Tech

The technology industry is worth in the vicinity of trillions of dollars, and its value seems only to be going up. In 2024, for example, Google's parent company, Alphabet, reported annual revenues of USD 350 billion, a 14 per cent increase in 12 months (Alphabet, 2025). In the same time frame, Meta, owner of Facebook, Instagram, and YouTube, among others, saw a 22 per cent increase in revenue, earning USD 164 billion in 2024 (Meta, 2025). Investment in AI alone is driving enormous amounts of spending: in 2023, the global AI market was valued at USD 200 billion; by 2030 it is expected to reach USD 2 trillion (Muldoon et al., 2024).

It is not an exaggeration to say that this growth depends on deception. Many of these technologies earn money by explicitly concealing how they work. As an example, take Google Search. Sometimes people perform searches using Google as a means to find the 'right' information or, at

[1] The term 'Big Tech' often refers to a small but powerful group of US-owned companies (Alphabet, Amazon, Meta, Apple, and Microsoft) as well as a handful of Chinese-owned companies (including Alibaba Group and Tencent). We use the term to refer to these companies and also to those with ties to Silicon Valley or Silicon-Valley-style thinking. On Silicon Valley's system of beliefs, see Adrian Daub's (2020) book, *What Tech Calls Thinking*.

least, good information. After all, Google's mission is "to organize the world's information and make it universally accessible and useful" (Google, n.d., para. 3). This might be a statement emblazoned on the wall of a local public library, but Google is the furthest thing there is from a public institution. Fundamentally, Google is a place to advertise (Fuchs, 2011; Noble, 2018; Vaidhyanathan, 2012). When a search is performed on Google, a person is most likely to see ads or websites that marketing professionals and algorithms ensure land on top. A bias towards Google's own digital properties is also likely to be noticeable since the company often makes its own sites and platforms more visible than others (Noble, 2018).

This happens against an economic backdrop called surveillance capitalism, the constant monitoring and tracking of our actions in order for companies "to predict and modify human behavior as a means to produce revenue and market control" (Zuboff, 2015, p. 75). Surveillance capitalism means that every time we click, like, search, bookmark, or comment, an opportunity for selling is created. Tech companies, however, do not publicise how deeply their products depend on and are funded by surveillance-capitalist activity. They prefer to promote the idea that their services are available to their users freely and harmlessly. This opacity can have fatal consequences. In *Algorithms of Oppression*, Safiya Umoja Noble discusses the 2015 massacre at a church in Charleston, South Carolina where the shooter, a white neo-Nazi nationalist, murdered nine Black people. The killings were partly motivated by the (dis) information the perpetrator found when he searched online for the history of crimes involving Black and white people. He took Google Search results as 'good' information rather than what they often are: sales and propaganda.

Just as deceitful language surrounding Google has had serious human consequences, harms are now being enacted on people in the Global South by the misleading language of AI. As an example, the term 'machine learning' obscures the fact that "roughly 80 per cent of time spent on training AI consists of annotating datasets" (Muldoon et al., 2024, p. 30), and annotation is an activity carried out by humans. More than that, it is an activity carried out by humans subject to exploitative and colonial labour practices (Muldoon et al., 2024). Often outsourced by tech giants such as OpenAI and Meta to firms in Ghana and Kenya, data annotators contend with rote tasks, high quotas, constant surveillance, menial pay, harassment, and inadequate resourcing to deal with the trauma of annotation work, which sometimes involves labelling content "from the darkest recesses of the internet … [including] child sexual abuse, bestiality, murder, suicide, torture, self harm, and incest" (Perrigo, 2023, para. 6). Deploying language in the field of AI that centres computers and erases the 'humans in the loop' is just one tool in an arsenal that renders technology's processes and aftermaths invisible.

These stories confirm that the language we use to talk about technology can wager no less than people's lives. This is emphasised time and again by the writers in this volume. Crucially, the lives, livelihoods, and life chances most often at risk are those of minoritised individuals.[2] What motivates us as editors of this book is a commitment to acknowledging that when we, members of a dominant group for whom technology is typically designed, discuss technology as it is marketed and deployed without signalling resistance, we tacitly accept, and are complicit in, its politics and outcomes. Citizens, scholars, and practitioners with a stated interest in social justice instead have a responsibility to intervene in the normative narratives surrounding digital technologies. Renaming them is one way to carry out this intervention.

3 Undoing Deception

Each chapter in this volume discusses a specific technology and, crucially, moves to rename it. We aim collectively to subvert Big Tech's careful branding and to rechristen popular technologies in ways that point explicitly to their problems.

When Big Tech rebrands, the goal is often the opposite: find new words or coin new phrases to minimise harms wrought by their products and platforms. Facebook's 'transformation' in 2021 is a case in point. Plagued by allegations about its failure to address misinformation, hate speech, and violence, Facebook rebranded as Meta. This was a move perceived largely as a public relations stunt at a fraught moment in the company's history (Isaac, 2021; Paul, 2021; Yohn, 2021). Rather than address complaints head-on, CEO Mark Zuckerberg shifted the conversation to the company's future, describing a vision of the 'metaverse'. The new vision landed uneasily because it was (and is) confusing

[2] We use 'minoritised' after Catherine D'Ignazio and Lauren F. Klein (2020, p. 26), who define 'minoritised groups' as "groups of people who are positioned in opposition to a more powerful social group".

(Ravenscraft, 2023; Yohn, 2021). In *Wired*, product writer and reviewer Eric Ravenscraft (2023, para. 1) quipped, "the metaverse is the future of the internet. Or it's a video game. Or maybe it's a deeply uncomfortable, worse version of Zoom? It's hard to say". Using language to sow confusion about technology is a deliberate move consistent with Big Tech's playbook. The confusion shifts the burden of understanding to us, as users, and helps to shield Big Tech from accountability (Nagy & Neff, 2024).

Our aim with this volume is to take popular technologies to task. Writers in this collection bring to the fore the politics that are swept aside by media spectacles and marketing strategies. We recentre them by renaming—and, therefore, reframing—the technology industry and the products it develops in terms of what they do, not simply what they appear to be. Our approach to renaming is rooted in this conviction: what something *is* is what it *does*. To understand a technology, its superficial properties should not be privileged or isolated over its inputs, by-products, outcomes, or aftermaths. Taking what Johanna Drucker (2013, para. 12) calls a performative-material approach, we aim to "shift from a concept of things as entities to a concept of them as events". We insist that digital technologies be understood as that which they enact, that which transpires as a result of their production and use, and that in which they are implicated, not just as the material objects they appear to be.

In his book *Reset,* Ronald Deibert (2020, p. 14) is similarly insistent when defining 'social media':

> Merriam-Webster defines social media narrowly as "forms of electronic communication… through which users create online communities to share information, ideas, personal messages, and other content"… But missing from this definition is the underlying business model, an appreciation of which is essential in order to fully understand the dynamics of social media. At their core, social media are vehicles for the relentless collection and monetization of the personal data of their users.

Deibert advocates for a definition of social media that encompasses its implications: that collecting and monetising data, one of social media's key functions, should be at the heart of how it is understood. This emphasis is important because it relates to technologies' 'dynamics': the types of interactions that technologies either make possible or foreclose. As José van Dijck, Thomas Poell, and Martijn de Waal (2018, p. 24) write, "platforms do not simply connect social and economic actors but fundamentally steer *how* they connect with each other. In this process, platforms construct new value regimes and economies". And, it is not only the materiality of technology with which we must be concerned but also its symbolic meaning. As media and communications scholars clearly point out, these technologies are 'doubly articulated': they are "uniquely, … the means (the media) whereby public and private meanings are mutually negotiated: as well as being the products themselves, through consumption, of such negotiations of meaning" (Silverstone et al., 1992, p. 28).

4 Doing Things with Words

Critical media and communications scholars call for new language to talk about technology (Boucher, 2021; Chown & Nascimento, 2023; Gillespie, 2017; Hwang & Levy, 2015; Jobin & Ziewitz, 2018; Lanier, 2011; Wallenborn, 2022; Wyatt, 2018, 2021). These calls are reminiscent of George Lakoff and Mark Johnson's landmark book, *Metaphors We Live By*, which holds that metaphors do not only structure language. They also structure thought. That is, we think about and relate to the world in terms of the metaphors that we use to describe it. Taking the example of 'argument as war', they argue that "we don't just *talk* about arguments in terms of war.… Many of the things we *do* in arguing are partially structured by the concept of war". For example, we believe that "we gain and lose ground. We plan and use strategies". There is "attack, defense, counterattack" (Lakoff & Johnson, 1980, p. 4). What is important to understand is that metaphors extend beyond cognitive frameworks. They influence behaviour. Metaphors facilitate some behaviours while foreclosing others. For instance, "we may lose sight of the cooperative aspects of arguing" (Lakoff & Johnson, 1980, p. 10), instead focusing on offence, defence, and gaining ground.

At stake in this particular example—argument as war—are human relationships. Lakoff and Johnson highlight the fact that metaphors can chart the horizon of possibilities for a relationship. If two conversation partners understand argument as battle, then a winner and a loser are likely to emerge. But, if another metaphor comes into play—argument as cooperative game, for instance—then another outcome becomes imaginable, and a potential fracture has been repaired. In Chap. 2, Melanie Baljko discusses repair at length. As she states, linguistic repair and relationship repair often go hand-in-hand.

In this way, language *does* things. It brings things into being. John Austin (1962/1975, p. 6) called this capacity of language 'performative'. A performative utterance is one wherein "the issuing of [the] utterance [is also] the performing of an action". By this definition, metaphors are almost always performative. At once, they provide 'shortcuts' (Boucher, 2021), embed assumptions (Hwang & Levy, 2015), "serve the interest of the metaphor's practitioners" (Gillespie, 2017, para. 11), and engender "potentially disruptive social consequences" (Black et al., 2006, p. 1). As Sally Wyatt asserts (2021, para. 3), "We have known about the performativity of language for getting on for a century ... there really is no excuse not to take seriously the power of words."

5 Symbolic Renaming

Amidst calls for new language, Anna Jobin and Malte Ziewitz (2018, para. 14) ask this crucial question: "What would it take to undo [existing technology metaphors]?". To that question, we add another: what would it take to bring into circulation new, reparative metaphors? Our answer is that it takes a collective will. It takes a movement, not a fight.

Big Tech is not our primary audience. We are not lobbying Silicon Valley to abandon its product names in favour of the ones we put forward here. Rather, this book does its work in service of symbolic renaming. This means being committed in our communities to adopting new language. By using new words, we can be 'linguistically disobedient' (Komska et al., 2019), signalling a commitment to public values over the values encoded by the technology industry: ableism, racism, extractivism, capitalism, and colonialism, to name a few.

What does symbolic renaming mean in practice? If a work team is considering investing in more 'predictive technologies', call them by Olivier Driessens' rename: 'automated predeterminations' (Chap. 8). If you are designing 'assistive technology', take seriously Melanie Baljko's notion that you might be designing 'ableist technology' (Chap. 2). If you are a professor, rebuff administrators pushing for AI use in the classroom, with Harriett Jernigan's claim that 'AI' is more aptly named 'digital settler colonialism' (Chap. 7).

If this seems challenging, consider historical precedents, and call to mind a host of words and phrases—which we do not reprint—that circulated in the public lexicon for decades. People in power did not put an end to them. People practising symbolic renaming did.

6 Renaming Matters Now

Big Tech's power and politics are clear. In 2024, million-dollar donations flowed from Amazon and Meta to Donald Trump's inauguration fund (Kim & Allyn, 2024). OpenAI's CEO, Sam Altman, personally wrote a cheque (Kim & Allyn, 2024). And Elon Musk, who owns X, donated USD 288 million in support of Trump's re-election (Thadani et al., 2025).

While Big Tech supports an increasingly authoritarian regime with cash, it is also supporting Trump's administration in-kind. In early 2025, Meta announced it was ending its fact-checking programme initially in the United States, a move regarded as pandering to Trump's desire for unmoderated speech online (Isaac & Schleifer, 2025). In the wake of executive orders that vilify minoritised individuals, Google, Amazon, and Meta have rolled back their equity, diversity, and inclusion initiatives. In February 2025, Google scaled back its ethical AI principles, trimming a former list of seven to three, which now allow the development of AI for weapons and military use (Assaad, 2025; epic.org, 2025).

Even if these moves are not the only cause, the consequences for democracies are real: the rise of mis/disinformation, a resurgence in far-right ideologies, and human rights violations. Yet these are obscured by language that positions technology as always helping, always altruistic, always at our service.[3] By renaming them, technologies can be recast as what they do *to* us in contrast to what Big Tech maintains they do *for* us.

Not all of the technologies examined in this book hail from Silicon Valley. D2L, for example, one of the learning management systems Kate Maddalena refers to in her chapter (Chap. 3), was the brainchild of Canadian John Baker while a student at the University of Waterloo (D2L, 2025). Gordon A. Gow discusses the often contested history of naming the radio 'spectrum', a global resource (Chap. 5). But no matter their origin, the names of all the technologies discussed in this book share a propensity for opacity. Far from revealing their logics and mechanics, the names they have been given by C-suites and marketing teams mislead, misrepresent, and misdirect. They emphasise the most charitable and least credible interpretations of what it is these technologies do.

[3] One of Google's newly minted 'AI Principles' is 'Bold innovation' (Google AI, n.d.), but as Adrian Daub (2020, p. 6) writes, "what if what goes by the name of innovation is ultimately just an opportunistic exploitation of regulatory gaps?"

What do we let stand when this kind of language endures? Simply put, we consent to hidden agendas, and we tolerate a system wherein language is contiguous with the goals of neo-imperialism and oppression (Baker-Bell, 2020; Lawrence, 2021). To create better futures, we need better language to scaffold them.

This is our long-term ambition, but as editors we have a shorter-term goal for you, the reader of this book. Our writers discuss technologies in ways they are rarely framed, distancing themselves from the prevailing messages about technology and society. In doing so, we aim to give you conceptual tools that break with Big Tech's branding. We hope that when you go to a town hall about adopting smart city technology in your part of the world, as Jess Reia and Luã Cruz describe (Chap. 6), or visit your doctor, who asks you to consent to having AI be integrated into your medical care, as Arun Jacob and Christina Boyles discuss (Chap. 4), you flinch, ever so slightly, and find there are questions that really must be asked before you comply.

7 How This Book Is Organised

This book is for readers everywhere who are interested in the power of language to mobilise social change. Our approach is to bring empirical research to bear on how a relatively simple renaming of familiar digital technologies helps to disrupt assumptions about them. The emphasis is on what a selection of today's popular technologies *actually* do, not Silicon Valley's (and other technology promoters') notions of what people should buy.

Fifteen contributor chapters follow. While each deals with a unique technology, they are grouped into five themes: '~~Knowing~~', '~~Optimising~~', '~~Predicting~~', '~~Saving~~', and '~~Socialising~~'. We use strikethroughs in section titles (and chapter titles) to indicate language and discourses we refuse. The works of Melanie Baljko, Kate Maddalena, and Arun Jacob and Christina Boyles constitute the section titled '~~Knowing~~'. Each of these chapters challenges how technologies tell users to 'know' the world, pushing back against epistemic violence. In '~~Optimising~~', Gordon Gow, Jess Reia and Luã Cruz, and Harriett Jernigan collectively assert how discourses of optimisation reinforce colonialist and capitalist relations. For their part, Olivier Driessens, Gillian Russell and Frédérik Lesage, and Eryk Salvaggio call into question what '~~Predicting~~' means in practice, emphasising the historical, discursive, and statistical processes that truly underlie 'predictive' tech. The chapters contributed by Anran Wang, Nathaniel Laywine and Victoria Simon, and Gemma Milne push back on technology developers' claims around '~~Saving~~'; the positioning of technologies as 'saviours' often masks something far more disconcerting. Finally, the works in '~~Socialising~~', written by Brooks DeCillia and Gabriela Perdomo, Evangeline Holtz-Schramek, and Zach Pearl, discuss the stakes, both physical and psychological, of participating in social platforms that, at the end of the day, are spaces only unequally open to all.

Together, as 22 authors of varying nationalities and mother tongues now working in Brazil, Canada, Denmark, England, Scotland, and the United States, we add our voices to the epigraph of this introductory chapter: "If we dwell differently among words, then we know different worlds" (Moss, 2000, p. 27). We hope you will lend your voice, too.

References

Alphabet. (2025, February 4). Alphabet announces fourth quarter and fiscal year 2024 results. *Alphabet*. https://abc.xyz/assets/a3/91/6d1950c148fa84c7d699abe05284/2024q4-alphabet-earnings-release.pdf

Assaad, Z. (2025, February 10). Google has dropped its promise not to use AI for weapons. It's part of a troubling trend. *The Conversation Canada*. https://theconversation.com/google-has-dropped-its-promise-not-to-use-ai-for-weapons-its-part-of-a-troubling-trend-249169#:~:text=In%20an%20update%20to%20its,directly%20facilitate%20injury%20to%20people

Austin, J. L. (1975). *How to do things with words*. Clarendon Press. (Original work published 1962).

Baker-Bell, A. (2020). *Linguistic justice: Black language, literacy, identity, and pedagogy*. Routledge.

Black, J., Downes, K., Field, F., Mozdzanowska, A., & Steel, K. (2006). *The metaphors of emerging technologies: Unpacking the disconnects between the "what" and the "how" in the world of "online shopping"* [Conference paper]. 9th International Conference on Technology Policy and Innovation, Santorini, Greece. https://dspace.mit.edu/bitstream/handle/1721.1/33003/santorini_paper_internal.pdf?sequence=1&isAllowed=y

Boucher, P. (2021, July 2). *What if we chose new metaphors for artificial intelligence?* European Parliamentary Research Service. https://epthinktank.eu/2021/07/02/what-if-we-chose-new-metaphors-for-artificial-intelligence-science-and-technology-podcast/

Chown, E., & Nascimento, F. (2023). *Meaningful technologies: How digital metaphors change the way we think and live*. Lever Press.

D'Ignazio, C., & Klein, L. F. (2020). *Data feminism*. MIT Press.

D2L. (2025). *Transforming the way the world learns*. https://www.d2l.com/about/

Daub, A. (2020). *What tech calls thinking: An inquiry into the intellectual bedrock of Silicon Valley*. FSG Originals.

Deibert, R. J. (2020). *Reset: Reclaiming the internet for civil society*. House of Anansi.

Drucker, J. (2013). Performative materiality and theoretical approaches to interface. *Digital Humanities Quarterly, 7*(1). http://www.digitalhumanities.org/dhq/vol/7/1/000143/000143.html

epic.org. (2025, February 5). Google rolls back responsible AI principles, breaking promise to limit military use of its products. *Epic*. https://epic.org/google-rolls-back-responsible-ai-principles-breaking-promise-to-limit-military-use-of-its-products/

Fuchs, C. (2011). A contribution to the critique of the political economy of Google. *Fast Capitalism, 8*(1), 31–50. https://fastcapitalism.journal.library.uta.edu/index.php/fastcapitalism/article/view/232/269

Gillespie, T. (2017, August 24). The platform metaphor, revisited. *Digital Society Blog*. https://www.hiig.de/en/the-platform-metaphor-revisited/

Google. (n.d.). *Our approach to search*. https://www.google.com/intl/en_us/search/howsearchworks/our-approach/#:~:text=Google's%20mission%20is%20to%20organize,height%20of%20the%20Eiffel%20Tower

Google AI. (n.d.). *Our principles*. https://ai.google/responsibility/principles/

Hwang, T., & Levy, K. (2015, January 15). 'The cloud' and other dangerous metaphors. *The Atlantic*. https://www.theatlantic.com/technology/archive/2015/01/the-cloud-and-other-dangerous-metaphors/384518/

Isaac, M. (2021, October 28). Facebook renames itself Meta. *The New York Times*. https://www.nytimes.com/2021/10/28/technology/facebook-meta-name-change.html

Isaac, M., & Schleifer, T. (2025, January 7). Meta sys it will end its fact-checking program on social media posts. *The New York Times*. https://www.nytimes.com/live/2025/01/07/business/meta-fact-checking

Jobin, A., & Ziewitz, M. (2018, March 6). Organic search: How metaphors help cultivate the web. *Digital Society Blog*. https://www.hiig.de/en/organic-search-metaphors-help-cultivate-web/

Kim, J., & Allyn, B. (2024, December 13). *Tech moguls Altman, Bezos and Zuckerberg donate to Trump's inauguration fund*. National Public Radio. https://www.npr.org/2024/12/13/nx-s1-5227874/trump-bezos-zuckerberg-amazon-facebook-open-ai-meta-inauguration-fund

Komska, Y., Moyd, M., & Gramling, D. (2019). *Linguistic disobedience: Restoring power to civic language*. Palgrave Macmillan.

Lakoff, G., & Johnson, M. (1980). *Metaphors we live by*. University of Chicago Press.

Lanier, J. (2011). *You are not a gadget: A manifesto*. Vintage Books. (Original work published 2010).

Lawrence, H. (2021). Siri disciplines. In T. S. Mullaney, B. Peters, M. Hicks, & K. Philip (Eds.), *Your computer is on fire* (pp. 179–198). MIT Press.

Meta. (2025, January 29). *Meta reports fourth quarter and full year 2024 results*. https://investor.atmeta.com/investor-news/press-release-details/2025/Meta-Reports-Fourth-Quarter-and-Full-Year-2024-Results/default.aspx

Moss, J. (2000). *Invisible among the ruins: Field notes of a Canadian in Ireland*. Cormorant Books.

Muldoon, J., Graham, M., & Cant, C. (2024). *Feeding the machine: The hidden human labor powering A.I.* Bloomsbury Publishing.

Nagy, P., & Neff, G. (2024). Conjuring algorithms: Understanding the tech industry as stage magicians. *New Media & Society, 26*(9). https://doi.org/10.1177/14614448241251789

Noble, S. U. (2018). *Algorithms of oppression: How search engines reinforce racism*. NYU Press.

Paul, K. (2021, October 28). Facebook announces name change to Meta in rebranding effort. *The Guardian*. https://www.theguardian.com/technology/2021/oct/28/facebook-name-change-rebrand-meta

Perrigo, B. (2023, January 18). OpenAI used Kenyan workers on less than $2 per hour to make ChatGPT less toxic. *Time*. https://time.com/6247678/openai-chatgpt-kenya-workers/

Ravenscraft, E. (2023, June 15). What is the Metaverse, exactly? *Wired*. https://www.wired.com/story/what-is-the-metaverse/

Silverstone, R., Hirsch, E., & Morley, D. (1992). Information and communication technologies and the moral economy of the household. In R. Silverstone & E. Hirsch (Eds.), *Consuming technologies: Media and information in domestic spaces* (pp. 15–31). Routledge.

Thadani, T., Morse, C. E., & Reston, M. (2025, January 31). Elon Musk donated $288 million in 2024 election, final tally shows. *The Washington Post*. https://www.washingtonpost.com/politics/2025/01/31/elon-musk-trump-donor-2024-election/

Vaidhyanathan, S. (2012). *The Googlization of everything (and why we should worry)*. University of California Press.

van Dijck, J., Poell, T., & de Waal, M. (2018). *The platform society: Public values in a connective world*. Oxford University Press.

Wallenborn, J.T. (2022, May 17). *AI as a flying blue brain? How metaphors influence our visions of AI*. Digital Society Blog. https://www.hiig.de/en/ai-metaphors/

Wyatt, S. (2018, October 18). Addiction: Apt metaphor for (over) use of digital technology? *Digital Society Blog*. https://www.hiig.de/en/addiction-apt-metaphor-for-overuse-of-digital-technology/

Wyatt, S. (2021). Metaphors in critical Internet and digital media studies. *New Media & Society*, *23*(2), 406–416. https://doi.org/10.1177/1461444820929324

Yohn, D. L. (2021, 2 November). Facebook's rebrand has a fundamental problem. *Harvard Business Review*. https://hbr.org/2021/11/facebooks-rebrand-has-a-fundamental-problem

Zuboff, S. (2015). Big other: Surveillance capitalism and the prospects of an information civilization. *Journal of Information Technology*, *30*(1), 75–89. https://doi.org/10.1057/jit.2015.5

PART I

~~Knowing~~

CHAPTER 2

Ableist Technology*

~~Assistive Technology~~

Melanie Baljko

1 Introduction

What is in a name? It can be many things, not least of all a window into sociotechnical imaginaries.[1] In this chapter, I explore the imaginaries surrounding the term 'assistive technology' (AT). I consider how this term is used to refer to figures that are diametrically opposed: digital artefacts born out of technoableist practice and technosocial interventions generated from within a disability justice framework. The name is problematic because it collapses their differences, thereby foreclosing the interrogation of the politics of AT.

[1] Peter Nagy and Gina Neff (2024, p. 4949) offer a definition of 'sociotechnical imaginary': "society's collective beliefs about the potential implications of technologies for their present and future lives". See also Jasanoff (2015).

M. Baljko (✉)
Department of Electrical Engineering and Computer Science, York University, Toronto, ON, Canada
e-mail: baljko@yorku.ca

C. Chokshi, R. Mansell (eds.), *The Need to Rename Tech*,
https://doi.org/10.1007/978-3-032-05155-4_2

AT, by its very name, presents itself as offering assistance. However, the term perpetuates the very ableism it seeks to combat. And this identifier, when mobilised in computing curricula, impacts the future design and application of the technology. It is not enough to point out a problem; I intend to address it. To do so, I draw principally upon a rich variety of scholarly traditions including critical disability studies, design studies, feminist philosophy, media and communications studies, and science and technology studies to address the problem. Rather than think in terms of a 'solution', I consider the concept of 'repair': both in terms of the correctness of a lexical referring expression and in terms of the social relations in its context of use.

2 Referring Expressions and Repair

The relationship between referring expressions and referents is contingent. Referring expressions are words, phrases, or other symbols that identify or point to something.[2] Referents are the 'somethings', be they concrete or abstract, that make up the shared world of interlocutors. Referring expressions and referents stand in a source-to-target relationship.

In his book, *Disability and Discourse Analysis*, Jan Grue (2015, p. 11–12) makes an important point about this contingency when he addresses

> the difficulty of talking, writing, and thinking about "disability" in the abstract ... "A disabled person" has no clearer referent than "A French person," but both phrases will tend to summon up, in the minds of readers, a referent of some sort. Is your "disabled person" the same as my "disabled person"? We won't know that until we've checked; if we can't check, the best we can do is provide an educated guess.

[2] In an analogous fashion to Gabriel Ignatow (2003), I use these two terms of referring expression and referent throughout. Ignatow used 'signifier' and 'referent', whereas I use 'referring expression' and 'referent'. This is a streamlining of substantial prior work and terminology: "For the purposes of this study, these terms are synonymous with Saussure's 'signifier' and 'signified' (Saussure, 1972 [1909]), Peirce's 'sign' and 'object' (Peirce, 1991), I.A. Richards' 'vehicle' and 'tenor' (Ogden and Richards, 1923), and Lakoff and Johnson's (1980) 'source domain' and 'target domain'" (Ignatow, 2003, p. 6).

How referring expressions are interpreted to identify their referents (also known as reference resolution) is a complex process about which much has been written. Suffice it to say, there are different ways that the process of reference resolution can go wrong. For instance, suppose I refer to 'the best pop song of the 80s'. You, my conversation partner, might understand this to mean Madonna's 'Like a Prayer', which is a good song, but not the one I meant. This type of 'wrong' indicates a failure to establish the common ground necessary for communication (Clark, 1996). And, for such a misunderstanding, humans have all sorts of linguistic mechanisms for effecting repair. Let us consider another case of 'wrong'. The reference resolution process might be 'successful' in the sense that interlocutors establish common ground, meaning both their understandings include the same intended referent. This is the 'yes' answer to Grue's rhetorical question on whether your 'disabled person' is the same as my 'disabled person'. But what about when that shared understanding is premised problematically? What kind of 'wrong' is this? Take, for example, the use of referring expressions to describe the internet: terms like 'information highway' and 'world brain', which are simultaneously metaphorical and selective, can be used politically to shape meaning and action (Wyatt, 2021). Referring expressions, when made up of figurative noun phrases, can be reductive, selective, misdirective, or otherwise inaccurate, especially in service of agendas of meaning. Grue (2015, p. 9) argues that:

> analysing disability from a discourse perspective is a matter of continually redirecting one's attention (and the reader's) to context and usage, partly because usage-in-context has real political implications ... [D]iscourse analysis is, besides other things, a tool for explicating political issues and conflicts.

The extent to which a referring expression is problematic is also a matter of epistemic stance: whose adjudication of reductiveness, selectiveness, misdirectiveness, or inaccuracy gets considered? For instance, it could be the interlocutors themselves, the observers of the discourse, or those who are impacted by the discourse—all of whom are connected to one another through a complex array of relationships. Thus, the relationship between referring expression and referent can be problematic in ways that are more complicated than reference resolution, through the baggage of metaphor and the entanglements of social relations.

If a referring expression is problematic, then repair should be sought. Here we can observe that this repair is not limited to the linguistic repair of a failure to establish common ground, but is also a kind of relationship repair. But sought by whom, for whom, what kind, and why? As E.V. Spelman (2002, p. 12) points out, "The English language is generously stocked with words [for the central human activity of repair] ... repair, restore, rehabilitate, renovate, reconcile, redeem, heal, fix, and mend ... These are distinctions that make a difference". In the next sections, I discuss a problematic relationship between the referring expression 'assistive technology' and its potential referents. Some aspects of this discussion will involve further breakdown and removal, which are forms of destruction, and others will involve transformation and the addition of new points, which are forms of creation. This discussion, therefore, takes place in what Spelman (2002) calls a 'blurry space', one that facilitates repair both as destruction and creation, involves interlinked processes that unfold over time, and reflects broader underlying attitudes towards maintaining and caring for our relationships and our society.

3 Assistive Technology (AT)

3.1 *Referring Expression and Referent*

The designator 'assistive technology' is often linked to two notable legislative acts in the United States (US) from over 30 years ago: the Technology-Related Assistance Act (commonly known as the Tech Act) of 1988, and the Individuals with Disabilities Act (IDEA) of 1990. Both defined AT as "any item, piece of equipment, or product system, whether acquired commercially off-the-shelf, modified, or customized, that is used to increase, maintain or improve the functional capabilities of individuals with disabilities" (Technology-Related Assistance for Individuals with Disabilities Act of 1988, 1988, Section 3.1). I first encountered this definition when I was a doctoral candidate in computer science in the early 2000s. I remember searching for a definition of AT that would be serviceable for my research needs. I made what I now recognise as a mistake: understanding the referring expression AT to presume a category of entity that already exists in the world and understanding these entities as available to be observed in action. I did not fully realise at the time that I was treating a socially-constructed concept as if it were of a *natural kind*—that is, an objectively-definable category of technology that "corresponds to a grouping that reflects the structure of the natural world rather than the interests and actions of human beings" (Bird & Tobin, 2024, para. 1). Scholars in science, technology, engineering, and mathematics (STEM) fields are perhaps particularly susceptible to this misunderstanding, which I argue arises from mistaking a 'label-for-natural-kind' type of relationship between referring expression and referent and, what is in actuality, a relationship shaped by social practices. We can illustrate this shaping by considering the imagined referents of the referring expression 'AT' using thought experiments.

3.2 *Assistive: In Actuality or Envisaged?*

Suppose we accept that the referents of AT correspond to a "grouping that reflects the structure of the natural world" (Bird & Tobin, 2024, para. 1). Then what structure provides the basis for the grouping of AT? Would membership in the category be contingent on the end result of 'assisting' as opposed to the design intention of providing assistance? If the former, then this means that AT refers only to those things that *actually have* positive impact, as opposed to the latter, which are things *intended to have* positive impact. But then, irrespective of actuality or intent, how would positive impact be established (as knowledge, as opposed to personal belief)? By which processes and by whom? What tests must these beliefs pass in order to be legitimated as knowledge? As Sandra Harding (1987) articulates, some subjects are systematically excluded as 'knowers' or agents of knowledge. Actual impact cannot easily be known and is difficult to adjudicate, so design intention is often imagined as a proxy for actual impact. The adjective 'assistive' is presumably intended to distinguish between these technologies and *assistive* ones, but this does not help to reveal the "paradoxical nature of technology: its simultaneous ability to open up but also to limit opportunities, access and inclusion" (Roulstone, 2016, p. 3).

Technologies can have positive and negative impacts. Positive impacts include reducing barriers in "environmental, interpersonal, virtual and psychosocial spaces", enhancing survival and recovery rates, opening new social horizons, and creating forms of recognition for new social and political identities (Roulstone, 2016, p. 6). There is a strong "discourse of technology as an equalizer of access" (Alper, 2015, p. 96). Negative impacts include alienation, marginalisation, stigmatisation, exclusion, and over-technologisation. In sum, as Goodley et al. (2021, p. 41) argue, "technological interventions should never be viewed as neutral nor benign". The referring expression acknowledges this non-neutrality even if only tacitly.

3.3 *Assistive to Whom?*

In considering the adjective 'assistive' in the expression AT, who or what is configured as the recipients of the assistance? The referents of AT are often characterised in a way that imagines the location of disability in the individual (which is tantamount to a rejected medical model of disability), as opposed to it being located relationally, as critical disability scholars such as Alison Kafer (2013) and Aimi Hamraie and Kelly Fritsch (2019) have convincingly demonstrated.

If the envisaged users of AT are 'individuals with disabilities', then the discursive construction of AT is built upon the discursive construction of disability:

> The category of "disabled" can only be understood in relation to "able-bodied" or "able-minded," a binary in which each term forms the borders of the other. As Rosemarie Garland-Thomson explains, this hierarchical division of bodies and minds is then used to "legitimat[e] an unequal distribution of resources, status, and power within a biased social and architectural environment." In this construction, disability is seen less as an objective fact of the body or mind and more as a product of social relations. (Kafer, 2013, pp. 5–6)

In Kafer's political/relational model, "the problem of disability no longer resides in the minds or bodies of individuals but in built environments and social patterns that exclude or stigmatize particular kinds of bodies, minds, and ways of being" (Kafer, 2013, p. 7). Hamraie's (2012) concept of the 'normate template' builds upon Garland-Thomson's concepts of the normate and mis-fit, and refers to the schema of the likely and 'normal' user as envisaged by the designers; in this work, Hamraie considered design fields such as architecture, industrial design, and assistive technology, but the concept of the normate template is applicable to other practices with design outputs that concern human experience. The normate template, when deployed in the design of 'space' and 'place' (i.e., not only the built environment and all the artefacts within it but also the time-based aspects of processes and places as well), is how we end up with the "built environments and social patterns that exclude or stigmatize particular kinds of bodies, minds, and ways of being" (Kafer, 2013, p. 7). Within these environments, disabled individuals often do not have the "comfortable and unremarkable majority experience of material anonymity, an unmarked subject position that most of us occupy at some points in life and that often goes unnoticed" (Garland-Thomson, 2011, p. 597). As Arseli Dokumacı (2023, p. 257) describes, it is within these environments "where we, as disabled people, eke out activist affordances" and "frictional practices of access production" take place (Hamraie & Fritsch, 2019, p. 3).

3.4 *Technology: Artefact and Process*

In considering the noun 'technology' in the expression 'assistive technology', what is configured as that which is doing the assisting? If the agent imagined to be doing the assisting is technology, then we have an instance of the discursive construction of AT being built upon the discursive construction of technology.

The reference resolution process involves recognising the conflation of 'technological artefact' and technology writ large, with the latter identifying a "spectrum of artifacts, techniques, organizations, and systems" (Woodhouse, 2013, p. 17).[3] For digital technology, this spectrum "is a collection—an extremely large vocabulary—of pieces and parts: hardware, software, transmission networks, protocols, languages, very large-scale integrated circuits, algorithms, and all components and practices that belong to these" (Arthur, 2009, p. 25). Brian Arthur (2009, pp. 25–26) argues that, as opposed to being merely a collection of artefacts, digital technology is a dynamic, evolving system, consisting of a

> repository of elements standing ready for particular uses. We could think of this repository as a toolbox of elements, or functionalities, available for use. But I prefer to think of it as a realm, a world within which certain things can be done. A world entered for what can be accomplished there.

So, digital technological artefacts fall within the spectrum of digital technology generally, but digital technologies are much more than artefacts, since they also include things such as techniques, practices, organisations, systems, and arenas of action. This conflation impacts the referents

[3] Woodhouse makes this point about technologies more generally. Thus, his remarks also apply to digital technologies.

of AT since they get imagined merely in terms of technological artefacts (e.g., as items or pieces of equipment), as opposed to being understood in terms of a broader concept of technology. Phrases such as 'product system', included in the IDEA legislation, hint at this broader spectrum. In this way, the referents of AT are shrunk down to end products as opposed to a broader spectrum of technology and its arenas of action. This is problematic because it is reductive. Peter Fuzesi (2019) applied the concept of 'maps of responsibilities' to the specific design realm of assistive technology. This concept, developed by Madeleine Akrich (1994) explains how technological objects carry embedded scripts that shape human actions and social interactions, where these scripts represent the designer's anticipation and prescriptive shaping of user behaviours. In recognising that AT development is a practice that joins the material world and the promises and imaginaries of AT, Fuzesi (2019, p. 30) makes the point that these "promises and imaginaries cannot be simply dismissed as naïve or imprecise representations; they are interventions into the ongoing figuring of contested bodies". Accepting Fuzesi's point means that we should not subscribe to a naïve view that AT has a definition that contains inaccuracies in need of correction. Instead, we should see that the naming of AT itself is wrapped up in the contested concept of disability itself.

We should turn away therefore from the label-for-natural-kind type of relationship between referring expression and referent. We see that common understandings of the referring expression AT are, at least in part, based in a sociotechnical imaginary, that is, a "collectively held, institutionally stabilized, and publicly performed visio[n] of desirable futures" (Jasanoff, 2015, p. 6). Both the 'assistive' part of the referring expression—the adjective of the noun phrase—and the 'technology' part of the noun phrases are embedded within this imaginary.

3.5 *Asking Questions*

Sara Hendren (2018) calls on designers to critically engage in and to interrupt cultural assumptions about enforcing so-called normalcy. For instance, consider the case of AT in the form of exoskeletons for those with mobility issues. To what extent does this much-hyped AT, or AT more generally, seek to disrupt the conditions that give rise to ableism? Ashley Shew (2023, pp. 11–12) proposes the term 'technoableism' to describe "a pattern disabled people see over and over... a belief in the power of technology that considers the elimination of disability a good thing, something we should strive for. ... often under the guise of empowerment". Similarly, Liz Jackson, Alex Haagaard, and Rua Williams describe some forms of ATs as disability dongles, "a techno-utopian (re)solution to the *design problem* [emphasis added]" and their place in "contemporary fairy tales that appeal to the abled imagination by presenting a heroic designer-protagonist" (Jackson et al., 2022, para. 1).[4] The designer-as-hero is a well-established trope in critical disability studies: "There's an extra helping of warm-hearted heroism attached to the stories about assistive technology—an emphasis on the gee-whiz quality of machinery, sentimentally wed to the experience of disability" (Hendren, 2020, p. 16). Mara Mills (2010) uses the term 'assistive pretext' to describe the use of disability as a precursor or pretense for engineering concerns. These are versions of "ableist accessibility" (Coombes et al., 2022, p. 4). The exoskeleton arises from ableist imaginaries: rather than ask the built environment to afford access to all individuals with diverse mobility capabilities, the design impetus is, instead, to attempt to mold the individual to the existing environment and 'fix' the disability. The history of technological intervention in the lives of disabled people has been associated largely with the concept of normality and with attempted 'restoration' to this state (Goodley et al., 2021; Oliver, 1990).

Such critiques from critical disability scholars open up questions about a seemingly benign term. Does the term AT imply any political commitments? Is AT concerned with power and privilege? Does it seek to intervene in ableism? Does it seek to displace the normate template? Does its design move forward through the use of value-based principles, such as the principles of disability justice and design justice (Costanza-Chock, 2020; Sins Invalid, 2019)? Typically, it does not. For these reasons, I argue the term AT is problematic.

4 Ableism-Reinforcing Technology in the Computing Curriculum

4.1 The Locale: The Baccalaureate Design Project

Postsecondary education is perpetuating the problematic use of the term 'assistive technology'. In their analysis of 'the abled imagination' that gives

[4] I added emphasis to 'design problem' because Jackson et al. (2022) are using the term here ironically, referring, in essence, to mis-fitting.

rise to disability dongles, Jackson et al. (2022, para. 9) identify issues of "misguided concerns about our [disabled] bodies" and "under-analyzed intentions and ambitions" and connect these issues quite pointedly to actors and sites within higher education. Specifically, they enumerate a list that includes design and engineering students and practitioners; Stanford University researchers; the 'Design and Innovation' workshops at the Massachusetts Institute of Technology; University of Texas students; Purdue University (specifically the Mechanical Engineering ME463 'Engineering Design' capstone courses, for which the Mallot Innovation Award is granted annually); the Human–Computer Interaction (HCI) lab at Cornell; and the Association for Computing Machinery (ACM) ASSETS conference organisers (ACM being a notable publishing venue for HCI scholarly outputs concerning assistive technology).[5]

Engineering capstone courses are a particular site of the problematic use of the term AT. In the US and globally, the Accreditation Board for Engineering and Technology (ABET) continues to require a capstone design project (ABET, 2023). In Canada, a senior (fourth-year undergraduate) capstone course is a requisite for an engineering programme to receive accreditation from the Canadian Engineering Accreditation Board (CEAB), the official body responsible for accrediting undergraduate engineering programmes. These capstone projects are often deployed as learning activities that bridge theory and praxis. As a professor of computer science in a School of Engineering for more than 20 years, I draw on my own knowledge to suggest that the student design project is a feature of many different undergraduate programmes, appearing not only in senior capstone courses in mechanical, electrical, software, and computer engineering, but also in many other courses in computer science (particularly HCI), design, and digital media. And, of the numerous student design projects that are instantiated, many of them end up with a design intention towards what Jackson et al. (2022) sceptically call an 'innovative' disability solution, or what we otherwise name as AT.

[5] In terms of actors and sites for innovating so-called solutions identified by Jackson et al. (2022), exceptions to higher education institutions include industrial labs/studios (e.g., Michael Graves Architecture and Design; Hewlett-Packard Labs); various start-ups (e.g., Lechal, Tec-Innovation, Ashirase/Honda's startup incubator); and entities that mount challenges and give out awards (e.g., the non-profit Cal Ripken Sr. Foundation, the host of the National STEM Challenge; Innovation Grand Prix at the Cannes Lions International Festival of Creativity; and Purdue University, granter of the Mallot Innovation Award).

4.2 *Assistive Technology in the Computing Curriculum*

The ACM, the world's largest educational and scientific computing society, and the Institute of Electrical and Electronics Engineers (IEEE), another professional association concerned with engineering, computer science, and related areas, have maintained a joint task force for developing curricula recommendations since the early 1990s. According to the joint task force's report, computing curricula exist in a wide array of baccalaureate disciplines, including computer engineering, computer science, cybersecurity, information systems, information technology, software engineering, and data science (CC2020 Task Force, 2020). The ACM Digital Library is a comprehensive repository of resources covering the fields of computing and information technology which can be treated as a data set that is reflective of the activities of each one of these baccalaureate computing disciplines. The term AT is found in every one of these disciplines, as summarised in Table 2.1.

The proliferation of the term AT across so many of the baccalaureate computing disciplines raises questions including: in which ways does computing education perpetuate or intervene in technoableism through references to AT? To what extent, if any, does computing education advocate for disability justice? Does computing education perpetuate or intervene in technoableism through the specific means of AT praxis? We can gather initial impressions from two key documents: 'Computing Curricula 2020: Paradigms for Global Computing Education', also known as CC2020 (CC2020 Task Force, 2020) and 'Computer Science Curricula 2023: Curriculum Guidelines for Undergraduate Degree Programs in Computer

Table 2.1 Evidence of the term AT mobilised within the full-text collection of the ACM Digital Library, which was gathered by performing a search of the ACM Digital Library using the name of the baccalaureate computing discipline and the term 'assistive technology'

Baccalaureate Computing Discipline	*Occurrences of the term assistive technology (Count)*
Computer Engineering	196
Computer Science	1231
Cybersecurity	95
Information Systems	844
Information Technology	534
Software Engineering	326
Data Science	119

Source: By author based on data in the ACM Digital Library as of March 2024

Science', also known as CS2023 (Kumar et al., 2023).[6] Both documents are the products of multi-year projects led by consortia of professional bodies representing hundreds of thousands of practitioners.[7] CC2020 is expansive and covers global curricula across all the baccalaureate disciplines identified above, whereas CS2023 focuses on the specific baccalaureate discipline of computer science. I have chosen the latter for closer inspection, since this is the field with which I am most knowledgeable. Additionally, this discipline contains the specific knowledge area of HCI, one of my primary research areas.

A content analysis of CC2020, which is the umbrella curriculum guide for computing, reveals silence on the issue of ableism.[8] The guide does not name ableism or other forms of oppression explicitly. In the places where it might be expected, the guide instead mobilises abstract language about "benefits [to] society" with the Knowledge-Skills-Disposition (KSD) Competency framework (CC2020 Task Force, 2020, p. 52).[9] In this framework, knowledge is understood as 'know-what', skills as 'know-how', and disposition as that which "moderate(s) the behavior of applying 'know-what' that becomes 'know-how' (p. 48). If one considers anti-ableism activism to fall under the category of a disposition in this KSD framework, then an anti-ableist curricular agenda could be considered to be generally compatible with CC2020, even though it, too, reproduces ableism by promoting the goal to "make all humans capable of living a normal life" (p. 77).

A content analysis of CS2023 focusing exclusively on curriculum guidelines for computer science, reveals a single acknowledgement of ableism, but not in the sense of indicating that computer science curricula should name it and intervene.[10] This sole mention of ableism occurs in a list of

[6] The CS2023 joint task force also included the Association for the Advancement of Artificial Intelligence (AAAI).

[7] The ACM was established in 1947 and is the world's largest educational and scientific computing society with over 100,000 members. The IEEE was founded in 1963 from the merging of two older societies (founded in 1884 and 1895, respectively). The IEEE Computer Society is one of the largest of its 39 technical societies, with a membership about half the size of ACM.

[8] Issues such as racism, colonialism, heteronormativity, and climate change are also not mentioned.

[9] Other examples include 'be in service to the welfare of society' and 'contribute constructively to society'.

[10] The methodology for the content analysis is briefly summarised here. A dictionary of curated terms was developed and used to identify relevant units of analysis (sentences and

reasons why students might not continue in the field of study, which results in a "lack of diverse identities within computer science" (Kumar et al., 2023, p. 285).[11] In terms of knowledge areas within computer science, there are no explicit mentions of ableism. The mention that has the closest connection is found in the knowledge area of Society, Ethics, and the Profession (SEP), which includes a core topic on the "theories describing the human creation and use of technology including instrumentalism, sociology of technological systems, disability justice, neutrality thesis, pragmatism, and decolonial models, including developing and using technology to right wrongs and do good" within a knowledge unit on "Professional Ethics" (p. 203). CS2023 "solicited articles" by "recognized experts" on how educators could address issues of "increased importance" that were identified in "[p]rior curricular guidelines [concerning] the design and delivery of computer science curriculum" (p. 339). "Teaching about Accessibility in Computer Science Education" (Ladner et al., 2023) was included as one such solicited article, but the article does not raise the issue of technoableism.

Knowledge about AT is identified as a core learning outcome for all computer science curricula in CS2023 as part of the knowledge area of HCI; specifically, learners are to "identify accessibility challenges faced by people with different disabilities, and specify the associated accessible and assistive technologies that address them" (Kumar et al., 2023, p. 177). Within the HCI knowledge area, a number of topics are listed to support this learning outcome, but the only ones that I found to engage with issues of power and ableism are listed as 'Unlearning and questioning' and 'Disability studies'.[12] In CS2023, of the 131 occurrences of 'accessibility',

paragraphs), which were then coded. Terms, denoted with quotes, included 'ableism', 'disability', and 'accessibility', and were detected with regular expressions. For instance, the expression 'accessib{ility|le}' matches both **accessib**ility and **accessi**ble, and the expression 'disab{ility|ilities|led}' matches with any of **disab**ility, **disab**ilities, **disab**led. Any match with the regular expression was counted as an occurrence, irrespective of the variant.

[11] "Despite being a creative, often highly compensated field with myriad job (and other) opportunities, racial, gender, and many other inequities in representation are pervasive in many regions. For too many students, their first computer science course is their last. There are many factors including the legacy of systemic racism, ableism, sexism, classism, and other injustices that contribute to the lack of diverse identities within computer science, and there is no single or quick fix." (Kumar et al., 2023, p. 285)

[12] Notably, these appear as sub-topics under the 'Background' topic which appeared in the 'non-core' part of the HCI knowledge area as opposed to the 'core' part.

essentially none interrogate the basis of inaccessibility.[13] Of the 30 mentions of 'disability', practically all are consistent with technoableism, except for the learning outcome which specifies that learners are to "identify developers' assumptions and values embedded in hardware and software design, especially as they pertain to usability for diverse populations including under-served and those with disabilities" (p. 201).[14] One would expect to find curricular guidance for teaching values-based technology design (including anti-oppression technology design) in the Knowledge Area of HCI. However, interestingly, it was the Knowledge Area of SEP—not HCI—which contained the curricular guidance best provisioned for intervening in technoableism.[15] It would be an interesting piece of future work to investigate the reasons for this gap in the curricular guidance provided in the HCI Knowledge Area. My preliminary speculation is that the 'reflective turn' in HCI scholarship has not yet propagated into the HCI undergraduate curriculum. This scholarship connected to 'third-paradigm' HCI (Harrison et al., 2011)—the paradigm that questions power structures and engages with social, cultural, and political dimensions and that followed its predecessor rationalist, cognition- and interaction-focused paradigms—has not yet reached computing curriculum guidelines. Another line of inquiry would be to investigate the extent to which SEP's focus can be seen as gradually shifting away from moral philosophy and towards values-based design, possibly influenced by recently popularised design thinking approaches.

[13] For instance, the CS2023 asserts that "[a]ccessibility, in the context of computer science, is about making computing products accessible to people with disabilities" (Kumar et al., 2023, p. 420). This statement is considered uncritical because it does not consider intervening in the underlying system that created the inaccessibility in the first place and fails to include a relational framing of inaccessibility.

[14] Mentions were detected for the expression 'disab{ility|ilities|led}', which matches with any of disability, disabilities, disabled.

[15] There are at least eight core topics, learning objectives, or dispositions, that may be considered critical. One is mentioned above (i.e., identifying assumptions and values embedded in hardware and software design). Also included is the advocacy disposition which identifies learners who "think, speak, and act in ways that … promote … equity … inclusion … in … product development (hardware and software)." Additionally, the core topic of "theories describing the human creation and use of technology including instrumentalism, sociology of technological systems, disability justice, neutrality thesis, pragmatism, and decolonial models, including developing and using technology to right wrongs and do good" (Kumar et al., 2023, p. 276) is also critical.

5 Rename and Repair

As indicated earlier, the referring expression AT is problematic because it neither implies the political commitments of intervening in ableism nor fully commits to technoableist AT, even though these are crucially different. This is especially problematic when the term is used in the educational pathways of early career digital practitioners. As Shew (2023, p. 48) remarks,

> On campus, I see my colleagues in engineering and computer science and 'helping' professions teaching narratives about technology as miraculous, holding up to young engineers in training various prosthetic and exoskeleton projects as 'life-changing' examples of humanitarian engineering, models of engagement with communities in need.

For disabled students who are presently in computing programmes, I cannot help but think that the term AT and the discourses around it do not support positive learning experiences. Many individuals with under-analysed imaginaries about AT will likely go on to be digital practitioners in Big Tech, where they will end up reproducing ableism in and through our technological systems.

But what to do? What would an 'ethics of care' have us do in this situation (Martin et al., 2015)? Who is doing the caring? I am aware of my own identity as a nondisabled person. I accept Shew's (2023, p. 14) assertion that "disabled people [are] the experts about disability. I'm no longer interested in what so-called experts (nondisabled scientists, physicians, therapists, and so on) have to say". As Spelman (2002, p. 44) notes, "[m]oral direction is something to be figured out by the moral travelers in the thicket of *their relations with others* [emphasis added], not something they can determine by reference to a sure and steady compass". I intend this chapter as an exercise in active listening which, in and of itself, is a form of action. Declining to use the problematic term AT is an acknowledgement of the many critiques of technoableism.

What term or terms should be used instead of AT? I argue that, in order to compel design practitioners to make their political commitments—or lack thereof—more explicit, the term AT should be replaced by the term *ableist technology* (whose acronym is also 'AT'), which is appealingly provocative. It is similar to the term 'ableist accessibility' (Coombes et al., 2022) in that it contains a jarring juxtaposition: a critique of ableism, alongside the helping-and-assisting connotation that comes from the more established acronym, which uses the 'assistive' adjective. The term 'disability dongle' has been introduced and explained by Jackson et al. (2022) and is also appealing, though it lacks the adjacency to the familiar acronym AT. The term 'ableist technology' is indeed missing the term 'assistive', which emphasises the point made by others: that the term 'assistive' in 'assistive technology' is redundant: "That's why the term assistive technology is easy shorthand but ultimately both redundant and misleading—because assistance is universal whenever we talk about tools" (Hendren, 2020, p. 44).

With this proposed renaming, am I saying that all assistive technologies are ableist? First, it is reductive to imagine a binary between ableist and non-ableist technologies; surely there is a continuum, as well as tensions and contradictions, between the two. How could this ever be adjudicated and by whom? Instead of attempting to answer, I am instead convinced by Shew's (2023, p. 43) call for us "all (disabled and abled alike) [to] think creatively about making adaptations so that everyone can participate in the world". These adaptations should also include adaptations in discourse and in referring expressions—hence, my call for renaming as a way to call out otherwise invisibilised ableism in much technology practice. I am not saying that all technology is ableist but rather that it is the formation of a 'special' category of technology, denoted by the 'special' term AT, which is steeped in ableism.

The next time you call upon the referring expression 'assistive technology' in your speech or writing, swap in the term *ableist technology* instead. The point that all technology is assistive technology is a good one, but it does not fully acknowledge the work that the term 'assistive technology' performs in our discourses. Assistive technology, if not renamed, permits ongoing unexamined design intentions to 'assist' users to conform to the normate without interrogating the causes of ableism in the first place. It permits the ongoing epistemic oppression that is already taking place in disability-related technology research (Ymous et al., 2020). Meryl Alper (2015, p. 3) encourages us to "listen more closely to the economic, social, and cultural logics that whisper through" the forms of assistive technology. With this renaming to ableist technology, these logics are not whispered but amplified. This renaming will likely feel uncomfortable; use the discomfort as a way to examine your basis for the marshalling of this term.

6 Conclusion

The term AT is misleading. I have explored why this is so. The term is typically presented as if it can be defined as a 'natural kind' of technological artefact via its defining property of 'assisting'. But this is not the case since the term connects to sociotechnical imaginaries. Naming techno-ableism in AT underscores crucial distinctions: there are technological processes that do harm through the perpetuation of ableist norms and practices under the guise of 'assisting'. We need to think critically about how to dismantle these norms through principles of disability justice and design justice.

Through the lens of higher education and the computing curriculum, I explored how AT is mobilised in the core curriculum guide for computing. This revealed a framing that belies a problematic engagement with digital technology's role in disability by the most important and influential bodies in the baccalaureate disciplines that are related to computing: the ACM and IEEE-CS. This framing impacts university students who are presently receiving their education in the computing disciplines. They are the future of tech design and application; as it stands, that future is as ableist as the present.

The call for renaming AT needs to be attentive to repair activity. As much as it is conventional for an argument to serve as a call to action, it is important to mark a time and place for listening too. What must be repaired is not only the relationship between referring expression and referent, but also relationships among those active in AT discourses. And this repair is nuanced: this is not a repair of human relations that once existed and are now fractured; this is a repair of systems for teaching, doing, and thinking that are made inaccessible by underlying normate templates. Repair needs to be accomplished through new relationships and new solidarities.

Acknowledgements I would like to express my sincere gratitude to the reviewers for their constructive feedback, which significantly improved the quality of this chapter. I am very thankful to my colleague Alice MacLachlan, who taught me about Spelman's work on the philosophy of repair. This work was supported by the 'Accessible Making for Assistive Technology' NSERC Discovery Grant (2018–2025).

References

Accreditation Board for Engineering and Technology (ABET). (2023). *Criteria for accrediting engineering programs, 2024–2025.* ABET. https://www.abet.org/wp-content/uploads/2023/05/2024-2025_EAC_Criteria.pdf

Akrich, M. (1994). The des-scription of technical objects. In W. E. Bijker & J. Law (Eds.), *Shaping technology / building society: Studies in sociotechnical change* (pp. 205–224). MIT Press.

Alper, M. (2015). Augmentative, alternative, and assistive: Reimagining the history of mobile computing and disability. *IEEE Annals of the History of Computing, 37*(1), 96–96. https://doi.org/10.1109/MAHC.2015.3

Arthur, W. B. (2009). *The nature of technology: What it is and how it evolves.* Free Press.

Bird, A., & Tobin, E. (2024). Natural kinds. In E. N. Zalta & U. Nodelman (Eds.), *The Stanford encyclopedia of philosophy.* Metaphysics Research Lab, Stanford University. https://plato.stanford.edu/archives/spr2024/entries/natural-kinds/

CC2020 Task Force. (2020). *Computing curricula 2020: Paradigms for global computing education.* Association for Computing Machinery (ACM), Institute of Electrical and Electronics Engineers-Computer Society (IEEE-CS). https://doi.org/10.1145/3467967

Clark, H. H. (1996). *Using language.* Cambridge University Press.

Coombes, E., Wolf, A., Blunt, D., & Sparks, K. (2022). Disabled sex workers' fight for digital rights, platform accessibility, and design justice. *Disability Studies Quarterly, 42*(2). https://doi.org/10.18061/dsq.v42i2.9097

Costanza-Chock, S. (2020). *Design justice: Community-led practices to build the worlds we need.* MIT Press.

Dokumacı, A. (2023). *Activist affordances: How disabled people improvise more habitable worlds.* Duke University Press.

Fuzesi, P. (2019). *Enabling access: Designing with and for dis/abled people in-between markets* [Doctoral dissertation, Lancaster University]. https://doi.org/10.17635/lancaster/thesis/787.

Garland-Thomson, R. (2011). Misfits: A feminist materialist disability concept. *Hypatia, 26*(3), 591–609. https://doi.org/10.1111/j.1527-2001.2011.01206.x

Goodley, D., Lawthom, R., Liddiard, K., & Runswick-Cole, K. (2021). Key concerns for critical disability studies. *International Journal of Disability and Social Justice, 1*(1), 27–49. https://doi.org/10.13169/intljofdissocjus.1.1.0027

Grue, J. (2015). *Disability and discourse analysis.* Ashgate.

Hamraie, A. (2012). Universal design research as a new materialist practice. *Disability Studies Quarterly, 32*(4), np. https://doi.org/10.18061/dsq.v32i4.3246

Hamraie, A., & Fritsch, K. (2019). Crip technoscience manifesto. *Catalyst: Feminism, Theory, Technoscience, 5*(1), 1–33. https://doi.org/10.28968/cftt.v5i1.29607

Harding, S. G. (1987). Is there a feminist method? In S. G. Harding (Ed.), *Feminism and methodology: Social science issues* (pp. 1–14). Indiana University Press; Open University Press.

Harrison, S., Sengers, P., & Tatar, D. (2011). Making epistemological trouble: Third-paradigm HCI as successor science. *Interacting with Computers, 23*(5), 385–392. https://doi.org/10.1016/j.intcom.2011.03.005

Hendren, S. (2018). All technology is assistive: Six design rules on disability. In J. Sayers (Ed.), *Making things and drawing boundaries: Experiments in the digital humanities* (pp. 139–146). University of Minnesota Press.

Hendren, S. (2020). *What can a body do? How we meet the built world.* Riverhead Books.

Ignatow, G. (2003). "Idea hamsters" on the "bleeding edge": Profane metaphors in high technology jargon. *Poetics, 31*(1), 1–22. https://doi.org/10.1016/S0304-422X(02)00042-6

Jackson, L., Haagaard, A., & Williams, R. (2022, April 19). *Disability dongle.* Platypus: The CASTAC Blog. https://blog.castac.org/2022/04/disability-dongle/

Jasanoff, S. (2015). Future imperfect: Science, technology, and the imaginations of modernity. In S. Jasanoff & S.-H. Kim (Eds.), *Dreamscapes of modernity: Sociotechnical imaginaries and the fabrication of power* (pp. 1–36). University of Chicago Press.

Kafer, A. (2013). *Feminist, queer, crip.* Indiana University Press.

Kumar, A. N., Raj, R. K., Aly, S. G., Anderson, M. D., Becker, B. A., Blumenthal, R. L., Eaton, E., Epstein, S. L., Goldweber, M., Jalote, P., Lea, D., Oudshoorn, M., Pias, M., Reiser, S., Servin, C., Simha, R., Winters, T., & Xiang, Q. (2023). *Computer science curricula 2023.* ACM Press, IEEE Computer Society Press and AAAI Press. https://doi.org/10.1145/3664191

Ladner, R. E., Ludi, S., & Domanski, R. J. (2023). *Teaching about accessibility in computer science education.* Article solicited by the ACM/IEEE-CS Joint Task Force on Computing Curricula, 2023. https://csed.acm.org/teaching-about-accessibility-in-computer-science-education/

Martin, A., Myers, N., & Viseu, A. (2015). The politics of care in technoscience. *Social Studies of Science, 45*(5), 625–641. https://doi.org/10.1177/0306312715602073

Mills, M. (2010). Deaf jam: From inscription to reproduction to information. *Social Text, 28*(1), 35–58. https://doi.org/10.1215/01642472-2009-059

Nagy, P., & Neff, G. (2024). Conjuring algorithms: Understanding the tech industry as stage magicians. *New Media & Society, 26*(9), 4938–4954. https://doi.org/10.1177/14614448241251789

Oliver, M. (1990). *The politics of disablement.* Palgrave Macmillan.
Roulstone, A. (2016). *Disability and technology: An interdisciplinary and international approach.* Palgrave Macmillan.
Shew, A. (2023). *Against technoableism: Rethinking who needs improvement.* W. W. Norton.
Sins Invalid (Ed.). (2019). *Skin, tooth, and bone: The basis of movement is our people: A disability justice primer* (2nd ed.). Sins Invalid.
Spelman, E. V. (2002). *Repair: The impulse to restore in a fragile world.* Beacon Press.
Technology-Related Assistance for Individuals with Disabilities Act of 1988 (Public Law 100-407). (1988). Congress.gov. https://www.congress.gov/100/statute/STATUTE-102/STATUTE-102-Pg1044.pdf
Woodhouse, E. (2013). *The future of technological civilization* (August 2013 Revised Ed.). Academia.edu. https://www.academia.edu/2910120/The_Future_of_Technological_Civilization
Wyatt, S. (2021). Metaphors in critical Internet and digital media studies. *New Media & Society, 23*(2), 406–416. https://doi.org/10.1177/1461444820929324
Ymous, A., Spiel, K., Keyes, O., Williams, R. M., Good, J., Hornecker, E., & Bennett, C. L. (2020). "I am just terrified of my future": Epistemic violence in disability related technology research. *Extended Abstracts of the 2020 CHI Conference on Human Factors in Computing Systems*, 1–16. https://doi.org/10.1145/3334480.3381828

CHAPTER 3

AIEEE!*

~~Learning Management System~~

Kate Maddalena

1 Introduction

If you teach at a university, you likely use a learning management system (LMS) such as Moodle, Canvas, or Blackboard (now Anthology) to keep your course materials online. Sometime around 2005, your employer invested in one of these platforms and integrated the software into the school's information technology and staffing infrastructure. You came to understand (or were forced to accept) that all university teaching was to become at least partially online teaching, and you went to a workshop that introduced you to the product your university had chosen. You uploaded your syllabus, made your first modular course schedule, linked up your course readings, and never looked back. Or, you held out until the 2020 global pandemic forced most university teaching and learning online, and you finally adopted the LMS. By now, preparing your course Moodle (or

K. Maddalena (✉)
Institute of Communication, Culture, Information and Technology, University of Toronto Mississauga, Mississauga, ON, Canada
e-mail: kate.maddalena@utoronto.ca

C. Chokshi, R. Mansell (eds.), *The Need to Rename Tech*,
https://doi.org/10.1007/978-3-032-05155-4_3

Canvas or Blackboard) page is unquestionably a normal and normative part of preparing for the next term.

If you are a university student in an increasing number of countries, you are so accustomed to these kinds of platforms that they are likely almost invisible to you. They are an unremarkable part of your learning and teaching experience. You may not even be aware that the generation before you had nothing like these portals that contain all of your course materials. If you are the parent of a university student in the United States (US) or Canada, you may have helped your child access their course materials online in high school. Now that they are in university, you may have hovered over your grown child's shoulder and said, 'when I was in school, we had to go to the Course Reserves section in the actual, physical library and make copies of articles so we could read them'. 'What's a Course Reserves section?' they might have asked, eyebrows pinched with scepticism. Course Reserves sections have been rendered nearly obsolete by LMS technologies.

Learning management systems, also known as course management systems (CMS) or learning platforms, are increasingly ubiquitous on university campuses, especially in Canada and the US, and they are widely touted by students, administrators, and teachers alike. They are expected to improve course accessibility for students, decrease repetitive labour for teachers, and allow for more standardised course management across large institutions, among other benefits. Though I acknowledge the convenience of LMS and the fact that their integration into higher education seems practically irreversible, the purpose of this chapter is to catalogue and critique their far-reaching and insidious utility as technologies of late capitalist oppression. LMS products are tools of surveillance capitalism that have introduced automated culture into higher education, enabling institutions to sell 'education' in bulk while reducing the presence of living, embodied teachers and students. I focus in this chapter on LMS affordances for surveillance and value extraction. I also explore secondary effects, such as deleterious environmental impacts and the de facto erasure of teaching and learning work—the very activities that LMS purport to facilitate.

I rename the CMS based on its oppressive affordances rather than its liberatory ones. We often think of Canvas, Blackboard, or Moodle as tools to be marketed for what we can do and make with them, but I want to write about what is done to us by these technologies and what they make us into. By 'us', I mean course instructors, students, and the classroom social space itself. Learning platform technology is lauded for its accessibility, which I concede, but it also enables harmful value extraction across time and space as well as totalising surveillance (of students by teachers, and of teachers by administrators). Under the ennobling guise of education, LMS technology renders human beings into capital for the university and the larger market. For that reason, instead of calling learning platforms LMS or CMS, I propose we call them AIEEE!: Accessible Insidious Extractive Everywhere Education.

AIEEE! (the exclamation point is part of the branding) evokes a cartoonish scream. Its cultural touchstone is the classic newspaper comic, *Calvin and Hobbes*, by Bill Watterson. During the boring days of summer, Calvin and his very real tiger friend, Hobbes, pass the time by riding a little red wagon down a hill. They board the wagon voluntarily, but are never able to keep control of it during the descent, screaming 'AIEEEE!' (Watterson, 1990) as they ride over cliffs, rocks, and streams. At the bottom of the hill, bruised and dusty, the friends ask each other why they got on the wagon in the first place. Then they climb the hill and do it again. It is a simplistic Sisyphean metaphor for technological determinism.

Universities in the US got on the AIEEE! (band)wagon in the early 2000s. The move made massive and fast philosophical and material changes to universities and in university pedagogy. It is worth noting that AIEEE! has produced its own interdisciplinary community of discourse—across the fields of education and writing studies, especially—that, in turn, has produced copious scholarship. Scholarship on AIEEE! and related software began with the advent of computer-assisted distance education, and it now comprises more than 30 years of research. Research in this field works to quantify and qualify the effects and efficacy of online education practices (Anderson, 2008; Blair, 2016; Blair & Monske, 2003; Means et al., 2010; Sherry, 1995) and evaluate student perceptions of online learning spaces (Fedynich et al., 2015; Williams et al., 2023;). It also documents AIEEE! affordances for innovative pedagogy (Anglesey, 2021; Schullo et al., 2003; Topacio, 2018) and strives to inform the design of courses hosted on AIEEE! to establish best practices (Crawley, 2021; Engvig, 2006; Gillam & Wooden, 2013; Ioannou & Hannafin, 2006; Kuhn, 2003).

The emergence of online education discourse as AIEEE! tools were developed and deployed illustrates a Foucauldian maxim: "[t]here is no power relation without the correlative constitution of a field of knowledge, nor any knowledge that does not presuppose and constitute at the same time power relations" (Foucault, 1977, p. 27). In this case, the new object of knowledge—online learning tools—produced its own academic discourse. But even more importantly, and although much of the scholarship listed above included critique, this discourse could never truly stand at a critical distance from its object of study; it presupposed a change that it worked to bring about. The study of online and digital forms of pedagogy has produced new teaching positions, working groups, and teaching and learning centres; it redirected budget lines, built new buildings, and most certainly made more machines to produce more online education. These discourses and spaces have become nodes of connection between the university and the corporate world, as the online journals, comment threads, and social media groups where the critical conversation occurred, both mirrored and connected directly to the corporate emergence of platform-based media markets. AIEEE! are proprietary goods developed for and sold to universities. Canvas, Blackboard, and Moodle are products of the corporate world.

2 Accessibility

One area of focus in the aforementioned autopoietic scholarship on AIEEE! is the learning platform's affordances for accessibility, and here is where I put my most careful qualification. AIEEE! are useful tools for making the geographically, biologically, economically, and socio-culturally delimited terrain of the university more accessible to people for whom barriers to education, often multiple intersecting ones, exist. My argument in this chapter is a polemical one, but here is my caveat: though the driving market force of digital education platforms may be corporate, capitalist, and inhumane, the spirit and value system of digital education discourse is not. Moreover, the COVID-19 pandemic has forced able-bodied and socio-economically privileged folks working in universities into an ad hoc disabled positionality. We have become, I hope, more-than-just-theoretically aware of pedagogy that centres accessibility. AIEEE! allow for accessible course design in multiple ways. They facilitate multimodal content, transcription, real-time closed-captioning of sound content, text chat functions for student backchannels, and remote access to course content or the classroom itself. They also afford temporal flexibility such as asynchronous engagement with the course and disembodied visibility via avatars that allow for a person to not be directly or primarily identified with their physical attributes. Finally, by capturing student–teacher interactions, they can serve as a mechanism for instructor accountability, a medium that requires self-reflective teaching. This list goes on and on. All of these affordances, when well-deployed, can allow for students and teachers to engage in an environment that is safer and more equitable for all human body-minds than the physical classroom—a box of human bodies at one point in geographical space and time—often is.

3 Insidiousness

Each of these access-promoting affordances, you may notice, also enables surveillance and data capture. Accessibility, unfortunately, is the Trojan horse of the AIEEE! apparatus. Accessibility as moral imperative provides these technologies their ethical cover; their extractive instrumentality is lying in wait, a part of their design. I take the term 'insidious' from Lisa Lane (2009, para. 3), who writes that CMS have "an inherent purpose implied in their design, and therefore a built-in pedagogy" that dates from the nineteenth century and privileges presentation and assessment over more active learning through participation and risk-taking. Insidiousness also comes in the form of the teleology I describe above: the assumption that the digital ship has sailed. An alternative 'A' for my acronym might be 'Already'; the assumption of already-ness is part of the technology's insidiousness.

4 Extraction

Teaching is part of most professors' workloads, and contemporary teaching in many universities requires working with AIEEE! Today, a professor is expected to design a website inside AIEEE! for every single course they teach. The Canvas page for a well-designed course is a lot like a textbook. It involves copious writing, the curation of readings and content, and editorial responsibility for permissions to that content—all labour associated with producing a pedagogical text. Student labour is also captured and preserved in an AIEEE!, producing data with potential to be mined and used for the platform's or the university's financial benefit. Jodi Dean's (2005) concept of 'communicative capitalism' articulates the relationship between online interpersonal communication and the passive labour of data production which produces value without remuneration to the labourer (here the student and teacher) as capital for a third party (in this case, the university and the corporations that own and maintain the AIEEE!).

Catherine D'Ignazio and Lauren F. Klein (2020) offer seven tenets of data feminism to articulate an ethos for feminist data hygiene and practice. The fourth tenet challenges binaries and hierarchies to make labour visible, and helps point to what cannot be seen or measured in an AIEEE!-centred learning apparatus. With reference to the work of Joni Seager, the authors ask what 'counts' and remind us that 'what gets counted counts'. D'Ignazio and Klein use non-binary gender as an example of a human experience that is not captured by discrete systems such as binary gender menu options. D'Ignazio and Klein's seventh tenet, 'show your work', refers to the feminist commitment to making invisible (digital) labour visible. AIEEE! shell design counts only as teaching in many academics' promotion and review processes, so they cannot, as the tenets of *Data Feminism* would require, 'show [their] work' in a way that is legible across a discipline in the way that a textbook might be. The labour involved in building an AIEEE! course page does not 'count' in most United States or Canadian universities in any meaningful way for the teacher who spends hours designing it.

The individual teacher's AIEEE! work does count, and returns dividends, for the university itself—the institution that, in most of North America, owns the teacher's work. Once a teacher has designed an AIEEE!, especially one that includes video, audio, and transcription elements (all best practices in terms of accessibility) that duplicate the instructor herself, the seating capacity of the course is greatly expanded. Large-format, AIEEE!-enabled courses, because they allow for larger classes with the same instructor, generate more tuition revenue for the institution and reduce human labour costs. Such courses usually depend on the lower-paid, precarious labour of sessional hires and grad students to manage any human-to-human interface, turning the professor of record into a managerial position, a boss to labourers under them.

One extreme example of this kind of labour-to-value extraction is the now-famous story of a deceased professor at Concordia University in Montreal, Québec, who 'taught' an Art History course during the COVID-19 pandemic. In fact, François-Marc Gagnon's lectures were used as a course tool, like a textbook, and the (online, asynchronous) course was managed by a different instructor and two teaching assistants. Tamara Kneese (2021), in a story for *Slate*, points out several reasons why those concerned with academic work conditions should pay attention to this very literal example of Marx's capital as dead labour. She describes Purdue University's move to define their relationship to their faculty's intellectual property such that the institution owned the rights to AIEEE! courses. Far beyond the simple sharing of a syllabus, a proprietary AIEEE! could ostensibly fill the role of the teacher-as-expert, with lower-paid, precariously employed labourers to manage tutorials and grading logistics. With the advent of artificial intelligence (AI), human labour could be disposed of altogether. Robert Ovetz (2021, p. 1066) describes the digital apparatus that would allow a dead man to teach as a "new technical composition of academic capital", one that deskills academic workers and gradually converts higher education to a modular, gig-worker economy.

Higher education's dependence on AIEEE! also works to extract data, which is arguably a currency itself (Hogan, 2021), from students and teachers alike. Data has value, of course, because it can be used to predict and control behaviour in order to produce even more value. In an educational context, data extracted from AIEEE! courses could be used to mine problem sets for the hardest problems in order to market new, automated tutorial products to schools and to students, or to train automated writing software to assist students writing prose. Such assistive software is a product that student and teacher labour have trained, but for which the student must also pay, after their labour is parlayed into new value. AIEEE! as a conduit to other media (documents, cloud-based applications, etc.) also make it a gateway to seamless AI integration and a source of data for AI training. As of 2022, AI was already being trained to design learning platform shells (Thongprasit & Wannapiroon, 2022). Aieeee! This last exclamation is not the acronym; it is me screaming.

Finally, AIEEE! require hardware to function, and the material resource requirements of twenty-first-century university servers are enormous. "The digital era," writes Mél Hogan (2021, p. 5), "is founded on data saturation," and so is education in the digital era. Hogan's work focuses on data production and maintenance in data centres as both an ecologically extractive practice and one that reconstitutes environments, from the draining of aquifers to the physical presence of data machines in buildings once devoted to human thriving. Data saturation requires infrastructure: non-renewable resources from the earth and the re-constitution of environments for the sake of data production and circulation.

5 Everywhere!

The final 'E' in my acronym stands for 'everywhere'. AIEEE! grants the classroom presence in any space (as long as the student has a mobile device and Wi-Fi), and it makes the teacher omnipresent in the digital classroom space. Everywhere-ness entails both the ability for teachers to surveil students and the implicitly mandatory submission to such surveillance as a natural function of pedagogy. A great deal of critical work on learning platforms supports the description of AIEEE! as spaces defined primarily by surveillance (Adams, 2010; Beetham et al., 2022; Kumar et al., 2019). This description makes them an extension of the already surveilled classroom space, with an even more frictionless interface because the AIEEE! space lacks bodies. In that space, students become, quite literally, their data (Kumar et al., 2019). The totalised surveillance of the digital classroom space prepares students to be equally submissive, docile-bodied contributors to circuits of power beyond the university (Packer et al., 2023). According to Ovetz (2021, p. 1069), "these technologies are designed to [transform] the assessment of comprehension of content knowledge [into] measurement of proficiency in task completion. The objective of these changes is to generate more productive self-disciplined students as labor power to meet the growing demand for precarious … work". The digital transformation of the university ostensibly meets the needs of a digitally transformed world.

In every way that the student becomes datafied and subject to surveillance, the teacher who works in an AIEEE! environment is also surveilled. The pedagogical tendency in such mediations is towards quantifiable and standardised measures of student engagement and learning. If I wonder if my student has been engaging with course materials, for example, I can look at the time they have spent logged on to the module (a measure that ignores any time spent with printed or otherwise unconnected materials). In place of verbal explanation and real-time (re)iteration of instructions, concepts, or other course content, the content on the AIEEE! becomes a definitive or 'master' rendition of the same and so begins to subtly discourage variation, questioning, and testing of the edges. In the same vein, students are aware that only work that fits within the framework of AIEEE! can 'count', and so are subtly discouraged from exploring, working, and discussing outside it. AIEEE!'s reliance on text-based, time-stamped communication in asynchronous discussion boards, for example, privileges mediated over embodied communication forms, and presumes the capture that the digital format affords; what is 'said' in a course discussion will persist and may be referenced later. The environment of surveillance forecloses the ephemerality of a risk taken in real-time conversation. If hate speech or harassment happens in the AIEEE!, it is pre-witnessed by the platform (i.e., recorded and time-stamped). The platform sanitises the teaching and learning space and profoundly transforms that space's possibility and politics.

Sarah Sharma's (2013) 'critical time' sees time as an axis on which political power is unevenly distributed. My use of the word 'everywhere' in the AIEEE! acronym is meant to imply a temporal and spatial ubiquity all of the time. The everywhere of highly mobile digital media operates on what Sharma (2013) might call, following communication historian Harold Innis, a spatial bias to manipulate time. By being everywhere in space, AIEEE! transform student and teacher temporality. In both cases, temporal manipulation attenuates energy and attention as it extends time for work. The everywhere of school/work imposes a sense of obligation: because I always could be doing work, I probably should be doing work. At the same time, ubiquity allows for postponement; because I always could be doing work, I can always do work later. The flexibility of asynchronicity becomes uneasy avoidance and constant deferral. Extension requests proliferate. Assignments languish unmarked. And when assignments are completed, they often remain in the digital space. Completion, as Ovetz (2021) observes, supersedes comprehension for both the student creating the work and the student apprehending it. The AIEEE! waits, a receptacle for the input of assignment and grade data.

Teacher and student also wait, uneasily negotiating the mediated manipulation of time. They are "tied together in time" (Sharma, 2013, p. 314) and separated by space, isolated and datafied. Part of this negotiation, it seems, is the perpetual question of who will exploit whom; because the AIEEE! is so temporally flexible, students can easily prevail upon a flexible teacher's mercy. But because the AIEEE! is so precise and surveillance-ready, inflexible teachers can police time much more easily. In either scenario, one person will have their temporal reality bent by the other. "The problem of difference and inequity is run through time … bodies are differently valued temporally and made productive for capital" (Sharma, 2013, p. 317). Recuperation or transformation from this mode in higher education will require a recognition of and reckoning with time as an axis of political power.

6 Can We Get Off This Runaway Wagon?

How realistic is an organised, intentional refusal or repurposing of AIEEE! technologies' extractive and everywhere affordances? Some scholars of teaching and learning are committed to concerted action. Ovetz (2021) proposes that students and increasingly precarious teachers should find class solidarity as the unpaid and underpaid producers of capital for the university. He sees faculty governance as an untapped source of power and calls for curricular refusal of online education as well as grade strikes. Ovetz's proposal is an ambitious one, but it has exciting implications for a transformation of the university into a site of resistance to the status quo, a role it has conceded to financially driven conservatism in the past half-century. Helen Beetham, Amy Collier, Laura Czerniewicz, Brian Lamb, Yuwei Lin, Jen Ross, Anne-Marie Scott, and Anna Wilson (2022) are part of an international working group that aims to observe and resist datafication and surveillance in higher education. Members of the working group, Amy Collier and Jen Ross, propose to imagine what post-secondary education looks like 'after surveillance', which requires "a willingness to speculate that some of the surveillance roles we have come to accept could be otherwise, along with an acknowledgment that we are implicated in [surveillance culture] in education. What can we do with that knowledge, and what culture shifts can we collectively provoke?" (Collier & Ross, 2020, p. 277). These perspectives demonstrate a growing will to refuse to climb the hill and jump back in the AIEEE! wagon, and to imagine a future that is more deliberate.

The important thing to remember when designing 'otherwise' is that there is one ethical value in the digital telos that is worth retaining: accessibility. I can imagine a dystopian future in which financially inaccessible boutique universities promise a nostalgic return to pre-digital pedagogies—small seminars, face-to-face classes—for the ultra-wealthy. The brochures are paper, a nostalgic novelty, and include photos of dark wood and vaulted, granite archways. Those with more modest means are educated in à-la-carte online modules that can be sold to thousands at a time. At the other end of a polarised spectrum of access, I can imagine a widespread refusal of higher education altogether, a turn that would render intellectual life inaccessible for the disenfranchised: a life of labour with no need for a life of the mind. Access will be, yet again, stratified for disabled folks. If you are differently abled and wealthy, I imagine, you may have access to an excellent online education; if you are not wealthy, you may have access to a poor online education, or none. I desperately hope that higher education can see itself through this moment to a wholesale transformation, one that might help to engender other ways of being for mainstream education and beyond, for everyone.

References

Adams, C. (2010). Learning management systems as sites of surveillance, control, and corporatization: A review of the critical literature. In D. Gibson & B. Dodge (Eds.), *Proceedings of SITE 2010 – Society for Information Technology & Teacher Education International Conference* (pp. 252–257). Association for the Advancement of Computing in Education (AACE).

Anderson, T. (Ed.). (2008). *The theory and practice of online learning* (2nd ed.). Athabasca University Press.

Anglesey, L. R. (2021). Social justice in an online classroom: A place-based approach to belonging. *Prompt: A Journal of Academic Writing Assignments, 5*(1), 34–41. https://doi.org/10.31719/pjaw.v5i1.73

Beetham, H., Collier, A., Czerniewicz, L., Lamb, B., Lin, Y., Ross, J., Scott, A.-M., & Wilson, A. (2022). Surveillance practices, risks and responses in the post pandemic university. *Digital Culture and Education, 14*(1) https://static1.squarespace.com/static/5cf15af7a259990001706378/t/61f83d6ce0107614753f858f/1643658607549/Beetham_etal_2022.pdf

Blair, K. L., & Monske, E. A. (2003). Cui bono? Revisiting the promises and perils of online learning. *Computers and Composition, 20*(4), 441–453. https://doi.org/10.1016/j.compcom.2003.08.016

Blair, K. L. (2016). MOOC mania? Bridging the gap between the rhetoric and reality of online learning. In D. Ruefman & A. G. Scheg (Eds.), *Applied pedagogies: Strategies for online writing instruction* (pp. 167–179). Utah State University Press.

Collier, A., & Ross, J. (2020). Higher education after surveillance? *Postdigital Science and Education, 2*(2), 275–279. https://doi.org/10.1007/s42438-019-00098-z

Crawley, K. L. (2021). Online writing instructors as strategic caddies: Reading digital landscapes and selecting online learning tools. In J. Borgman & C. McArdle (Eds.), *PARS in practice: More resources and strategies for online writing instructors* (pp. 19–29). WAC Clearinghouse.

Dean, J. (2005). Communicative capitalism: Circulation and the foreclosure of politics. *Cultural Politics, 1*(1), 51–74. https://doi.org/10.2752/174321905778054845

D'Ignazio, C., & Klein, L. F. (2020). *Data feminism.* MIT Press.

Engvig, M. (2006). *Online learning: All you need to know to facilitate and administer online courses.* Hampton Press.

Fedynich, L., Bradley, K. S., & Bradley, J. (2015). Graduate students' perceptions of online learning. *Research in Higher Education Journal, 27*. https://eric.ed.gov/?id=EJ1056187

Foucault, M. (1977). *Discipline & punish*. Random House Digital, Inc.

Gillam, K., & Wooden, S. R. (2013). Re-embodying online composition: Ecologies of writing in unreal time and space. *Computers and Composition, 30*(1), 24–36. https://doi.org/10.1016/j.compcom.2012.11.001

Hogan, M. (2021). The data center industrial complex. In M. Jue & R. Ruiz (Eds.), *Saturation: An elemental politics*. Duke University Press.

Ioannou, A., & Hannafin, R. (2006). Improving web-based learning by using improved and well designed course management systems. In *Proceedings of SITE 2006—Society for Information Technology & Teacher Education International Conference, 2005*(1), 3444–3449. https://www.learntechlib.org/p/22625/

Kneese, T. (2021, January 27). How a dead professor is teaching a university art history class. Slate. https://slate.com/technology/2021/01/dead-professor-teaching-online-class.html

Kuhn, V. (2003). A review of *Virtual education, real educators: Issues in online learning* [by B. Froese-Germain]. *Kairos: A Journal of Rhetoric, Technology, and Pedagogy, 8*(2). https://kairos.technorhetoric.net/8.2/binder.html?reviews/kuhn/index.htm

Kumar, P. C., Vitak, J., Chetty, M., & Clegg, T. L. (2019). The platformization of the classroom: Teachers as surveillant consumers. *Surveillance & Society, 17*(1/2), 145–152. https://doi.org/10.24908/ss.v17i1/2.12926

Lane, L. M. (2009). Insidious pedagogy: How course management systems affect teaching. *First Monday, 14*(10). https://doi.org/10.5210/fm.v14i10.2530

Means, B., Toyama, Y, Murphy, R., Bakia, M., & Jones, K. (2010). *Evaluation of evidence-based practices in online learning: A meta-analysis and review of online learning studies*. United States Department of Education, Office of Planning, Evaluation, and Policy Development. https://www.ed.gov/sites/ed/files/rschstat/eval/tech/evidence-based-practices/finalreport.pdf

Ovetz, R. (2021). The algorithmic university: On-line education, learning management systems, and the struggle over academic labor. *Critical Sociology, 47*(7–8), 1065–1084. https://doi.org/10.1177/0896920520948931

Packer, J., Nuñez de Villavicencio, P., Oswald, K., Monea, A., Maddalena, K., & Reeves, J. (2023). The prison house of the circuit: Politics of control from analog to digital. University of Minnesota Press.

Schullo, S., Siekmann, S., & Szydlo, S. (2003). Synchronous distance education systems, choosing the right solution?. In *Proceedings of E-Learn 2003--World Conference on E-Learning in Corporate, Government, Healthcare, and Higher Education*, 2003(1), 2421–2428. Association for the Advancement of

Computing in Education (AACE). https://www.learntechlib.org/primary/j/ELEARN/v/2003/n/1/
Sharma, S. (2013). Critical time. *Communication and Critical/Cultural Studies, 10*(2–3), 312–318. https://doi.org/10.1080/14791420.2013.812600
Sherry, L. (1995). Issues in distance learning. *International Journal of Educational Telecommunications, 1*(4), 337–365. https://www.learntechlib.org/primary/p/8937/
Thongprasit, J., & Wannapiroon, P. (2022). Framework of artificial intelligence learning platform for education. *International Education Studies, 15*(1), 76–86. https://doi.org/10.5539/ies.v15n1p76
Topacio, K. N. M. (2018). Exploring the use of online educational platforms in teaching writing among ESL students. *Journal of Language and Linguistic Studies, 14*(1), 86–101. https://www.jlls.org/index.php/jlls/article/view/549/346
Watterson, B. (1990, August 10). *Calvin and Hobbes* [comic strip]. https://www.gocomics.com/calvinandhobbes/1990/08/10
Williams, T. L., Walker, E., Ludlum, M., Edwards, M., & Gregory, K. (2023). Online learning during the Covid crisis: Student views. *Journal of Higher Education Theory and Practice, 23*(2). https://doi.org/10.33423/jhetp.v23i2.5818

CHAPTER 4

HealthcAIre*

~~Healthcare~~

Arun Jacob and Christina Boyles

1 Introduction

The Apple TV+ science fiction series Foundation (2021–), based on the Isaac Asimov (1951) novel of the same name, mobilises 'psychohistory', a fictional scientific concept that uses history, sociology, and statistical analysis to predict the future behaviours of large populations. The idea holds that while individual behaviour may not be predictable, the behaviour of populations might be. Asimov's literary world features powerful computers and big data sets that are able to predict everything, including the rise and fall of empires. In the real world, Asimov's vision played out when the journal *Science* dedicated a 2017 special issue to the application of predictive modelling algorithms. These were examined in contexts ranging from

A. Jacob (✉)
Faculty of Information, University of Toronto, Toronto, ON, Canada
e-mail: arun.jacob@mail.utoronto.ca

C. Boyles
Department of Library and Information Science, Indiana University Bloomington, Bloomington, IN, USA
e-mail: clboyles@iu.edu

C. Chokshi, R. Mansell (eds.), *The Need to Rename Tech*,
https://doi.org/10.1007/978-3-032-05155-4_4

armed conflict to urban fire and health inspections to optimise the use of data-driven decision-making (Athey, 2017; Jasny & Stone, 2017).

The Asimovian fictional premise came even closer to our lived experiences over the course of the COVID-19 pandemic, when we witnessed an assemblage of media techniques and technologies come together to measure and manage human capacities, predict tendencies, and control bodies in space and time using what historian and philosopher Michel Foucault (1976/1990) calls technologies of biopower. Since the onset of the pandemic, for example, many patients can be 'seen' by AI-enabled telehealth technologies that interface with clients and perform diagnostics, changing the ways in which health and human services are provided. The promise of AI's application to medicine is its life-saving potential; it increases the pace at which diagnostics can be run and conclusions can be drawn. The practical application of these tools, however, often fails to live up to this promise (Chakravorti, 2022). Like psychohistory in Asimov's Foundation narratives, real-world predictive systems prioritise population-level data over the bodily experience of individual patients. They approach digital health data as an asset to transform the operations of healthcare systems and services. Additionally, AI enables private sector health providers to bill for more patients since the tool reduces the time each patient spends interacting with medical professionals.

In contemporary capitalist society, knowledge and wisdom now reside squarely within the purview of big data, predictive data analytics, and information management. When knowledge is capital and information is a commodity, wisdom is the capacity to forecast earnings from data (Committee on Energy and Commerce, 2023; House Committee on Energy and Commerce, 2023). The big data stockpiles generated by smart systems make up the building blocks of the information economy, combining technology, commercial interests, and social operations. Just as flora convert carbon dioxide exhaled by fauna into oxygen, we think data processing plants such as Acxiom, Epsilon, and Experian convert the data exhaust made by people into information commodities, which are then traded in the market economy in pursuit of profit and power.

Digital health informatics companies are no exception. They are shaping up to be, above all, data tomb raiders, amassing medical information and health data to accrue wealth and morph into computational powerhouses as public health services deteriorate (Committee on Energy and Commerce, 2023). And, they are doing so in an environment where AI is largely unregulated in many countries. For these reasons, we propose renaming healthcare as *healthcAIre*, a rhetorical move that highlights how our health needs are increasingly being addressed by disembodied actors whose large data sets are programmed in opaque and problematic ways. Extending Anne Balsamo's (1995, p. 57) argument that medical imaging technologies do not simply produce images of the body, but rather they "transform the material body into a visual medium", we see these technologies as media that determine how the material body is perceived and how in the process the body becomes a medium to render, collect, and procure data from. Operating within the same Western logics that enable police brutality and instrumental reason, the development of healthcAIre technologies in the wake of COVID-19 is a form of what Naomi Klein (2008) terms 'disaster capitalism', under which healthcare providers can justify the implementation of a far-reaching health surveillance system while patients are being stripped of their access to social safety nets and as global conglomerates seize the means of health data production (Lorinc, 2022; Robertson & Hannay, 2024). As Klein observes in *The Shock Doctrine* (2008, p. 168), "In moments of crisis, people are willing to hand over a great deal of power to anyone who claims to have a magic cure".

2 HealthcAIre Tech

To think through the kind of data-based technologies that might be considered healthcAIre tech, it is helpful to trace the types of telehealth technologies, including pharmacy management software systems and electronic medical and health record-keeping systems, that have been brought together through numerous corporate mergers and acquisitions. Consider a Canadian example: Loblaw Companies Ltd.'s purchase of the pharmacy group Shoppers Drug Mart Corporation for USD 12.4 billion in 2014, the electronics medical records firm QHR Corporation for CAD 170 million in 2016, and the Lifemark Health Group for CAD 845 million in 2022, plus its investment of CAD 75 million in the virtual healthcare provider Maple highlight how the company is piecing corporate entities together into a digital health platform that is actively reshaping how public healthcare services are provided in Canada (Robertson & Hannay, 2024). Loblaw's digital health infrastructure stack optimises and leverages its distribution network of pharmacies located throughout the country, along with AccuroEMR, its electronic health records software, and Medeo, the telemedicine virtual care software that it acquired from QHR technologies. The company has also inked partnership agreements with Canada

Health Infoway, the federal digital health solutions provider, to adopt the national e-prescription platform PrescribeIT, while retaining its in-house digital prescription and messaging software, FreedomRX.

The health software services that Loblaw has acquired and developed over the years have accelerated the adoption of telemedicine services across multiple public and private health provider networks, laying the groundwork for widespread virtual appointment and consultation services. Health Clinic by Shoppers Drug Mart, a primary-care and family practice clinic that yokes together Loblaw's entire digital health services infrastructure, is currently being piloted at select locations in the Greater Toronto Area. These private health clinics leverage the company's suite of technology-enabled and virtual care services to offer a much more convenient service through which people can access a new tier of healthcare services. The stay-at-home mandates of the COVID-19 pandemic, in particular, have made virtual walk-in clinics a palatable option compared to in-person primary care services.

TELUS Health is another Canadian corporation reshaping healthcare practices through its various buyouts, mergers, acquisitions, and partnerships. With the purchase of Emergis Inc. in 2007 for CAD 763 million, TELUS entered Canada's health claims processing and pharmacy management systems market. TELUS Health Solutions, launched in 2008, licensed Microsoft's HealthVault platform to provide electronic record management for Canadian healthcare providers. With the acquisition of Quebec-based KinLogix and the western Canadian electronic medical records company Wolf Medical Systems in 2012, followed by Ontario's largest electronic medical records provider, PS Suite EMR, in 2013, TELUS Health emerged as a leading provider of electronic medical and health records. Agreements drawn up with Tunstall Healthcare Group in 2017 have allowed the company to offer remote monitoring and video-conferencing telehealth software solutions. TELUS Health has also invested in the United Kingdom (UK)-based digital health company Babylon Health to offer Canadians a digital healthcare app that allows them to access virtual care and health information solutions. TELUS Health's acquisition of Akira Health in 2019 further bolstered its on-demand virtual care capabilities. By leveraging its core business—selling access to its telecommunication infrastructure and data lines—TELUS Health has positioned itself strategically in the digital health services market.

However, the pivot to virtual care and telehealth consultations comes at a significant cost. As data-driven decision-making practices take centre stage in the health sector lexicon, terms such as 'precision medicine' and 'personalised medicine' also gain currency. As patients are responsibilised to use AI-driven health assessment tools to generate their own medical history, these telehealth medical consultation apps accumulate troves of information about people's material and subjective lives. As such, these corporations are able to operate without guardrails or accountability measures in place, which might include asking for patient permission to collect data, undertaking data audits, working to establish regulatory bodies, and more. Friedrich Kittler's (1999, p. xi) claim that "What remains of people is what media can store and communicate" is particularly true in the era of AI. This media determinism highlights the cultural logic underlying digital health systems. We become the data that is collected about us. HealthcAIre entities take this to an extreme, further reducing the need for human interaction and nuanced thinking in medicine.

3 Risks of AI

Nuanced thinking is, precisely, AI's weakness. While we advocate for healthcare solutions to address COVID-19 and other public health emergencies, we argue that the healthcAIre solutions currently being implemented exacerbate existing inequalities by over-relying on algorithmic solutions, which are rife with problems. Scholars such as Cathy O'Neil (2016), Virginia Eubanks (2018), and Safiya Umoja Noble (2018) demonstrate that the problems with algorithms are not inherent to the models themselves but rather stem from issues within our broader social systems. As a result, issues surrounding gender, race, and sexuality—among others—become hard coded as binary categories or weighted values. The 'binary prediction' that underlies algorithms is also present in healthcAIre. Patients are often triaged using classification systems that label them as well/unwell, urgent/non-urgent, saveable/unsavable, or acute/chronic. The problem with binary categorisation is that it fails to recognise nuance in health data (or other contexts). Codifying binaries into our healthcAIre systems risks reinscribing and reinforcing harmful practices of the past—both by reducing or ignoring individual experiences because they do not fit a statistical pattern or by invisibilising issues that need to be addressed. As Catherine D'Ignazio and Lauren Klein (2020, p. 171) argue,

> The bottom line for numbers is that they cannot speak for themselves. In fact, those of us who work with data must actively prevent numbers from

> speaking for themselves because when those numbers derive from a data setting influenced by differentials of power, or by misaligned collection incentives … and especially when the numbers have to do with human beings and their behavior, then they run the risk of not only being inherently grandiose and empirically wrong, but also of doing real harm in their reinforcement of an unjust status quo.

To outline the problem of such binary thinking, we use the term healthcAIre explicitly to highlight the risks and dangers of these tools. For example, in the United States (US), the Veterans Health Administration (VHA), the integrated healthcare system for US veterans, implemented an AI-assisted suicide risk prediction algorithm, Recovery Engagement and Coordination for Health–Veterans Enhanced Treatment (REACH VET), in 2017. REACH VET was touted as a success because it lowered the overall rate of suicide among veterans (Carey, 2020; Ravindranath, 2019). However, the algorithm's effort to lower the rate of suicides among veterans who were at high risk programmatically favoured male-identifying veterans over their female-identifying peers (Glantz, 2024). This outcome reflects many other earlier findings about the use of AI—namely that it exacerbates existing cultural biases by encoding them into far-reaching formulas (Buolamwini, 2023; Eubanks, 2018; Noble, 2018). In Sect. 4, we examine BlueDot, a Toronto-based healthcAIre start-up, to demonstrate how AI impacts the care received by marginalised populations and how healthcAIre, in particular, emulates harmful power structures by prioritising profit and investors over patient wellness.

4 BlueDot

COVID-19 was not only a pivotal moment for health informatic surveillance; it also highlighted many of the inequities in Western culture, including health inequity, police violence, workplace injustice, and discrimination. During this time, communities in Canada and the US documented an increase in racist sentiments. According to Stop Asian-American and Pacific Islander (AAPI), Hate, an organisation tracking incidents of racism during the pandemic, over 1400 incidents were reported in 2020 between March 19 and April 9 in the US (Huang, 2020).

In addition to increased hate, marginalised communities experienced higher infection rates of the disease itself. According to a study by epidemiologist Gregorio Millett and co-authors (2020, p. 37), "nearly 20% of

US counties are disproportionately black, and they accounted for 52% of COVID-19 diagnoses and 58% of COVID-19 deaths nationally". In other words, COVID-19 has exacerbated existing inequalities by prompting increased racial violence and worse health outcomes for Black, Indigenous, and people of colour (BIPOC) communities. Thomson Reuters' chief legal officer Thomas Kim (2020, para. 2) observes that "some have referred to this unbridled bias as the shadow pandemic—the racism that has raised its ugly head and spread across the country as fear and blame become the false cure for the ignorant".

The violence and injustice brought to light by the COVID-19 pandemic cannot be separated from the technological solutions used to manage it. One such tool is Toronto-based AI start-up BlueDot, which, on December 30, 2019, alerted its clients to a mysterious illness that appeared in Wuhan, China. The digital healthcare start-up flagged an unusual surge of cases of pneumonia in the Chinese city nine days before the World Health Organization reports would be released (Heaven, 2020; Niiler, 2020; Stieg, 2020; Vendeville, 2020). Dr. Kamran Khan, an infectious disease physician with training in public health and preventive medicine from the University of Toronto, built BlueDot to monitor infectious disease outbreaks around the world using machine learning. As the algorithm scours through news reports, airline ticketing data, animal and plant disease networks, and more, mining these information sources to develop actionable intelligence, it furthers the widespread reorganisation of medical knowledge in the twenty-first century. The scale, pace, and capacity for pattern recognition of BlueDot's algorithmic medical gaze accelerates the dehumanising medical separation of the patient's body from the patient's identity and exacerbates the power interests of the material and intellectual infrastructures that make the corporeal analysis possible. Hence, the algorithmic medical gaze here is capable of penetrating surface illusions and revealing hidden truths from very large non-traditional data sets, signaling an epistemological break with respect to the history of medicine.

BlueDot's software-as-a-service platform is powered by Amazon Elastic Compute Cloud (EC2), which is a part of Amazon Web Services (AWS), the cloud computing services infrastructure that undergirds the operations of the digital health services venture. Using AWS' natural language processing and machine learning systems, the BlueDot platform provides an alluring techno-solution: infectious disease modelling, outbreak detection, and pathogen data surveillance systems (AWS Events, 2020). The automated work of collating, correlating, and corroborating data is done by BlueDot's proprietary "disease surveillance analytic program" (Gomes et al., 2022, p. 58), extending the doctor's gaze of the body from a corporeal to an algorithmic domain. The differential diagnosis of the patient, namely the systems and methods used to identify possible disease entities, is deferred to the algorithm based on its capacity to determine symptoms, illness, and cause (Adam et al., 2022; Poursabzi-Sangdeh et al., 2021; Yang et al. 2023). The overconfidence in AI's capabilities for disease diagnosis creates a political climate eager to install AI as the diagnostic tool of choice, funnelling public monies from proven initiatives to these unproven technology entities (United States Government Accountability Office, 2022).

The suicide prediction statistical model implemented in REACH VET, as described above, for example, gave preference to male-identifying veterans over their female-identifying counterparts. Among the variables that were not accounted for by the algorithm were military sexual trauma and intimate partner violence—both of which are linked to a very high risk of suicide among female-identifying veterans (Glantz, 2024). Furthermore, employing healthcAIre tools can limit or eradicate the possibility of human intervention into healthcare decisions. Marzyeh Ghassemi et al. (2021), in their critique of the use of machine learning to generate health and medical recommendations, detail how human practitioners over-trust AI systems when they believe the algorithm performing the task is much more efficient, effective, accurate, and precise than they are (Ghassemi et al., 2021; Manrai & Beam, 2023; Schwartz Reisman Institute, 2021).

This also happens if there is an expectation that employing the technological solution will enable risk mitigation. In the case of BlueDot, one can witness an emergent epistemological rupture within the contemporary practitioner's medicalised gaze. Just as the question, 'What's the matter with you?' gave way to 'Where does it hurt?', the question posed by the contemporary medical practitioner is epidemiological, as evidenced by the common COVID-19 screening question: 'Have you lived in, worked or travelled from China within the past 14 days?' The question is meant to gather quantitative information about a patient's virus exposure history in order to calculate a corresponding risk assessment. Medical investigations, diagnoses, and treatments rely on software-defined criteria, exemplifying both the media determinist and epistemological shift in medical practice. Moreover, the impetus of the question is "to help minimize the negative economic impact" caused by the spread of the virus (Gilles, 2018, para. 5). With the use of big data to surveil and predict the global spread of infectious diseases, the spatial configuration and conceptualisation of disease is being reconfigured. Predictive analytics and big data are not only expanding medical practice, but also tying it to market forces and global flows of capital, people, and information.

These processes are not being undertaken by healthcAIre alone but are part and parcel of existing digital economies. Data brokers—organisations that specialise in collecting and amassing data from both public and private sources—have long been profiting from the legal, but sometimes unethical, collection of data. Data from these sources fuels platforms like BlueDot, whose algorithm has the scale, pace, and capacity for pattern recognition, accelerating the dehumanising separation of the patient's body from the patient's identity. Similarly, cleaving the patient from their body increases the power of those who own the material and intellectual infrastructure enabling the analysis. We must pay particular attention to the increased use of data-harvesting health technologies in contemporary healthcAIre systems, which, by capturing, processing, storing, and transmitting diagnostics, also "interpenetrate human bodies … [and] shape human experience in the name of solving problems" (Packer et al., 2023, p. 6).

5 HealthcAIre in a Colonial Context

The issues underlying healthcAIre, which existed well before the development of AI and smart health, are rooted deeply in the colonial logics of conquest and extraction. According to Nick Estes (2020, p. 87),

> Debates about the epidemiological vulnerability of Indigenous people first came to prominence in the 1970s as historians backed away from narratives of European cultural superiority in search of more scientific explanations. This biological turn identified microbes as a primary culprit in the mass death of the Indigenous.

In other words, the diseases introduced by European colonists came to be understood as tools that furthered colonisation and conquest.

This example highlights the failure of scholars and medical practitioners to understand the health of Indigenous peoples and of those operating outside the colonial context more broadly. Since the 1970s, these conversations have expanded to include colonised peoples across the globe as well as other communities whose positionality is marginalised within the larger culture (Adam et al., 2022; Nadis, 2022). For example, health surveillance initiatives in North America are disproportionately targeted towards BIPOC patients (Chen et al., 2019; Nadis, 2023; Ouyang, 2023). These programmes often fail to address how (settler) colonialism and discriminatory policies are responsible for health disparities—particularly by limiting access to the resources needed to ensure health and well-being. Instead of addressing the structural inequalities underlying health surveillance, corporate enterprises are developing tools that profit from them. These tools are trained on existing health data, which include the historical biases outlined above, and are then deemed suitable to supplement or replace other healthcare interventions (Giovanola & Tiribelli, 2023). Believing that healthcAIre will reduce loads on medical facilities and improve healthcare outcomes, many states and provincial governments have purchased access to algorithms that claim to reduce the abuse of public funds and services.

Upon further examination, many of these programmes limit rather than expand access to public health services, particularly for those who are most vulnerable (Eubanks, 2018). As healthcAIre becomes the hegemonic mode of health services operation, it is essential to ensure equity is built into the training data of these systems and to inform the public about the techne and technologies used to reduce healthcare disparities caused by biases. To understand the impact of healthcAIre on these groups, we rework the term 'immunological Other', understood as a member of a historically marginalised group whose biological and biometric information is used to justify increased mistreatment. As Byung-Chul Han (2015) elucidates in *The Burnout Society*, an immunological Other functions as the incomprehensible, uncontrollable, irreducibly different, and, at times, dangerous Other. This immunological Other, Han argues, threatens the health of the physical body and the body politic, making it necessary to reorganise the world via a particular topology. The immunologically organised world is pockmarked by borders, fences, and walls in both the real and virtual worlds always already monitoring the movement of the Other, placing them in proximity to a locational data-gathering apparatus (Han, 2015; Noone & Jacob, 2024). The preoccupation with such Others is gaining traction through both the rise of healthcAIre—the design of which exacerbates the coding of patients into binaries—and increased climate vulnerability, which is leading to upticks in disease, natural disasters, and migration. In other words, healthcAIre and disaster capitalism work in tandem, each producing conditions that fuel the other.

6 Implications

Our information ecosystems are rife with systems designed to aid and abet data acquisition and surveillance technologies. For example, electronic medical records, which can be mined by pharmaceutical companies to upsell drugs and generate new revenue streams using patient assistance programs (PAPs), have come under increased scrutiny for distorting the decision-making processes of patients and clinicians (McLean & Bruser, 2017). In 2017, drug companies paid TELUS Health to manipulate their software so that branded medication would be pushed by the software, overriding the generic drugs that pharmacists would opt for. As payment assistance vouchers and brand cards for prescription drugs become digitised, baked into the electronic health record software system, doctors and pharmacists lose their agency as medical decision-makers. If the physician writes the generic name of the drug 'methylphenidate HCl' in a prescription, TELUS's electronic health record software does not initialise the payment assistance voucher; however, if the doctor writes the brand name of the drug Concerta®, the software recognises the brand name and processes the voucher. This makes the branded drug cheaper than the generic drug for the patient.

Although savings are made by the individual consumer, these savings are not passed on to employers and employees who pay into the insurance plan. The price of the higher-cost branded drug is offloaded onto the employees, who have to negotiate and pay for a much more expensive insurance plan on the whole. Therefore, individual savings perversely eat away at collective benefits, and this perversion has been conceived by the corporations that own this proprietary software that are programmatically inserted into the system. As and when AI systems are used to improve the accuracy and precision of financial assistance eligibility assessments, the automation of information collection and verification processes, executed at unprecedented speeds and scales, introduces new vagaries into the patient financial assistance experience. New forms of economic value generation and social control are being embedded into the technoscape, collecting our digital fingerprints, codifying our preferences, and sorting our habits—with or without our knowledge—to bolster the system's predictive analytics capacities. The commodification and privatisation of the medical information infrastructure, accompanied by the appropriation and co-optation of people's social relations, knowledges, habits of mind, and beliefs, are unfolding within the contemporary infoscape as they have once before in the ethnoscape.

Biodata is increasingly being weaponised by these systems. For example, in the UK and the US, migration policy now involves DNA analysis. The fallout from these programmes is clear. In the UK, members of the Windrush generation (migrants from the Caribbean who emigrated between 1948 and 1971) were being expelled from the country at alarming rates, based on DNA test results submitted to companies like Ancestry.com and 23&Me (Lammy, 2020). In the US, a proposed policy seeks to denaturalise or expel close to 11 million residents using the same data sources (Finnegan, 2016). As Angela Saini (2019, p. 19) argues, DNA testing is one tool that has contributed to the resurgence of race science, a flawed school of thought in which some people are denoted as biologically, and, therefore, immunologically, superior to others. "One team of scientists," Saini writes, "claimed that the tiny peppering of Neanderthal DNA may have given Europeans different immune systems from Africans. Another published paper linked Neanderthal DNA to a whole host of human differences."

Using (bio)data to enact or exacerbate discrimination is highly problematic. The cultural history of medicine that Michel Foucault (1963/2003) elucidates in *The Birth of the Clinic* points us to epistemic shifts that have led to corresponding changes in the medical gaze. Reading Foucault alongside media coverage of the Canadian AI epidemiologist, Dr. Kamran Khan, who sent early warnings of the COVID-19 outbreak, reveals how our contemporary understandings of disease are embroiled in discourses of our social reality, biology, political economy, geography, and language. BlueDot and services like it extend the premise of the Foucauldian medical gaze to the contemporary big data landscape, deploying natural language processing and machine learning algorithms to predict the spread of dangerous infectious diseases the world over.

7 Conclusion

The persistence of the algorithmised medical gaze is particularly alarming as capitalists continue touting the value of applying technological solutionism to large-scale human problems.[1] The COVID-19 pandemic is one defining example of such an approach, and can be understood as a turning

[1] Evgeny Morozov (2013, pp. 327–328) defines the term 'technological solutionism' as "the idea that given the right code, algorithms and robots, technology can solve all of mankind's problems, effectively making life 'frictionless' and 'trouble-free'".

point in the institution of the biosurveillance state. BlueDot, as one of the earliest tools utilised in response to COVID-19, serves as a generative starting point from which to understand the risks and harms of AI in healthcare. BlueDot brings together an assemblage of techniques and technologies to measure and manage human capacities, predict tendencies, and control bodies in space and time using evermore intrusive technologies of biopower. The emergence of profit-driven medical practices that are bound up in predictive analytics and big data both extend the scope, size, and scale of medical practice and yoke it to the global flow of capital, peoples, and information. Notably, BlueDot has received millions of dollars in seed funding from venture capitalists who were particularly interested in "explor[ing] opportunities to use BlueDot's robust data aggregation, artificial intelligence, and predictive analytics capabilities to help insurance clients make informed decisions around the prevention of infectious diseases" (BlueDot Inc., 2019, para. 2).

As healthcAIre vendors such as BlueDot proselytise the emancipatory potential of their computational technologies, their infrastructural circuits of socialisation, interaction, and identification are profoundly warping the concept of real/virtual life and real/virtual relations. The datafication and digital transformation of the economy are rapidly morphing healthcare providers into technology service providers. An agile health management programme accessible to the general public has to be reliable, nimble, and scalable to offer just-in-time in-personal health coverage to the user base and prepare for massive surges in caseloads. In order to offer Healthcare-as-a-Service (HaaS), gaps in access to public health data have to be filled with a rich data set of health and economic data that is collated and curated by public–private partnerships in order to create a robust electronic health record database. This sort of techno-solutionist approach to health services unspools health work from its care work legacies and histories.

Healthcare practitioners are seeing healthcAIre technologies and platforms renegotiate what care-based praxis can look like and how these new technologies differ from what many might consider the traditional tools of the trade. For example, personalised health information can be furnished accurately and precisely by the Internet of Healthcare Things (IoHT). IoHT relegates care to a top-level domain name such as .care (orDot-Care), which is available to corporations that can identify themselves as care-giving or -taking service providers, or .health (DotHealth), the exclusive domain name available to trusted health industry brands. The world of digital health, virtual care, and bioinformatics technologies is governed by the logics of data-driven decision-making. Clinical practitioners are being sidelined for cost-effective, AI-embedded technological solutions that supercharge the privatisation and corporatisation of healthcare through large-scale datafication. Biomedical equipment manufacturers that suffuse medical hardware with AI, health informatics companies that engineer the AI software, and pharmaceutical companies that back the development of wetware [i.e., biological technology that influences the body (Winthrop-Young, 2010)] coalesce to create the infrastructural stack that powers the smart digital health services and virtual care systems that we term healthcAIre.

These healthcAIre systems suture the bond between metrics and power. Pairing metrics with power is a key step in creating algorithmic value through datafication technologies and exploring economic opportunities arising from implementing smart systems. In other words, the problems inherent to healthcAIre tools like BlueDot will only scale up, expanding their scope in ways that will impact more lives. Such risks become all the more problematic when the quality of healthcare is measured solely via key performance indicators and metrics, when patient compliance is attained by non-human actors, and when healthcare can be delivered remotely through mediated technology solutions, in the absence of healthcare workers who are thought to decrease operational efficiencies and effectiveness. HealthcAIre coverage increasingly encompasses a stack of digital health infrastructures, platforms, and services, accessible to responsibilised subjects who participate in the health market economy by making timely updates to their electronic health records, upgrading their body sensor networks, and purchasing adequate wearable technologies.

Separated from human care and empathy by design, these tools cannot respond to patient needs with the nuance required to ensure safe medical experiences for all. As one of us, Christina Boyles et al. (2023, p. 182) note, "If we fail to intervene in harmful surveillance practices, we risk replicating and iterating on discriminatory systems through new technological innovations". The data surveillance embodied by healthcAIre tools like BlueDot is particularly problematic because it is built upon the historical legacies of colonialism and conquest. By taking advantage of a global health crisis like COVID-19, healthcAIre tools are proliferating—filling in the gaps left by a weakened healthcare system, and generating profits for tech entrepreneurs and investors.

Before healthcAIre fully pervades public health, we need to be explicit about the role of AI in medicine, the risks to patients and providers, and the protections (or lack thereof) being built into these systems. Given that AI can and does exacerbate existing social and cultural biases, how can we best protect patients' health and safety in the AI context? Can we? The lack of data transparency and accountability for those AI products currently in use exacerbates existing normative problematics and practices, as evidenced by the case of REACH VET (Glantz, 2024). We already have information about the harms caused by AI, including increases and amplification of misinformation, the biases in training data and AI model outputs, and the erosion of user privacy as data is scaped typically without consent (Ryan-Mosley, 2023). These risks should give us pause, especially since AI is likely to aggravate existing issues in public health. By renaming healthcare as healthcAIre, we hope to bring attention to its risks and problems, emphasise the biases of these technologies, and encourage public health patient advocacy. Knowing that healthcAIre exists and how it functions helps drive social, organisational, and policy changes that can produce a more equitable healthcare system.

References

Adam, H., Balagopalan, A., Alsentzer, E., Christia, F., & Ghassemi, M. (2022). Mitigating the impact of biased artificial intelligence in emergency decision-making. *Communications Medicine, 2*(1), 1–6. https://doi.org/10.1038/s43856-022-00214-4

Athey, S. (2017). Beyond prediction: Using big data for policy problems. *Science, 355*(6324), 483–485. https://doi.org/10.1126/science.aal4321

AWS Events. (2020, July 22). *Powered by AWS, BlueDot uses machine learning to detect and respond to infectious disease risks* [Video]. *YouTube*. https://www.youtube.com/watch?v=cLB-cixa-Io

Balsamo, A. M. (1995). *Technologies of the gendered body: Reading cyborg women*. Duke University Press.

BlueDot Inc. (2019, August 7). Digital health company BlueDot secures $7M USD series A financing. *CISION: PR Newswire*. https://www.prnewswire.com/news-releases/digital-health-company-bluedot-secures-7m-usd-series-a-financing-300894210.html

Boyles, C., Boyles Petersen, A., & Jacob, A. (2023). Operationalizing surveillance studies in the digital humanities. In M. K. Gold & L. F. Klein (Eds.), *Debates in the digital humanities 2023* (pp. 176–190). University of Minnesota Press. https://doi.org/10.5749/9781452969565

Buolamwini, J. (2023). *Unmasking AI: My mission to protect what is human in a world of machines*. Penguin Random House.

Carey, B. (2020, November 23). Can an algorithm prevent suicide? *The New York Times*. https://www.nytimes.com/2020/11/23/health/artificial-intelligence-veterans-suicide.html

Chakravorti, B. (2022, March 17). Why AI failed to live up to its potential during the pandemic. *Harvard Business Review*. https://hbr.org/2022/03/why-ai-failed-to-live-up-to-its-potential-during-the-pandemic

Chen, I. Y., Szolovits, P., & Ghassemi, M. (2019). Can AI help reduce disparities in general medical and mental health care? *AMA Journal of Ethics, 21*(2), E167–E179. https://doi.org/10.1001/amajethics.2019.167

Committee on Energy and Commerce, 18th Congress. (2023, April 19). *Who is selling your data: A critical examination of the role of data brokers in the digital economy*. United States Government Publishing Office. https://www.congress.gov/118/chrg/CHRG-118hhrg55269/CHRG-118hhrg55269.pdf

D'Ignazio, C., & Klein, L. F. (2020). *Data feminism*. The MIT Press.

Estes, N. (2020). The empire of all maladies: Colonial contagions and Indigenous resistance. *The Baffler, 52*, 86–92. https://www.jstor.org/stable/26922855

Eubanks, V. (2018). *Automating inequality: How high-tech tools profile, police, and punish the poor*. St. Martin's Press.

Finnegan, M. (2016, August 22). Trump sticks to hard line on deporting 11 million immigrants. *LA Times*. https://www.latimes.com/politics/la-na-pol-trump-immigration-deportation-20160822-snap-story.html

Foucault, M. (1990). *The history of sexuality: An introduction* (Vol. 1). Vintage Books. (Original work published 1976).

Foucault, M. (2003). *The birth of the clinic: An archaeology of medical perception*. Psychology Press. (Original work published 1963).

Ghassemi, M., Oakden-Rayner, L., & Beam, A. L. (2021). The false hope of current approaches to explainable artificial intelligence in health care. *The Lancet Digital Health, 3*(11), e745–e750. https://doi.org/10.1016/S2589-7500(21)00208-9

Gilles, B. (2018, June 20). *Join BlueDot in confronting global outbreaks with big data*. MaRS Discovery District. https://www.marsdd.com/our-story/join-bluedot-in-confronting-global-outbreaks-with-big-data/

Giovanola, B., & Tiribelli, S. (2023). Beyond bias and discrimination: Redefining the AI ethics principle of fairness in healthcare machine-learning algorithms. *AI & Society, 38*(2), 549–563. https://doi.org/10.1007/s00146-022-01455-6

Glantz, A. (2024, May 23). Artificial intelligence: Vveteran suicide prevention algorithm favors white men. *The Fuller Project*. https://fullerproject.org/story/artificial-intelligence-veteran-suicide-prevention-algorithm-favors-men/

Gomes, B. M., Rebelo, C. B., & de Sousa, L. A. (2022). Public health, surveillance systems and preventive medicine in an interconnected world. In J. C. Prata, A. I. Ribeiro, & T. Rocha-Santos (Eds.), *One health: Integrated approach to 21st century challenges to health* (pp. 33–71). Academic Press. https://doi.org/10.1016/B978-0-12-822794-7.00006-X

Han, B.-C. (2015). *The burnout society*. Stanford University Press.

Heaven, W. D. (2020, March 12). AI could help with the next pandemic—but not with this one. *MIT Technology Review*. https://www.technologyreview.com/2020/03/12/905352/ai-could-help-with-the-next-pandemicbut-not-with-this-one/

House Committee on Energy and Commerce. (2023, April 19). Who is selling your data: A critical examination of the role of data brokers in the digital economy [Video]. *YouTube*. https://www.youtube.com/live/dVx-hObuS0Y

Huang, J. (2020, 9 April). Verbal abuse, assault, shunning: Coronavirus 'hate' tracker now includes more than 1,400 reports of Anti-Asian racism. *LAist*. https://laist.com/news/coronavirus-tracker-anti-asian-racism

Jasny, B. R., & Stone, R. (2017). Prediction and its limits. *Science, 355*(6324), 468–469. https://doi.org/10.1126/science.355.6324.468

Kim, T. (2020, July 30). How to fight anti-Asian hate during the era of COVID-19. *Thomson Reuters*. https://www.thomsonreuters.com/en-us/posts/news-and-media/fight-anti-asian-hate-covid-19/

Kittler, F. A. (1999). *Gramophone, film, typewriter*. Stanford University Press.

Klein, N. (2008). *The shock doctrine: The rise of disaster capitalism*. Penguin Books.

Lammy, D. (2020, February 10). Two years after Windrush, we're deporting people who've only known Britain as home. *The Guardian*. https://www.theguardian.com/commentisfree/2020/feb/10/windrush-deporting-people

Lorinc, J. (2022, March 16). From bakery to 'tech behemoth': How Loblaw became a titan of the private health-care industry. *Toronto Star*. https://www.thestar.com/business/from-bakery-to-tech-behemoth-how-loblaw-became-a-titan-of-the-private-health-care/article_327a75b8-e366-5013-afbd-00cb44639b36.html

Manrai, A., & Beam, A. (Hosts) (2023, June 28). Can AI be harmful? A conversation with MIT's Dr. Marzyeh Ghassemi [Audio podcast episode]. In NEJM AI Grand Rounds. https://ai-podcast.nejm.org/e/can-ai-be-harmful-a-conversation-with-mit-s-dr-marzyeh-ghassemi/

McLean, J., & Bruser, D. (2017, July 29). Doctors use this software during patient visits. Now Big Pharma is tapping it to sell their drugs. *Toronto Star*. https://www.thestar.com/news/canada/2017/07/29/doctors-use-this-software-during-patient-visits-now-big-pharma-is-tapping-it-to-sell-their-drugs.html

Millett, G. A., Jones, A. T., Benkeser, D., Baral, S., Mercer, L., Beyrer, C., Honermann, B., Lankiewicz, E., Mena, L., Crowley, J. S., Sherwood, J., & Sullivan, P. S. (2020). Assessing differential impacts of COVID-19 on black communities. *Annals of Epidemiology, 47*, 37–44. https://doi.org/10.1016/j.annepidem.2020.05.003

Morozov, E. (2013). *To save everything, click here: The folly of technological solutionism.* PublicAffairs.

Nadis, S. (2022, December 16). Subtle biases in AI can influence emergency decisions. *MIT News.* https://news.mit.edu/2022/when-subtle-biases-ai-influence-emergency-decisions-1216

Nadis, S. (2023, August 17). How machine-learning models can amplify inequities in medical diagnosis and treatment. *MIT News.* https://news.mit.edu/2023/how-machine-learning-models-can-amplify-inequities-medical-diagnosis-treatment-0817

Niiler, E. (2020, January 25). An AI epidemiologist sent the first alerts of the coronavirus. *WIRED.* https://www.wired.com/story/ai-epidemiologist-wuhan-public-health-warnings

Noble, S. U. (2018). *Algorithms of oppression: How search engines reinforce racism.* New York University Press.

Noone, R., & Jacob, A. (2024). Bad boundaries: Geofences and the intimacies of location data. *TOPIA: Canadian. Journal of Cultural Studies, 48*, 76–92. https://doi.org/10.3138/topia-2023-0035

O'Neil, C. (2016). *Weapons of math destruction: How big data increases inequality and threatens democracy.* Crown Publishers.

Ouyang, A. (2023, September 13). How an archeological approach can help leverage biased data in AI to improve medicine. *MIT News.* https://news.mit.edu/2023/how-archeological-approach-can-help-leverage-biased-data-ai-improve-medicine-0913

Packer, J., de Villavicencio, P. N., Monea, A., Oswald, K., Maddalena, K., & Reeves, J. (2023). *The prison house of the circuit: Politics of control from analog to digital.* University of Minnesota Press.

Poursabzi-Sangdeh, F., Goldstein, D. G., Hofman, J. M., Vaughan, J. W. W., & Wallach, H. (2021). Manipulating and measuring model interpretability. In *CHI '21: Proceedings of the 2021 CHI Conference on Human Factors in Computing Systems* (pp. 1–52). https://doi.org/10.1145/3411764.3445315

Ravindranath, M. (2019, June 25). *How the VA uses algorithms to predict suicide. Politico.* https://www.politico.com/story/2019/06/25/va-veterans-suicide-1382379

Robertson, S. K., & Hannay, C. (2024, August 9). Loblaw's health care empire is growing. But can it earn the trust of Canadian patients? *The Globe and Mail.* https://www.theglobeandmail.com/business/article-loblaw-shoppers-drug-mart-health-care/

Ryan-Mosley, T. (2023, June 12). It's time to talk about the real AI risks. *MIT Technology Review.* https://www.technologyreview.com/2023/06/12/1074449/real-ai-risks/

Saini, A. (2019). *Superior: The return of race science.* Beacon Press.

Schwartz Reisman Institute. (2021, August 18). *Marzyeh Ghassemi | Don't expl-AI-n yourself: Exploring healthy models in machine learning for health.* [Video]. YouTube. https://www.youtube.com/watch?v=TWNrnctqrzc

Stieg, C. (2020, March 3). *How this Canadian start-up spotted coronavirus before everyone else knew about it.* https://www.cnbc.com/2020/03/03/bluedot-used-artificial-intelligence-to-predict-coronavirus-spread.html

United States Government Accountability Office: Report to Congressional Requesters. (2022, September 29). *Artificial intelligence in health care: Benefits and challenges of machine learning technologies for medical diagnostics.* United States Government Accountability Office. https://www.gao.gov/products/gao-22-104629

Vendeville, G. (2020, March 27). U of T infectious disease expert's AI firm now part of Canada's COVID-19 arsenal. *University of Toronto News.* https://www.utoronto.ca/news/u-t-infectious-disease-expert-s-ai-firm-now-part-canada-s-covid-19-arsenal

Winthrop-Young, G. (2010). Hardware/software/wetware. In W. J. T. Mitchell & M. B. Hansen (Eds.), *Critical terms for media studies* (pp. 186–214). University of Chicago Press.

Yang, Y., Zhang, H., Katabi, D., & Ghassemi, M. (2023). Change is hard: A closer look at subpopulation shift. In *Proceedings of the 40th International Conference on Machine Learning*, *202*, 39584–39622. https://proceedings.mlr.press/v202/yang23s.html

PART II

Optimising

CHAPTER 5

Spectrumscape*

~~Radio Spectrum~~

Gordon A. Gow

1 Introduction

> Like no other, the radio spectrum is the first form of world property. (Smythe, 1981, p. 302)

> All media are active metaphors in their power to translate experience into new forms. (McLuhan, 1964, p. 57)

The radio spectrum is integral to our daily lives, powering everything from smartphones and Global Positioning System (GPS) receivers to aviation beacons and radio telescopes. It is, in the words of Rachel O'Dwyer (2013, p. 499), "a core apparatus in the digital economy". However,

G. A. Gow (✉)
Media and Technology Studies, University of Alberta, Edmonton, AB, Canada
e-mail: ggow@ualberta.ca

C. Chokshi, R. Mansell (eds.), *The Need to Rename Tech*,
https://doi.org/10.1007/978-3-032-05155-4_5

despite its centrality in our lives today, most of us rarely consider it.[1] This chapter explores the language used to talk about the *radio spectrum* and how efforts to (re)name it have shaped our awareness and understanding of the resource that makes wireless communication possible.

Cultural, economic, and political discourse about wireless communication has long been guided by what J. P. de Vries (2008, p. 3) labels the "spectrum-as-territory" metaphor. In more general terms, policymakers and radio engineers refer to specific regions of the spectrum as 'beachfront property' or to less valuable frequencies as 'vacant'.[2] A territorial metaphor is evident in the critical political economy literature, most notably in Dallas Smythe's (1981) comparison of the radio spectrum to other natural resources and how these are "the subject of constant power struggles, given the relentless efforts to transform a world public property into one where private ownership and control dominates" (as cited in Mazepa & Mosco, 2016, p. 163).

In this chapter, I consider how the spectrum-as-territory metaphor has persisted within the discourse of wireless communication, even as other groups have sought to (re)name it. With recent advances in digital technology and the increasing profitability of the wireless industry, three historical terms have resurfaced in the contemporary political economy of wireless communication to invoke normative claims around ownership and access rights to this precious resource. I discuss how the Māori label spectrum as a *taonga*, or treasured resource, to assert their cultural claims to traditional radio and television broadcasting and, more recently, to fifth-generation (5G) wireless communication. I highlight how the ancient Greek term *ether* was taken up in the late Edwardian period and early

[1] The Oxford English Dictionary (n.d.) states that the term 'radio spectrum' occurs "about 0.1 times per million words in modern written English" (Frequency section, para. 1). By contrast, the word 'radio' occurs about 40 times per million words and "is one of the 2000 most common words in modern written English" (Frequency section, para. 1).

[2] In at least one case, the metaphor has been applied literally by regulators in New Zealand, where "the Management Rights Regime (MRR) that was established to facilitate a spectrum market ... is explicitly a system for land transactions" (De Vries, 2008, p. 4).

twentieth century as a popular name for spectrum among a growing community of radio amateurs. The term then fell out of favour, only to return in the 1970s when computer scientists in Silicon Valley sought to describe a new design concept for local area networks (LANs)—what we now refer to as the Ethernet. Finally, I consider how the agrarian-era term *commons* was recast as a *supercommons* in the early 2000s by the open spectrum movement (OSM) in response to neoliberal efforts to privatise radio spectrum in the United States (US) and elsewhere.

In presenting these three examples, I demonstrate how different naming efforts convey an underlying "ontological metaphor" (Lakoff & Johnson, 2003, p. 23) that continues to influence public understanding and policy discourse around wireless technologies. I then look to Peter Schaefer's (2013) distinction between a metaphor's cognitive and normative dimensions to show how the spectrum-as-territory metaphor has provided an historically stable referent for various (re)naming movements that have unfolded over more than a century of radio regulation and spectrum policy history. In its normative dimension, I argue, this spatial metaphor has provided an interpretive flexibility (Pinch & Bijker, 1984) that has enabled social groups to express distinctive views on how spectrum should be allocated and managed, ranging from radically open models to those advocating for exclusive private property rights. Finally, I point to Zita Joyce's (2007) term *spectrumscape* as representing a renaming effort that reconciles the persistence of the cognitive dimension of the spatial metaphor with its variable and contested normative dimension.[3]

2 Spectrum Is a Taonga

> So the spectrum is a taonga. There's just no doubt about it. (Walker, 2022, para. 24)

New Zealand's national holiday, Waitangi Day, is observed annually on the 6th of February. The Māori, the Indigenous peoples of the land they call *Aotearoa*, refer to this day as *Te Rā o Waitangi*. The day commemorates the 1840 signing of the Treaty of Waitangi (*Te Tiriti O Waitangi*), an agreement between the British Crown and more than 500 Māori tribal chiefs that ultimately led to the declaration of British sovereignty over New Zealand.

[3] The author respectfully acknowledges Joyce's use of the term 'spectrumscape' which informs the renaming proposal in this chapter and is reflected in this chapter's main title.

Te Rā o Waitangi in 2022 was especially notable because it marked the culmination of a series of sustained efforts by the Māori to be granted the right to participate directly in radio spectrum management in New Zealand (Walker, 2022). Just a few days earlier, the Māori had signed an agreement with the Crown in which the New Zealand government agreed to set aside 25 per cent of high-value radio spectrum designated for next-generation wireless broadband services. This was in addition to an ongoing allocation of 20 per cent of future national commercial spectrum allocations to be administered by a Māori Spectrum Entity. With this agreement, the Crown acknowledged that the "Māori have some legitimate claim on spectrum ownership and that this will endure into the future" (Howell & Tang, 2023, p. 5). The agreement was considered a significant breakthrough for Māori decolonisation and as potentially precedent-setting for Indigenous peoples in other countries.

Despite this achievement, the New Zealand government refused to accede to the terminology in the Māori claims in which the radio spectrum is named as a *taonga* (Howell & Tang, 2023). The meaning of taonga is nuanced and complex, associated linguistically with similar terms in other Eastern Polynesian languages. The *Te Aka Māori* dictionary defines it as "treasure, anything prized—applied to anything considered to be of value including socially or culturally valuable objects, resources, phenomenon, ideas and techniques" (Māori Dictionary, n.d.). The word *taonga* does not appear in Article Two of the English-language version of the Treaty of Waitangi, which refers instead to "the exclusive and undisturbed possession of their lands and estates, forests, fisheries, and other properties". By contrast, as conveyed in the Māori language version, the treaty "confirmed and guaranteed the rangatira 'te tino rangatiratanga'—the exercise of chieftainship—over their lands, villages and 'taonga katoa'—all treasured things" (Orange, 2023, Interpretations section, para. 5).

Whether these rights extend to the radio spectrum was first raised when the Waitangi Tribunal declared the Māori language, *te reo,* as a taonga, resulting in the passage of the Māori Language Act in 1987. The claim leading to that decision was launched partly to establish support for Māori language broadcasting, citing te reo as a culturally valuable resource to be protected under the provisions of the Treaty of Waitangi. When the New Zealand government later proposed to auction portions of the radio spectrum for use by high-value wireless communication services, the Māori, citing a treaty breach, applied for an injunction. This resulted in subsequent claims reasserting that the radio spectrum itself is a taonga and that the Crown and Māori must act in partnership for its management. In 1990, the Waitangi Tribunal made this statement (p. 41):

> The taonga of the spectrum is different in essence, in terms of its discovery, its development and its usage from any other taonga known by or used by any of the tribes. Even though the spectrum was not evident at the time of the signing of the Treaty, in hindsight we know that it has been part of the universe since the time of creation …
>
> Furthermore, the spectrum is a natural resource, enveloping the whole of the earth at the same time. As such, it is for the whole of mankind. It cannot be possessed by one person or by one group; it can only be used by them. The available right is the right of access shared with all other members of the human race. The spectrum is a taonga to be shared by the tribes and by all mankind. Neither of the Treaty partners can have monopoly rights to this resource.

The position taken by the Tribunal set in motion a contentious debate that illustrates the role of language in the political economy of wireless communication. According to Joyce (2020, p. 38), "The story of New Zealand radio spectrum is … about the right of the state to create property rights in previously unpropertized resources, posing traditional forms of knowledge and resource use against state discourse of technology and material value."

The struggle over spectrum as a taonga can be seen as a (re)naming movement led by the Māori, pitting an alternative worldview against the Crown's efforts to promulgate a property rights regime rooted in a colonial interpretation of a treaty that predates the invention of radio. The (re) naming effort was an act of reterritorialisation, wherein "decolonizing the radio spectrum means understanding that it is a space and a resource, a common socially-constructed asset" (Bravo, 2018, para. 15) and not a right *in rem* to be assumed by the Crown. By asserting that spectrum is a taonga, the Māori challenged policymakers to reconsider the intersection of the natural world and radio technology in the light of Indigenous epistemologies.

3 The Luminiferous Aether

Fifty years after the signing of The Treaty of Waitangi, an Italian inventor, Guglielmo Marconi, began successfully to use radio waves for human communication.[4] When we speak of 'wireless' or 'radio' today, we refer to a diverse and growing category of technologies that transmit and receive electromagnetic radiation between 3 Hz and 3000 GHz.[5] Advances in technology over the past century mean that the usable bandwidth of the radio spectrum is now 5000 times larger than in the early 1930s (Werbach, 2004). The International Telecommunication Union (ITU), established nearly a century ago, is the official world body that works closely with 193 member states and other stakeholders to coordinate the management of the radio spectrum. The ITU allocates spectrum into groups of frequencies ('bands') intended for specific applications, much like zoning is applied to land for development purposes (Figs. 5.1 and 5.2).

The spatial dimension of electromagnetic energy has been of great interest throughout history. During the late Victorian period, leading up to the invention of radio, it was widely believed that this form of energy required some type of physical medium for its propagation in space. That medium was referred to variously as the 'ether', 'aether', or the 'luminiferous aether'. The ether's mythological origins date back to Ancient Greece when it was regarded as "the element breathed by the gods", with some early Platonic philosophers believing it to be "a constituent element of the soul" (Muri, 2007, p. 63). In early modern Europe, natural philosophers adopted the term to describe "an elastic and subtle substance permeating all of space between the planets, between particles of air, and between all elementary particles of matter" (Muri, 2007, p. 63). Allison Muri (2007) observes that both Huygens and Newton postulated different versions of ether to account for the propagation of light and gravitation. Victorian-era

[4] In 1897, Marconi used radio waves to send the message 'C A N Y O U H E A R M E' in Morse code across the Bristol Channel (Holmes, 2022).

[5] Radio transmissions are periodic waveforms typically measured as units of frequency in cycles per second. Under the International System of Units (ISU), this is designated as Hertz (Hz), named after the scientist Heinrich Hertz. Hz can be prefixed under the metric system, and commonly used multiples for radio are kHz (kilohertz, or 1000 Hz), MHz (megahertz, or 1×10^6 Hz), and GHz (gigahertz, or 1×10^9 Hz). For example, AM radio operates between 535–1605 kHz, FM radio between 88 MHz and 108 MHz, and Wi-Fi systems operate in the 2.4 GHz and 5 GHz frequency bands.

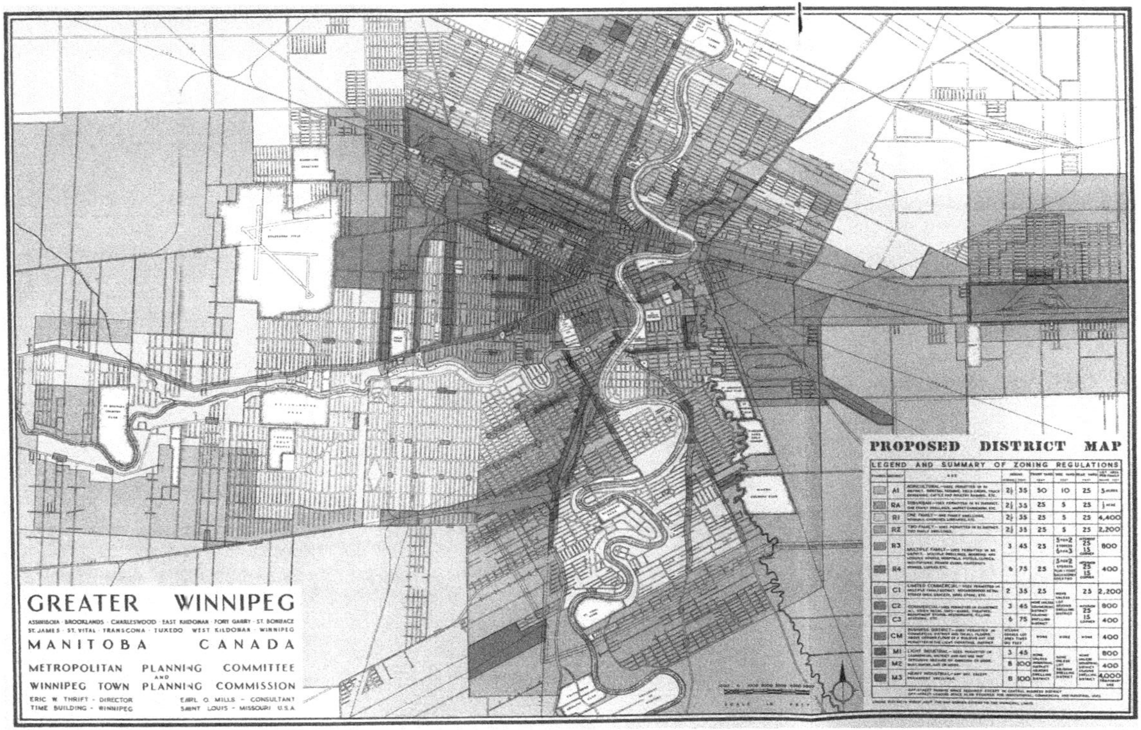

Fig. 5.1 An historic zoning map for the Greater Winnipeg District (ca. 1947). Wikimedia Commons (n.d.)

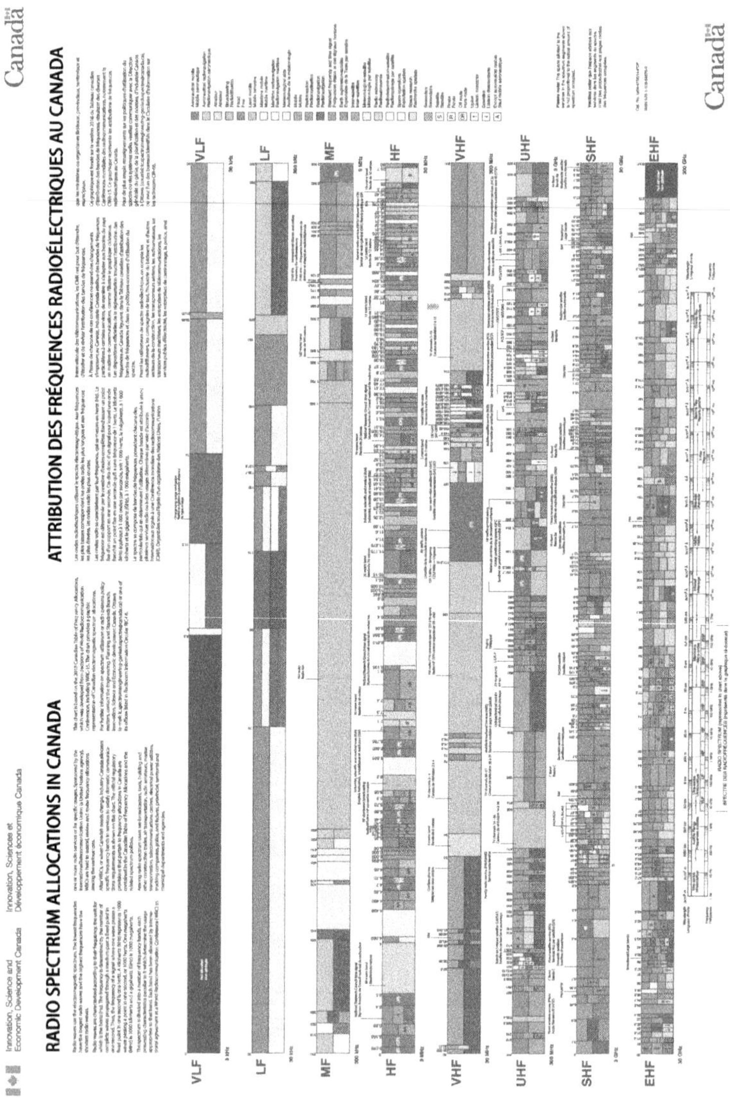

Fig. 5.2 Chart showing radio spectrum allocations in Canada. Innovation, Science and Economic Development Canada (2018)

science considered ether an "electrical fluid" (Muri, 2007, p. 64) that could help explain the mysterious forces of electromagnetism.

Despite the failure of the famous Michelson–Morley experiment in 1887 to detect an 'ether wind'—hypothesised as an effect that would result from the Earth's motion through the universal ether—and the further discrediting of the existence of the ether by Einstein's theory of relativity, the term continued to be used during the popularisation of wireless technology in the 1920s. During this period, do-it-yourself radio kits became widely accessible to active amateur hobbyists, and radio receivers were marketed to the general public. These conditions created a demand for clear, simple explanations for that "imponderable, elastic, all-pervading medium which is assumed to exist in order to explain the transmission of energy in the form of electro-magnetic waves" (Navarro, 2016, p. 471).

An emerging industry of radio manufacturers and broadcasters popularised the term (sometimes spelled as 'aether') through its frequent use in periodicals like *The Wireless World* (see Fig. 5.3). This supported a movement among commercial interests to "[legitimize] wireless as a serious, scientific activity" (Navarro, 2016, p. 468) and bolstered efforts to regulate the airwaves, aiming to prevent unruly amateurs from interfering with commercial broadcasting signals. As Joe Milutis (2006, p. 78) writes in his book *Ether*, "the beginning of the twentieth century … was marked by a conceptualization of ether as property", leading to a concerted and globally coordinated effort in radio frequency standardisation. A metaphor was being invoked that would pave the way for a territorialisation of the radio spectrum as government entities increasingly made "the gradations of the ether their business" (Milutis, 2006, p. 78).

The term 'radio spectrum' first began to circulate in the late 1920s, gradually displacing the term 'ether' in official documents and popular scientific discourse.[6] However, ether made an unexpected return in the mid-1970s when an American engineer named Robert Metcalfe conceived of a decentralised network design that came to be known as Ethernet (Schaefer, 2013). Metcalfe's use of this term (see Fig. 5.4) evoked an essential aspect of the territorial metaphor that is continuous with the

[6] The Oxford English Dictionary (n.d.) traces the first use of 'radio spectrum' to comments made by an American politician in December 1927: "During 1928 the spotlight of public interest in radio will turn upon the long reaches of the radio spectrum below the broadcasting band" (Meaning & use section, para. 2).

THE
WIRELESS WORLD
THE OFFICIAL ORGAN OF THE WIRELESS SOCIETY OF LONDON
VOL. VIII. No. 2. APRIL 17TH, 1920 FORTNIGHTLY

AETHER

THE SUBSTRATUM OF THE UNIVERSE.

By PHILIP R. COURSEY, B.Sc., A.M.I.E.E.

WHAT is the Aether—using the word not in its chemical sense of ether the anæsthetic, but with the meaning commonly assigned to it by the physicist? Much has been written about this universal medium (for such we may call it for want of more exact knowledge of its ultimate nature) and many are the theories that have been built up around the hypothesis of its existence. The term aether is generally used to designate this omnipresent universal medium which fills all space and is in, between, and around, all bodies and substances.

Some three centuries ago, at a time when the foundations of modern astronomy were being more surely laid upon the subsoil of fact and accurate observation, the first inkling became evident of the need for some medium in space to act as a connecting link for the transmission of light between the Stars, the Planets, the Earth, and the other bodies of the cosmos. The earliest ideas of the nature of light seem very crude when examined from the view point of modern knowledge. Descartes, for instance, about 1640, in his theories of the universe, proposed the idea that light was simply a statical pressure transmitted through some medium (which he regarded as a form of matter) between say the Sun and the Earth. He assumed that force cannot be transmitted from one point to another except by actual pressure or impact, and thus was led to the enunciation of the principle that interplanetary space must be occupied by "matter" imperceptible to the touch but capable of serving as the vehicle of force and light. His basis of all things was a primitive, elementary, unique type of matter, boundless in extent and infinitely divisible. According to his theory the sun is the centre of a huge vortex so that the parts of the medium surrounding it and forming the vortex are straining away from the centre around which they turn. There is thus established an outward pressure in all directions, which was assumed to constitute the light which was evidently radiated from the sun in all directions in space.

Needless to say such postulates are not accepted at the present day, as it is generally recognised that light is really a form of wave motion. It is interesting, however, to recall these old ideas of light being a force, in conjunction with the more modern observations on the *pressure* of light.

An idea of light more in accordance with modern views, was set out by R. Hook in his *Micrographia* published in 1667. He recognised the fact that the parts of all luminous bodies are in rapid motion, and hence inferred that it was much more reasonable to suppose light also to be a vibratory motion rather than a statical pressure or force. To quote from

37

Fig. 5.3 The term 'ether' or 'aether' continued to be used in popular science writing and amateur radio periodicals well into the 1920s. The Wireless World (1920)

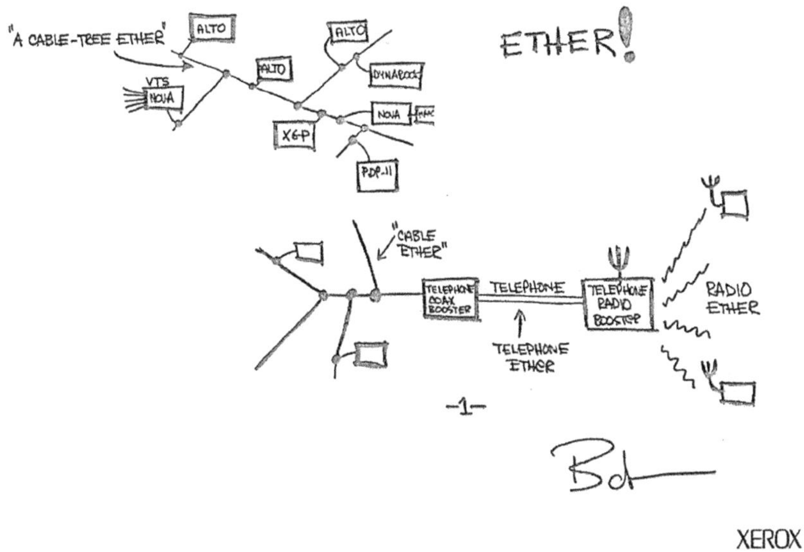

Fig. 5.4 Composite of sketches of Ethernet, drawn by Bob Metcalfe while a researcher at Xerox PARC in the early 1970s. Metcalfe (1973)

Victorian notion of a luminiferous ether. As Schaefer (2013, p. 2016) explains:

> The elusive qualities of the ether within the discourse of late nineteenth-century physics worked well as a means to promote the similar ambiguities of the ether network. The lack of point-to-point transmission in packet-switching, the flexible but nonrepresentational dimension to the LAN's [Local Area Network] topology, and the indirect means by which message transmission could be verified all share qualities similar to the Victorian notion of 'ether' referenced by the Ethernet architects.

Metcalfe even named two of his Alto desktop computers 'Michelson' and 'Morley' in homage to the two physicists who had searched in vain for proof of the ether (Schaefer, 2013).

'Ether' continued to be used throughout the twentieth century and into the twenty-first century as a spatial metaphor for expressing ideas of territoriality in communication networks—whether to justify setting aside frequencies for commercial broadcasters in the early 1920s, to convey the concept of a decentralised LAN architecture, or for the name of Vitalik Buterin's blockchain-based cryptocurrency platform, Ethereum. The name endures partly because it conveys a mutable concept of territoriality that acts as a placeholder of sorts, expressing a relationship between technology, science, and socio-political interests "as they shift and transform, century after century" (Milutis, 2006, p. xi).

In addition to serving as a cognitive 'placeholder' for engineers who were imagining an architecture of distributed computing networks, the term 'ether' also resonated with a set of values shared among those who worked with Metcalfe at Xerox PARC and in Silicon Valley during the 1970s. As Schaefer (2018, p. 2018) notes:

> The 'ether' in Ethernet not only explained [in a territorial sense] how the network moved information to any place in the facility but also helped to reinforce the norms of the institution ... [that] information [should] be universally accessible and that the ideas be shared on an equal basis. ... The culture of the PARC was one of information accessibility, and the values held by community members were built into its network.

Serving as more than a cognitive metaphor, ether provided Metcalfe and his team with a useful technomorphism to promote an interdisciplinary workplace culture that valued information technology for its socially transformative potential. This mindset reflected a broader social movement emerging out of Southern California at the time (Wyatt, 2004), one that would embrace the openness and non-hierarchical cooperation of 'virtual' communities facilitated by an internet-inspired metaphor of the 'digital commons'.

4 The Spectrum Fallacy

> Spectrum can be defined as a perfectly renewable resource but just as easily framed or managed as a rival good. (O'Dwyer, 2013, p. 512)

A commonly held contemporary view among policymakers and others in the wireless industry is that the radio spectrum is a natural resource like air, water, or land. From a historical perspective, it may be useful to think of it in Heideggerian terms as something 'present-at-hand' that has always existed in the world. Spectrum becomes 'ready-to-hand' when radio technology enables it to serve as a medium for distant communication.[7] A version of this conception informs part of the Māori's claim to spectrum as a taonga existing before colonisation. As a natural resource, spectrum is infinitely reusable, but that use is limited by the technical requirements of radio systems. This limit on usability is circumscribed by *interference*, which the ITU Radio Regulations (2024, para. 1) define as:

> the effect of unwanted energy due to one or a combination of emissions, radiations, or inductions upon reception in a radiocommunication system, manifested by any performance degradation, misinterpretation or loss of information which could be extracted in the absence of such unwanted energy.

In other words, interference refers to the degree of unwanted noise in a system that adversely affects the ability to communicate a message. It is categorised into three types: permissible, acceptable, and harmful. The looming problem of harmful interference, especially in high-demand frequencies, is what is deemed to create scarcity in those bands (Global System for Mobile Communications Association, 2017). Managing this scarcity, as such, is a primary rationale for government regulation and oversight of the radio spectrum.

As commentators have observed, however, the designation of 'harmful' interference in radio systems is a social construct. It is not a naturally-occurring phenomenon in spectrum's present-at-hand status, but, rather, it is an unwanted artefact—a negative externality—caused by natural forces (e.g., atmospheric conditions) or competing radio systems operating contiguously in space and time. In other words, the source of scarcity is associated with the technical properties of the 'radiocommunication system' and with decisions taken about its use, and not with the spectrum as a naturally occurring form of energy. In emphasising this point, David Reed suggests we consider a spectrum-as-colour metaphor, commenting that "there's no scarcity of spectrum anymore than there's a scarcity of the colour green" (as cited in Weinberger, 2003, para. 5).

[7] Heidegger (1962, p. 100) writes, for instance, "'Nature' is not to be understood as that which is just present-at-hand, nor as the power of Nature. The wood is a forest of timber, the mountain a quarry of rock; the river is water-power, the wind is wind 'in the sails'. As the 'environment' is discovered, the 'Nature' thus discovered is encountered too. If its kind of Being as ready-to-hand is disregarded, this 'Nature' itself can be discovered and defined simply in its pure presence-at-hand".

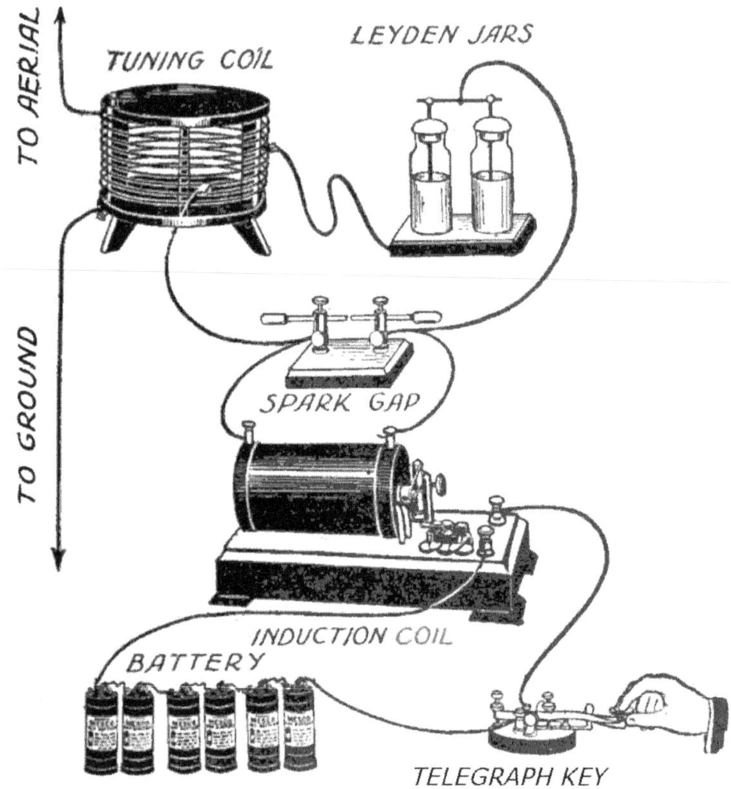

Fig. 5.5 Pictorial diagram of a simple spark-gap transmitter from a 1917 boy's hobby book. Seton (1917)

The origins of harmful interference, as manifested in radio systems today, can be traced to the rudimentary spark gap method used by Marconi in 1901 to make the first transatlantic radio transmission. Figure 5.5 shows a simple spark-gap transmitter from a 1917 boy's hobby book, typical of the low-power transmitters built by thousands of amateurs during the early period of radio. This spark-gap technique incorporates a telegraph key into an electrical circuit to produce intermittent transmissions that energise a broad and indiscriminate swath of frequencies. Over time, improvements in radio systems eventually enabled transceivers to operate in more discrete frequency divisions that reduced (but often did not eliminate) harmful interference, permitting listening stations to filter out unwanted transmissions by 'tuning in' to a desired signal while ignoring others. Kevin Werbach (2004, p. 869) characterises this frequency division method of transmission as a "design choice". This design choice had far-reaching consequences for spectrum management, even as new frequency-sharing methods became increasingly available.

Leading up to the First World War, a chief concern for government regulators "was not congestion or overoccupancy but rather protocols by which radio operators could locate and communicate with each other in what was virtually empty terrain" (Aitken, 1994, p. 689). By the mid-1920s, however, harmful interference was becoming a widespread problem for listeners trying to tune in to their favourite programmes. Commercial radio stations would cut into each other's broadcasts, and owners of these stations sometimes sought to overpower competitors who were transmitting in the same market.[8] When television emerged in the mid-twentieth century, the US government implemented a set of rules known as 'UHF taboos'. These regulations were designed to limit the spacing of TV transmitters in both physical distance and frequency (Marcus, 2020). While this approach was essential to reduce unwanted interference, it left significant portions of valuable spectrum idle and underutilised.

The Ultra High Frequency (UHF) TV taboos symbolise the inefficiencies created by the need to mitigate harmful interference. This led economists of the Chicago School persuasion, notably Ronald Coase, to put forward an influential case for treating spectrum like private property. This meant assigning its uses through a pricing mechanism using exclusive licences to maximise efficient use (Hazlett et al., 2011; Taylor, 2013). Economists typically assume that radio frequencies are a 'rivalrous' resource like tracts of fenced-in farmland. Economic arguments derived from this claim about spectrum would persuade policymakers in New Zealand in the early 1990s—followed by all other major economies worldwide—to introduce a competitive bidding process to award high-value spectrum use licences (O'Dwyer, 2013). Auctions continue to be used to

[8]Thomas Hazlett (2017), former chief economist at the Federal Communications Commission, contests this historical account, arguing that interference was a pretence for the federal US government to assert its influence over a burgeoning commercial market for broadcast radio.

assign blocks of frequencies most coveted by commercial interests and to meet the growing demand for advanced wireless services.

In the early 2000s, the Open Spectrum Movement (OSM) emerged, led by academics and policy advocates in the US such as David Reed at MIT, Yochai Benkler at Harvard, Lawrence Lessig at Stanford, and Kevin Werbach, then at the Federal Communications Commission. The OSM sought new metaphors for spectrum that would be applied to criticise long-standing assumptions about harmful interference and scarcity. OSM proponents suggested spectrum-as-an-ocean or spectrum-as-public-right-of-way to highlight its status as a common pool resource (De Vries, 2007, 2008). The rhetorical strategy of OSM did not aim to displace the territorial meaning as much as it challenged the reification of the radio spectrum in regulatory discourse.

Open spectrum advocates questioned existing methods for mitigating harmful interference by highlighting radio equipment designs that are not dependent on discrete and exclusive frequency assignments and which allow multiple users to use the same frequency bands with minimal interference. Citing these innovations, Werbach (2004, p. 882) declared that "spectrum is a fallacy" and suggested that, in its role as a cognitive metaphor, it distracts policymakers from the possibilities of an open commons-based approach to wireless radio policy.

Open spectrum proponents cite a variety of successes with licence-exempt approaches to wireless technology, suggesting that it is a sustainable approach to managing the radio spectrum as a common pool resource (Weiss & Gomez, 2020). Examples of successful efforts at spectrum sharing include amateur radio, citizens band (CB) radio, and the wave of innovations enabled by the open spectrum allocated for Wi-Fi and Bluetooth devices (Blevins, 2023).

The OSM emphasises that new radio technologies and alternative governance processes can transform the radio spectrum into a non-rivalrous public commons that minimises unwanted interference through innovative frequency-sharing methods. Some argue that this approach has the potential to flip spectrum into an anti-rival resource, suggesting the term "cooperation gain" to describe how frequency-sharing techniques can lead inversely to growth in bandwidth capacity by using smart radios and mesh network designs (Werbach, 2004, p. 928).

In effect, the OSM draws on the spectrum-as-commons model to reject arguments for spectrum privatisation and calls, instead, for a governance regime premised on open access as a first principle. For instance, Werbach (2004, pp. 930–931) suggests that we consider an approach where:

> the commons would be the baseline, with property encompassed within it, rather than the reverse. The initial legal rule for wireless communication should be universal access. Anyone would be permitted to transmit anywhere, at any time, in any manner, so long as they did not impose an excessive burden on others … To a first approximation, this regime collapses to the system we have today, but it allows for expansion, potentially in radical directions.

Going further, Werbach proposes the term 'supercommons' as an inclusive spatial metaphor that de-emphasises the properties of the radio spectrum itself and redirects attention to the capabilities of devices such as software-defined radio and cooperative architectures for wireless systems.

The normative function of the supercommons metaphor is, however, less clear. O'Dwyer (2013, p. 499, 521), for instance, suggests that even as the OSM advocates for "a greater communality of the radio spectrum", there is the looming possibility of "a much more draconian form of enclosure dressed in the 'socialist' garb of 'the commons'". Specifically, she points to a paradox in which "new forms of regulation appropriate to the commons" could facilitate "a shift from autonomous radios, to one in which some central authority has the power to remotely monitor or even switch off a device" (O'Dwyer, 2013, p. 522). To illustrate this threat, O'Dwyer cites a series of consultations held by the US National Telecommunications and Information Administration (NTIA) regarding standards to enable dynamic spectrum sharing for software-defined radio systems. These 'tethered' systems rely on centralised databases and remote monitoring and control by corporations or state entities to manage their use. Such systems may become more commonplace as commercial interests confront spectrum scarcity as a barrier to deploying 5G wireless systems.[9] "Here", says O'Dwyer (2013, p. 522), "we encounter a commons

[9] Nokia (2024) positions fifth-generation (5G) wireless systems as providing fast mobile broadband connectivity for a myriad of networked devices and as essential infrastructure for the so-called Internet of Things (IOT). The design of 5G systems utilises distinct bands of spectrum: low- and mid-band spectrum (between 1 and 6 GHz) for efficient geographic coverage and capacity, in addition to high-band spectrum (24–40 GHz) for high speed over shorter distances. All of this spectrum is considered commercially valuable and many countries are or will soon be auctioning it to private operators.

with a new kind of enclosure. The frequency band becomes open, but various draconian interventions in the networked architecture constrain access". In other words, the supercommons may promise a spectrum windfall only to become subject to a reconfiguration of exclusive access rights through software and networked connectivity.

5 A Proposed Renaming: Spectrumscape

> As much as I enjoy naming the names, it is even more exciting to find something I cannot name. (Maloof, 2008, p. 17)

Metaphors are powerful tools for naming because they simultaneously reveal and conceal, shaping how we perceive and relate to concepts (Lakoff & Johnson, 2003). The radio spectrum is often framed as a scarce natural resource subject to the tragedy of the commons. Elinor Ostrom (1999, p. 498) identifies common-pool resources—such as lakes, forests, and the atmosphere—as "natural or manmade resources from which it is difficult to exclude or limit users once the resource is provided". Such resources face appropriation challenges, requiring users to coordinate their use to avoid over-exploitation. Framing the spectrum as a natural resource has served as an ontological metaphor, enabling policymakers, engineers, and users to conceptualise electromagnetic energy in terms of land or property (Lakoff & Johnson, 2003). However, this metaphor can be misleading by obscuring the power dynamics and inequalities inherent in spectrum allocation and management (De Vries & Westling, 2017; Reid, 2018).

As Viktor Smith (2021, p. 12) observes, "New names are not always for labelling entirely new phenomena. They may also categorise and present things that have been around us all along in a new way." Yet even when new names are adopted, the metaphors underpinning them often endure, continuing to influence understanding in subtle but significant ways. These metaphors can become entrenched as hegemonic assemblages, resisting efforts to redefine or reframe them. The persistent metaphor of the radio spectrum as territory exemplifies this, shaping discourse even as new terms are introduced.

For example, Werbach's (2004) term 'supercommons' was proposed to inspire a transformative approach to radio regulations. Yet, it remains rooted in the spectrum-as-territory metaphor, demonstrating the enduring cognitive appeal of this framing. Particularly for policymakers and the public, geographic metaphors provide a familiar and effective way to express the intangible qualities of the radio spectrum. This persistence underscores the metaphor's cognitive resonance, even as normative debates around spectrum use and regulation evolve. In other words, spectrum-as-territory is likely to influence discourse about wireless communication for the foreseeable future:

> (t)he persistence of [a] metaphorical system through time and across cultures suggests that it represents a significant, entrenched part of the human conceptual system. And the consistency of this metaphorical system across categories ... indicates that there is a common human rationality at work. (Winter, 2003, p. 55)

Even for radio system engineers and physicists, for whom the operational reality of spectrum is expressed extensively in mathematical terms, a spatial metaphor continues to be useful as conversational shorthand and in structuring mental models for this kind of work (Sfard, 1994).

A renaming effort must, therefore, propose a term that preserves the cognitive resonance of the spectrum-as-territory metaphor but also acknowledges that "radio waves do not merely exist or define 'space'; they are transmitted for specific purposes, shaped by decisions made by individuals wielding varying levels of political and economic power" (Joyce, 2007, p. 91). Moreover, it must address the competing normative claims this metaphor generates, particularly in the "antagonisms between openness and enclosure" (O'Dwyer, 2013, p. 499) that underlie ongoing debates about the regulation of radio technology. In essence, any renaming effort must account for both the cognitive and normative dimensions of the spectrum metaphor as they have evolved over time.

To this end, I propose adopting Joyce's (2007, p. 91) term *spectrumscape*, which incorporates Arjun Appadurai's (1996) spatial metaphor of the '-scape' to represent "the movement of people, media, technology, money, and ideas around the world" enabled by wireless technology. This term is particularly compelling because it retains the widely accepted cognitive reference of spectrum-as-territory while acknowledging its status as a historically and contemporarily contested resource shaped by "complex intertwinings of culture, economics, and politics across the globe" (Joyce, 2007, p. 91). In this way, *spectrumscape* offers a shared cognitive model that also highlights the diverse normative claims it generates.

In the case of the Māori, a *spectrumscape* renaming emphasises how *taonga* imbues the spectrum-as-territory metaphor with deep cultural significance predating the invention of radio technology. Today, it functions as a normative challenge to the colonisation and privatisation of radio waves by the Crown, instead, asserting collective ownership grounded in Indigenous values. The spectrumscape concept also underscores the continuity of the cognitive role of the spatial metaphor, exemplified by the historical term 'ether', which described radio energy as an all-pervasive medium accessible to all. In the 1970s, Robert Metcalfe revived the term to describe the spatial design of the Ethernet protocol, reflecting a normative perspective that championed open access and sharing, principles he promoted at Xerox PARC. These values later shaped the OSM of the early 2000s. In each instance, the spectrum-as-territory metaphor is cognitively consistent, even as its normative claims evolved to reflect changing visions of access, ownership, and regulation.

In summary, *spectrumscape* is a valuable term because it captures the enduring essence of an ontological metaphor—the spectrum as radio energy—an ever-present, intangible resource that flows "through and around human presence" (Joyce, 2007, p. 91). The suffix '-scape' further emphasises the historically specific and contested political economy of radio technology, where ongoing conflicts persist over the entitlements of private and public actors to determine the uses of this vital resource. By merging the timeless metaphor of spectrum as a pervasive medium with the competing aims of institutions and divergent human interests, *spectrumscape* draws attention to the need for decision-making that upholds community values and collective aspirations. As wireless communication technologies continue to expand, the term can encourage critical thinking and informed debate about how radio frequencies are allocated and managed to serve the common good.

References

Aitken, H. G. J. (1994). Allocating the spectrum: The origins of radio regulation. *Technology and Culture, 35*(4), 686–716. https://doi.org/10.2307/3106503

Appadurai, A. (1996). *Modernity at large*. University of Minnesota Press.

Blevins, J. (2023). The policy origins of Wi-Fi. *Indiana Law Journal, 98*(2), 529–574. https://www.repository.law.indiana.edu/ilj/vol98/iss2/5

Bravo, L. (2018, July 9). Decolonizing communication media and digital technologies. *Ritimo*. https://www.ritimo.org/Decolonizing-Communication-Media-and-Digital-Technologies#nb12

De Vries, J. P. (2008). De-situating spectrum: Rethinking radio policy using non-spatial metaphors. *2008 3rd IEEE Symposium on New Frontiers in Dynamic Spectrum Access Networks.* https://colab.ws/articles/10.1109%2Fdyspan.2008.63

De Vries, J. P. (2007). Imagining radio: Mental models of wireless communication. *InterMedia, 35*(3), 25–29. https://www.iicom.org/wp-content/uploads/23_PDFsam_Intermedia-Volume-35-No-3.pdf

De Vries, J. P., & Westling, J. (2017). *Not a scarce natural resource: Alternatives to spectrum-think.* SSRN. https://doi.org/10.2139/ssrn.2943502

Global System for Mobile Communications Association. (2017). *Introducing radio spectrum: Spectrum primer series.* GSMA. https://www.gsma.com/spectrum/wp-content/uploads/2017/04/Introducing-Radio-Spectrum.pdf

Hazlett, T. W. (2017). *The political spectrum: The tumultuous liberation of wireless technology, from Herbert Hoover to the smartphone.* Yale University Press.

Hazlett, T. W., Porter, D., & Smith, V. (2011). Radio spectrum and the disruptive clarity of Ronald Coase. *The Journal of Law & Economics, 54*(4), S125–S165. https://doi.org/10.1086/662992

Heidegger, M. (1962). *Being and time* (J. Macquarrie & E. Robinson, Trans.). Blackwell Publishers.

Holmes, J. (2022, May 12). Marconi's first radio broadcast made 125 years ago. *BBC.* https://www.bbc.com/news/uk-england-somerset-61327062

Howell, B., & Tang, X. (2023). Using spectrum allocations to address indigenous rights claims: The case of New Zealand. *Telecommunications Policy, 47*(10), 1–15. https://doi.org/10.1016/j.telpol.2023.102642

Innovation, Science and Economic Development Canada. (2018). *Radio spectrum allocations in Canada* [Chart]. Government of Canada. https://ised-isde.canada.ca/site/gestion-spectre-telecommunications/sites/default/files/attachments/2022/2018_Canadian_Radio_Spectrum_Chart.PDF

International Telecommunication Union (ITU). (2024). *Radio interference.* ITU, United Nations. https://www.itu.int/en/mediacentre/backgrounders/Pages/radio-interference.aspx#:~:text=1003%20of%20the%20ITU%20Constitution,in%20accordance%20with%20Radio%20Regulations%2

Joyce, Z. (2020). Radio spectrum as indigenous space: Property rights and traditional knowledge in New Zealand's spectrum. In G. Taylor & C. Middleton (Eds.), *Frequencies: International spectrum policy* (pp. 19–45). McGill-Queen's University Press.

Joyce, Z. (2007). Spectrumscape: The space of wirelessness. *Media International Australia, 125*(1), 83–93. https://doi.org/10.1177/1329878X0812500110

Lakoff, G., & Johnson, M. (2003). *Metaphors we live by.* University of Chicago Press.

Maloof, J. (2008). The naming of things. *Environmental Philosophy, 5*(2), 17–20. http://www.jstor.org/stable/26167980

Māori Dictionary. (n.d.). Taonga. In *Te Aka:* Māori Dictionary. Retrieved January 31, 2025 from https://maoridictionary.co.nz/

Marcus, M. J. (2020). Spectrum sharing. In G. Taylor & C. Middleton (Eds.), *Frequencies: International spectrum policy* (pp. 187–206). McGill-Queen's University Press.

Mazepa, P., & Mosco, V. (2016). A political economy approach to the internet. In J. M. Bauer & M. Latzer (Eds.), *Handbook on the economics of the internet* (pp. 163–180). Edward Elgar Publishing.

McLuhan, M. (1964). *Understanding media: The extensions of man*. McGraw-Hill.

Metcalfe, R. (1973, May 22). *Ether!* [Original ethernet sketch]. DigiBarn ComputerMuseum.https://www.digibarn.com/collections/diagrams/ethernet-original/composit-ethernet-sketch.jpg

Milutis, J. (2006). *Ether: The nothing that connects everything*. University of Minnesota Press.

Muri, A. (2007). *The enlightenment cyborg: A history of communications and control in the human machine, 1660–1830*. University of Toronto Press.

Navarro, J. (2016). Ether and wireless: An old medium into new media. *Historical Studies in the Natural Sciences, 46*(4), 460–489. https://www.jstor.org/stable/26413621

Nokia. (2024). *5G spectrum bands explained — low, mid and high band*. https://www.nokia.com/thought-leadership/articles/spectrum-bands-5g-world/

O'Dwyer, R. (2013). Spectre of the commons: Spectrum regulation in the communism of capital. *Ephemera, 13*(3), 497–526. https://ephemerajournal.org/contribution/spectre commons-spectrum-regulation-communism-capital

Orange, C. (2023). Te Tiriti o Waitangi—The treaty of Waitangi. *The Encyclopedia of New Zealand*. http://www.TeAra.govt.nz/en/te-tiriti-o-waitangi-the-treaty-of-waitangi/print

Ostrom, E. (1999). Coping with tragedies of the commons. *Annual Review of Political Science, 2*, 493–535. https://doi.org/10.1146/annurev.polisci.2.1.493

Oxford English Dictionary. (n.d.). Radio spectrum. In *Oxford English Dictionary*. Retrieved March 14, 2025, from https://doi.org/10.1093/OED/2324546867

Pinch, T. J., & Bijker, W. E. (1984). The social construction of facts and artefacts: Or how the sociology of science and the sociology of technology might benefit each other. *Social Studies of Science, 14*(3), 399–441. http://www.jstor.org/stable/285355

Reid, B. E. (2018, September 11). Spectrum, analogy, and the line from physics to policy. *Blake E. Reid*. https://blakereid.org/spectrum-analogy-and-the-line-from-physics-to-policy/

Schaefer, P. (2013). Why is "ether" in Ethernet? *International Journal of Communication, 7*(17), 2010–2026. https://ijoc.org/index.php/ijoc/article/view/1866/984

Seton, E. T. (1917). [Spark gap transmitter diagram]. *Wikimedia Commons.* https://commons.wikimedia.org/wiki/File:Spark_gap_transmitter_diagram.png

Sfard, A. (1994). Reification as the birth of metaphor. *For the Learning of Mathematics, 14*(1), 44–55. https://www.jstor.org/stable/40248103

Smith, V. (2021). *Naming and framing: Understanding the power of words across disciplines, domains, and modalities.* Routledge.

Smythe, D. W. (1981). *Dependency road: Communication, capitalism, consciousness, and Canada.* Ablex Publishing.

Taylor, G. (2013). Oil in the ether: A critical history of spectrum auctions in Canada. *Canadian Journal of Communication, 38*(1), 121–137. https://doi.org/10.22230/cjc.2013v38n1a2600

Waitangi Tribunal. (1990). *Report of the Waitangi Tribunal on claims concerning the allocation of radio frequencies.* https://forms.justice.govt.nz/search/Documents/WT/wt_DOC_68476762/Allocation%20of%20Radio%20Frequencies%201990.pdf

Walker, P. (2022, February 20). The spectrum – The battle to reclaim a taonga. *E-Tangata.* https://e-tangata.co.nz/media/the-spectrum-the-battle-to-reclaim-a-taonga/

Weinberger, D. (2003, March 12). The myth of interference. Salon. https://www.salon.com/2003/03/12/spectrum/

Weiss, M. B. H., & Gomez, M. (2020). Polycentric governance for spectrum sharing. In G. Taylor & C. Middleton (Eds.), *Frequencies: International spectrum policy* (pp. 208–236). McGill-University Press.

Werbach, K. (2004). Supercommons: Toward a unified theory of wireless communication. *Texas Law Review, 82*(4), 863–973. https://web.archive.org/web/20160328032422id_/http://werbach.com/research/supercommons.pdf

Wikimedia Commons. (n.d.). *Greater Winnipeg proposed zoning regulations district map (1947)* [Map]. https://commons.wikimedia.org/wiki/File:Zoning-maps-winnipeg-9370554-o.jpg

Winter, S. L. (2003). *A clearing in the forest: Law, life, and mind.* University of Chicago Press.

The Wireless World. (1920, April 17). *The Wireless World* [Volume VIII, issue 2 of electronics journal]. https://www.worldradiohistory.com/UK/Wireless-World/20s/Wireless-World-1920-04.pdf

Wyatt, S. (2004). Danger! Metaphors at work in economics, geophysiology, and the Internet. *Science, Technology, & Human Values, 29*(2), 242–261. https://doi.org/10.1177/0162243903261947

CHAPTER 6

Technosolutionist Urbanism*

~~Smart City~~

Jess Reia and Luã Cruz

1 Introduction

Calling an urban space a 'smart city' implies that it is efficient, resilient, and aligned with visions of the future. Cities rarely want to be considered the opposite of smart. Local governments, therefore, are increasingly adopting technologies, rankings, and partnerships that engage in urban intelligence competitions, even though these pursuits are often misaligned with residents' priorities. This chapter discusses the need to rename the claims of smartness in cities that present technology as the primary solution for long-standing problems. Our study primarily focuses on Brazilian municipalities that have been adopting systems advertised as 'smart'—that is, which received awards in smart city rankings or drafted smart city

J. Reia (✉)
School of Data Science, University of Virginia, Charlottesville, VA, USA
e-mail: reia@virginia.edu

L. Cruz
Brazilian Institute for Consumer Protection (IDEC), São Paulo, Brazil
e-mail: lua.cruz@idec.org.br

C. Chokshi, R. Mansell (eds.), *The Need to Rename Tech*,
https://doi.org/10.1007/978-3-032-05155-4_6

master plans in partnership with the private sector (Reia & Cruz, 2021, 2023).[1] We propose renaming smart cities as *technosolutionist urbanism*.

In the course of our research, we identified several corporations providing misleading metaphors to lure municipalities into 'smartness' via unregulated lobbying. Overlapping with other vague but attractive words—such as artificial intelligence (AI), Internet of Things (IoT), and big data—the smart city hides corporate interests that seek to privatise urban digital infrastructures (Söderström et al., 2014; Voorwinden, 2021). Transparency and accountability are rarely part of the equation when it comes to smart cities and AI, or these initiatives are opaque (Ananny & Crawford, 2018; Jacobs et al., 2020; Novelli et al., 2023; Reia & Cruz, 2021; Wylie, 2022). This shift towards privatisation prompts municipalities to adopt proprietary, non-interoperable solutions or to introduce one-size-fits-all technosolutionist products in different cities, regardless of their unique needs and characteristics. *Technosolutionism* is the belief that technology is objective and can address all problems universally from poverty to climate change. We argue that this dangerous perspective oversimplifies complex problems and ignores the social, historical, and cultural contexts in which technology operates, often exacerbating existing inequalities.

The so-called urban intelligence market is a prosperous one, encompassing real-time data flows and optimisation in urban spaces and imaginaries (Mattern, 2014; Reia & Belli, 2021). Expos and fairs dedicated to smart cities are abundant across the globe.[2] They often follow a similar setup. In the exhibition area, companies and governmental agencies showcase the latest technology solutions such as drones and smart cameras. Beyond the exhibition lies a restricted area, accessible only to those with the appropriate credentials (which may cost a hefty fee). In this space, workshops, panels, and networking opportunities take place. In even more restricted areas, such as VIP rooms and lounges, mayors and companies negotiate and make deals. Similar to border, defence, and security fairs,

[1] We consulted the Ranking Connect Smart Cities (n.d.), focusing on the three highest-ranked municipalities in 2017: Rio de Janeiro, São Paulo, and Curitiba. The cities that drafted smart city master plans were Juazeiro do Norte, Vitória, Salvador, and Campinas. Although our focus is primarily on Brazilian cities, given the nature of our work, we situated the study within the broader context of Latin American cities, where many advocates have been questioning harmful 'smartness', such as facial recognition technologies (Al Sur, 2021).

[2] Famous examples include the Smart City Expo Barcelona, which branched out to other countries, including Brazil.

urban intelligence expos are "a transmission belt for knowledge, technology and capital transfer, and simultaneously a platform and institution that produces meaning and action" (Stockmarr, 2016, p. 189). They shape knowledge, fields and discourses around and about technology, being "positioned and portable" at the same time (Baird, 2017, p. 200).

Cities are often perceived as messy spaces that must be tamed and rationalised (Mattern, 2017a). Hence, the argument for efficiency and futurism advanced by smart city evangelists becomes very attractive (Yigitcanlar, 2021)—especially when these evangelists promise quick turnarounds, publicity, and solutions to problems such as crime rates, mobility, and climate crisis. Even when some projects fail (O'Kane, 2022), they help advance the smart city agenda.

On top of these shortcomings lie the human rights-based concerns associated with the gathering of large amounts of data from people in dense urban areas. As such, residents are subject to surveillance that, in the absence of clearly defined and robust digital rights frameworks and a responsible (and ethical) approach to big data, can lead to the over-policing (Maynard, 2017; Taylor, 2017) or control of marginalised communities whose visibility as data points can reproduces historical inequalities (Benjamin, 2019; Silva, 2023).

In this chapter, we position the smart city agenda as a problematic corporate-led agenda that conceals the privatisation of urban digital infrastructures, often via unregulated lobbying and opaque partnerships. First, we present a brief overview of the relations between urban spaces and technologies; we then explore how the idea of 'smartification' of everything is applied to all facets of urban life. Next, we examine how corporate power can undermine democratic processes in the smart city context and then we address threats to fundamental rights. In the final section we propose to rename the smart city based on what it often represents: *technosolutionist urbanism*.

Our reflections are rooted in fieldwork carried out in three Brazilian cities (São Paulo, Curitiba, and Rio de Janeiro) between 2017 and 2021; participant observation at smart city expos in São Paulo and Curitiba; and a multistakeholder map we created containing information on relevant government, industry, academic, and civil society organisations in each city studied.[3] Our study involved policy and legal analysis of master plans,

[3] We visited the Smart City Expo Curitiba in 2018 and 2019, the Connected Smart Cities event in 2018, and the Smart City Business America Congress in 2018 and 2019.

legislation, reports, white papers, public policies, investment plans, official press releases, procurement processes, and contracts from 2017 to 2023; nine in-depth interviews with policymakers, civil servants, company representatives, and specialists in Rio de Janeiro, São Paulo, and Curitiba; and Freedom of Information Act (FOIA)-equivalent (*Lei de Acesso à Informação*) requests to keep track of investments, contracts, and privacy compliance made by the city governments included in the study.

2 Urban Spaces and Technology

Technologies and cities have shared a common history for millennia as evidenced by historical and contemporary relationships that humans establish with the built environment and various technical devices. Technological advancements, from the electrification of public spaces in the early nineteenth century (Nye, 2018) to the high-performance computing and AI of the early twenty-first century (Brandusescu & Reia, 2022), have reshaped urban spaces and changed how humans and non-humans interact with them. As a result, unique names have been used in an attempt to describe the city's emerging attributes, signalling what these attributes ostensibly offer residents. The 'informational city' (Castells, 1989), 'media city' (McQuire, 2008), 'communicative city' (Gumpert & Drucker, 2008), and 'autonomous city' (Cugurullo, 2021) are examples of the naming of tech-integrated urban spaces. 'Smart city' is a recent iteration of this practice of naming.

The definition of a smart city originated as an often vague and opaque narrative conceptualised by and for a private sector in which the public interest is not a central concern as indicated by Henrique Frota, director of Instituto Polis (and see Ruhlandt, 2018).[4] The words 'smarter cities' were trademarked by IBM in 2011, and have since been adopted by industry, municipal governments, academia, and civil society organizations worldwide (Söderström et al., 2014). The pervasiveness of the language is demonstrated by its inclusion in the preparatory documents leading to the United Nations New Urban Agenda (NUA).[5] Despite the first-ever

[4] Instituto Polis, founded in 1987, is one of Brazil's leading organisations conducting public-interest research and advocacy work on various aspects of the right to the city. Frota was interviewed by the authors, 9 May 2019.

[5] The NUA, signed in Quito, Ecuador in 2016, provides global urban planning guidelines for the next two decades.

inclusion of the 'right to the city' in the text (Lefebvre, 1968; Maricato, 1985), the corporate-led vision seems to prevail in item 66: "We commit ourselves to adopting a smart-city approach that makes use of opportunities from digitalization, clean energy and technologies" (United Nations Conference on Housing and Sustainable Urban Development, 2017, p. 19).[6]

The eagerness to incorporate technology in urban development is tied to new metaphors to rationalise cities, as demonstrated by Shannon Mattern (2017a, para. 13), who argues that "our current paradigm, the *city as computer*, appeals because it frames the messiness of urban life as programmable and subject to rational order". By likening the city to a computer, one can erase various subjective social, economic, and environmental issues that do not belong in the efficient, innovative urban machine. Rodrigo Firmino, drawing upon experience in Brazil, shared in an interview that "most of these municipal projects are more concerned about efficiency than the right to the city".

The corporate storytelling in smart city initiatives that emphasises efficiency also contributes to the hierarchisation of cities in rankings and awards, according to their purchase and adoption of specific technologies. These rankings generate 'smartmentalities' that influence urban identities (Vanolo, 2014). In this context, the smart city agenda prioritises short-term, short-lived responses to the complexities of our territories by gathering big data in real time, selling the promise of efficiency and governance mechanisms that promote the automation of public services, while they monitor and control the urban territory (Kitchin, 2015; Kitchin et al., 2018; Meijer & Bolívar, 2016; Niaros, 2016).

In their efforts to be perceived as more intelligent and fulfill a global agenda revolving around 'smart' technologies and devices, municipal governments adopt a technosolutionist approach to historical problems (Morozov, 2013). These technological shortcuts cannot fix centuries of inequalities and this is not necessarily their goal. Examples of such shortcuts include the adoption of technologies like facial recognition technologies (FRT) used for surveillance and biased crime prediction algorithms

[6] David Harvey (2008, para. 2) described the right to the city this way: "The right to the city is far more than the individual liberty to access urban resources: it is a right to change ourselves by changing the city. It is, moreover, a common rather than an individual right since this transformation inevitably depends upon the exercise of a collective power to reshape the processes of urbanization. The freedom to make and remake our cities and ourselves is, I want to argue, one of the most precious yet most neglected of our human rights."

or, in the realm of education, the use of ChatGPT to prepare classes and educational websites owned and operated by governments and which send the personal data of children to technology companies.

These off-the-shelf, one-size-fits-all proprietary solutions abound, roping cities into arrangements that neither benefit the public interest nor the cities' own fiscal stress (van Loon & Toshkov, 2015). The technosolutionism behind the acquisition of certain technologies ignores the fact that "[urban] intelligence is simultaneously epistemological, technological, and physical; it's codified in our cities' laws and civic knowledge and institutions, hard-wired into their cables and protocols, framed in their streets and architectures and patterns of development" (Mattern, 2017b, p. xii).

As we move towards large language models, generative AI, supercomputers, and massive underground data storage (Murphy, 2022), the problematic relationship between technology and urban planning must be renamed—or at least exposed for what it is and what it does.

3 The Smartification of Everything

Our research identifies the misguided adoption of data-centric systems in cities as a form of 'smart-washing' of urban planning and governance, a process that drives increased privatisation of digital public infrastructure and urban services (Reia & Cruz, 2025).[7] One example is São Paulo's Smart Sampa programme, whose goal is to rent cameras and deploy algorithms to assist in combatting crime. The programme gives priority to privatised, data-driven solutions like surveillance systems, ultimately reinforcing existing inequalities and neglecting the needs of marginalised communities while presenting itself as a step toward progress. The smart city agenda is technopolitical with consequences that permeate residents' public and private lives (Kurban et al., 2017; Winner, 1980).

Another example of smart-washing is based on sustainability claims made when projects promise green energy products and improved efficiency in services provided to residents. As the datafication of our cities increases, and as developments in AI promise a better future, the underlying environmental costs of urban smartification are rarely made visible (Obringer & Nateghi, 2021). Data centres and supercomputers use natural resources to operate, leaving a significant carbon footprint (Brierley,

[7] The term is adapted from similar concepts like greenwashing in environmental issues and ethics washing in Big Tech (de Freitas Netto et al., 2020; Bietti, 2020).

2023). Electric vehicles and other devices require materials mined in the Global South, such as in South America's 'lithium triangle' (Argento & Slipak, 2021). There are hidden environmental and social costs embedded in the smartification and datafication of the world around us (Vera et al., 2019).

The emergence of rankings and competitions for smartness are facilitators of technosolutionist urbanism. Even when certain cities rank highly and receive awards for their smartness, the public perception might be mismatched with the idealisation of a smart city, given that these perceptions are deeply connected to residents' everyday needs and what they see as a priority in terms of policy or investment. As Henrique Frota, director of Instituto Polis, states "the use of technology in cities does not need to be framed by the smart cities agenda; it needs to be implemented based on the notion of the right to the city and the radicalization of democracy—questioning who are these technologies serving? And why?"[8]

The lack of meaningful civic engagement in technology-related decision-making and policy undermines trust in both governments and technologies (Brandusescu & Reia, 2022). The smart city of today—as well as the projected smart areas of the future—fails more than it succeeds at achieving change-making citizen participation.[9] Participation in smart cities unfolds in a variety of ways, frequently based on the "instrumentality of the neoliberal ideals of 'citizen-centric' smart city approaches with the slipping away of citizen as a political subject holding a set of rights and entitlements to much weaker socio-economic and legal positions" (Cardullo & Kitchin, 2019, p. 10). Fragmented examples of successful civic engagement activities do exist.[10] They include the public Wi-Fi in São Paulo and the Barcelona City Council technological sovereignty guide (Ajuntament de Barcelona, 2017).[11] However, there is a long way to go in the Brazilian cities we studied to achieve smart citizenship, especially given the limitations and risks of current participation methods (Birhane et al., 2022). Pro-forma public hearings and consultations that engage residents

[8] Frota made this comment in an interview with the authors, 9 May 2019.

[9] See, for example, Songdo in South Korea or the new concept of urban living in Saudi Arabia (https://www.neom.com/en-us/regions/theline)

[10] The term 'fragmented' here refers to the fact that these examples of successful civic engagement activities are not part of a cohesive or widespread strategy that is consistently implemented across various cities or regions. Instead, they represent isolated instances or initiatives within specific locations.

[11] See more information about the project at https://wifilivresp.github.io/

only later in the process often fail to genuinely incorporate feedback and create change (Arnstein, 1969).

4 The Pervasiveness of Corporate Interests in Democratic Processes

Research has shown that, internationally, smart cities are both an agenda and a marketing device (Stockmarr, 2016). In this section, we contribute to critical scholarship on smart cities by illustrating how smart city projects can undermine democracy and participatory local governance.

Our study identified companies and consultancy firms of all sizes as leading policy and lawmaking at the local level in Brazil. These organisations sell smart city plans, sometimes called master plans for smart cities and innovation, to city governments; these plans later become municipal laws.[12] Juazeiro do Norte, Salvador, and Vitória are examples of municipalities that hired consultancy firms to make their cities smarter. Drafted by the private sector, often in public–private partnerships and costing millions of Brazilian reais, these plans that become municipal laws rarely open up opportunities for meaningful civic engagement or social participation. However, when they do, such democratic possibilities are frequently more performative than effective (Cardullo & Kitchin, 2019).

When companies lead policy and lawmaking, they overrun the democratic processes in which citizens elect their representatives, creating a dangerous precedent. Research demonstrates that these dynamics are worrisome since they can exacerbate existing inequalities, compromise (frail) public trust in governments and technologies (Dwork & Minow, 2022; Nunes et al., 2023), or serve to intensify the power of authoritarian governments (Ricaurte et al., 2024). In Brazil, lobbying is unregulated, facilitating the participation of private stakeholders in policy and lawmaking in both visible and invisible ways. Beyond the technology sector, lobbying is a pervasive problem with consequences for other urban governance laws in the country (Rodrigues, 2014).

The privatisation of digital infrastructures—such as data centres, fibre-optic cables, sensors, and telecommunication apparatus—that we call smart-washing results in reduced oversight, and, thus, decreasing accountability mechanisms. Brazilians may not have had direct control over

[12] For the cooperation agreement, see Juazeiro do Norte (2017); for the municipal law, see Juazeiro do Norte (2018).

communication and media infrastructure in the past, but there were more well-established accountability mechanisms in place such as regulatory agencies and participatory budgets. In the case of smart tech, this privatisation process also generates closed, proprietary, non-interoperable systems that cannot be integrated with other systems already deployed by the government—and which become dependent on a company for maintenance and updates (International Bank for Reconstruction and Development, 2019; Lerner et al., 2020). In more alarming cases, cities acquire technology that can be harmful to historically marginalised communities, such as FRT (Raji et al., 2020; Souza & Zanatta, 2021) and automated decision-making in social services (Eubanks, 2018; Ranchordás, 2022).

The Brazilian smart cities market involves a complex web of corporate interests, and 'techno-optimism' permeates various networks in the business and public sectors (Issaka, 2023). Beyond the big international players, small national companies—even those under investigation for corruption (Rebello, 2023)—provide an attractive narrative on urban modernisation. Some of these companies use foreign software, often from Russia, China, Israel, and the United States (Pisanu et al., 2021), raising questions about digital sovereignty and cybersecurity (Belli, 2021; Hurel, 2023). The prioritisation of certain public services over others is also warped by the search for smartness at all costs. In Brazil, congresspeople are allocating millions of Brazilian reais to FRT instead of to much-needed basic water and sewage management in Goiás. In Bahia and São Paulo, other needs of the population, such as more hospitals and ambulances, are dismissed when purchasing smart tech, as indicated by investigative journalists, civil society advocates, such as Coalizão Direitos na Rede and Al Sur, and by scholars who play an important role in uncovering these issues and bringing them to public debate.[13]

5 A Threat to Fundamental Rights

Brazil for many years has been considered a global leader in technology policy (Arnaudo, 2017), from mobilisation around copyright law reform and the free-culture movement to the groundbreaking Brazilian Civil Rights Framework for the Internet (*Marco Civil da Internet*) and a data

[13] See, for example, the series "Quem paga a conta?" [Who pays the bill?] on corruption, lobbying and technology in Brazilian cities, published by The Intercept Brasil in 2023.

protection regulation (Mendes & Keller, 2020). The changes taking place in cities that are embracing the recommendations of smart city consultancies conflict, however, with the broader digital rights agenda (Digital Freedom Fund, 2020; Shaw & Graham, 2017). For instance, FRT and other surveillance technologies are under public scrutiny because of the harm created by their false positives which lead to human rights violations (Durães, 2024).

Like other Global South communities, Brazilian cities struggle with varying levels of inequality, a lack of public funding, and security issues. With over 5500 municipalities, Brazil is an attractive market for technosolutionism. Civil society organisations are left with the challenging task of safeguarding the human rights threatened by smart systems—by using strategic litigation, acting in coalitions and regional networks of support, and engaging in public interest lobbying (Cruz, 2022). While the smart narrative promises efficiency and security, the implementation of smart city models leads to constant monitoring of people's movements and the mass collection of personal data, restricting freedom of movement and expression and also endangering the privacy and autonomy of the most vulnerable communities, such as people of colour, LGBTQIA+ individuals, sex workers, immigrants, and the unhoused (Corrêa, 2021).

As explained in an open letter from a campaign led by Brazilian civil society organisations to ban the use of FRT by police forces (Tire Meu Rosto da Sua Mira, 2022), the dangers of deploying large-scale surveillance systems in Latin America are frightening. These technologies are used to identify and track individuals, posing a significant threat to fundamental rights such as privacy and freedom of assembly and expression (Cetic.br, 2022). Consequently, they exacerbate Brazil's challenges in addressing mass incarceration and racial biases in the criminal justice system, eroding the presumption of innocence and, in some cases, leading to wrongful arrests (Silva, 2023).[14] These violations underscore the urgent need for greater transparency and improved regulatory frameworks as smart cities become increasingly popular (Perego, 2021).

The real-life smart city (as opposed to its utopian versions) can pose a threat to fundamental rights and undermine democratic processes. By

[14] These tools have led to serious human rights abuses globally, including wrongful arrests or jailing due to misidentification, exemplified by cases in Argentina and in the United States (The Associated Press, 2023; Naundorf, 2023). In response to these concerns, cities in these countries have opted to ban the use of FRT altogether.

delegating digital infrastructures and their management to the private sector, municipalities deprioritise the democratic values of accountability, transparency, and social participation (Goodman & Powles, 2019; Santos et al., 2023).

6 Renaming the Smart City: Technosolutionist Urbanism

The current smart city agenda in the Global South is extractivist and corporate-led, facilitating the privatisation of crucial digital infrastructures and the maintenance of power through data colonisation (Ricaurte, 2019). By proposing quick technological solutions to hundreds of years of inequality, smart tech may advance a few steps in some directions—such as providing better services to residents relying on social benefits or real-time app tracking of the bus schedules—but, on the whole, it barely scratches the surface of deeper urban problems.[15] As the thriving technology market—now further invigorated by the promise of AI—consolidates around urban governance, we rename the smart city by depicting it for what it is: *technosolutionist urbanism.*

Technosolutionist urbanism often disregards or downplays concerns related to privacy, climate crisis, the digital divide, and social inequality, favouring a technocratic and oversimplified view of urban problems (Coleman, 2023). This further marginalises vulnerable communities, exacerbates environmental issues, increases indiscriminate surveillance, and threatens citizens' fundamental rights, raising significant ethical and political concerns about the future of cities and society at large.

To depart from technosolutionist urbanism approaches, the deployment of data-centric technologies in urban spaces must, we argue, address five key issues. First, policies and practices involving advanced technologies should meaningfully include residents' voices before making substantial decisions, leveraging the benefits of participatory approaches, while avoiding risks of co-optation (Birhane et al., 2022). Local knowledge and expertise shared by community spokespeople can offer fresh perspectives to policymakers. Second, climate justice must be a central component of

[15] While these apps may provide convenience and efficiency, they do not address systemic challenges such as economic disparity, unequal access to resources, or insufficient public transportation infrastructure. As a result, the apps may be helpful on a surface level but do not lead to comprehensive changes that address the broader, pressing societal issues.

the urban tech agenda, avoiding misleading greenwashed metaphors that disguise new technologies as 'sustainability' initiatives (de Freitas Netto et al., 2020) and tackling environmental issues holistically, from the natural resources needed to keep data centres running to the hidden costs of AI and the electrification of vehicles (Coleman, 2023; Hogan, 2015). Third, data justice and digital rights considerations must be key components of tech design and deployment instead of an afterthought to, or an unaddressed element of, the smartness equation (Costanza-Chock, 2020). Fourth, cities need affordable technology, favouring replicable, open source, and collaborative solutions—thereby anticipating or preventing future issues with obsolescence, discontinuity, and instability of local politics. Fifth, a transdisciplinary approach to both technology and urban governance is needed; one that focuses on specific aspects of the city (such as mobility and waste management) and brings other dimensions of urban life to light. Specifically, such an approach should foreground cultural policy and the role of cultural institutions in the ever-changing relationship between spaces, technologies, and people.

References

Al Sur. (2021). Facial recognition in Latin America: Trends in the implementation of a perverse technology. *AlSur*. https://www.alsur.lat/en/report/facial-recognition-latin-america-trends-implementation-perverse-technology

Ajuntament de Barcelona. (2017). *Policy on technological sovereignty and guidelines for its implementation*. https://ajuntamentdebarcelona.github.io/ethical-digital-standards-site/tech-sovereignty/0.1/policy.html

Ananny, M., & Crawford, K. (2018). Seeing without knowing: Limitations of the transparency ideal and its application to algorithmic accountability. *New Media & Society, 20*(3), 973–989. https://doi.org/10.1177/1461444816676645

Argento, M., & Slipak, A. M. (2021). Litio en Sudamérica, más extractivismo en la acumulación por desfosilización. *Grupo Editorial Energía y Equidad; Energía y Equidad, 3*, 70–75. https://ri.conicet.gov.ar/handle/11336/207758

Arnaudo, D. (2017). Brasil e o Marco Civil da Internet: O Estado da Governança Digital Brasileira. *Artigo Estratégico, 25*, 1–57. https://igarape.org.br/marco-civil/assets/downloads/igarape_o-brasil-e-o-marco-civil-da-internet.pdf

Arnstein, S. R. (1969). A ladder of citizen participation. *Journal of the American Institute of Planners, 35*(4), 216–224. https://doi.org/10.1080/01944366908977225

The Associated Press. (2023, September 25). Black plaintiffs file lawsuits for wrongful arrests or jailing due to facial recognition technology. *NBC News*.

https://www.nbcnews.com/news/nbcblk/black-plaintiffs-file-lawsuits-wrongful-arrests-jailing-due-facial-rec-rcna117168

Baird, T. (2017). Knowledge of practice: A multi-sited event ethnography of border security fairs in Europe and North America. *Security Dialogue, 48*(3), 187–205. https://doi.org/10.1177/0967010617691656

Belli, L. (2021). BRICS countries to build digital sovereignty. In L. Belli (Ed.), *CyberBRICS* (pp. 271–280). Springer. https://doi.org/10.1007/978-3-030-56405-6_7

Benjamin, R. (2019). *Race after technology: Abolitionist tools for the new Jim code*. Polity.

Bietti, E. (2020). From ethics washing to ethics bashing: A view on tech ethics from within moral philosophy. In *Proceedings of the 2020 Conference on Fairness, Accountability, and Transparency* (pp. 210–219). https://doi.org/10.1145/3351095.33728

Birhane, A., Isaac, W., Prabhakaran, V., Diaz, M., Elish, M. C., Gabriel, I., & Mohamed, S. (2022). Power to the people? Opportunities and challenges for participatory AI. In *Proceedings of the 2nd ACM Conference on Equity and Access in Algorithms, Mechanisms, and Optimization (EAAMO '22)* (pp. 1–8). Association for Computing Machinery. https://doi.org/10.1145/3551624.3555290

Brandusescu, A., & Reia, J. (Eds.). (2022). *Artificial intelligence in the city: Building civic engagement and public trust*. Centre for Interdisciplinary Research on Montreal, McGill University. https://www.mcgill.ca/centre-montreal/projects/completed-projects/ai-city

Brierley, C. (2023). *Big data's hidden cost: The carbon footprint of computational science*. University of Cambridge Stories, Green Algorithms. https://www.cam.ac.uk/stories/green-algorithms

Cardullo, P., & Kitchin, R. (2019). Being a 'citizen' in the smart city: Up and down the scaffold of smart citizen participation in Dublin, Ireland. *GeoJournal, 84*(1), 1–13. https://doi.org/10.1007/s10708-018-9845-8

Castells, M. (1989). *The informational city*. Blackwell.

Cetic.br. (2022). *Privacidade e proteção de dados pessoais 2021: Perspectivas de indivíduos, empresas e organizações públicas no Brasil*. https://cetic.br/pt/publicacao/privacidade-e-protecao-de-dados-2021/

Coleman, J. (2023, December 7). *AI's climate impact goes beyond its emissions*. Scientific American. https://www.scientificamerican.com/article/ais-climate-impact-goes-beyond-its-emissions/

Connected Smart Cities. (n.d.). *Ranking connected smart cities 2024*. https://ranking.connectedsmartcities.com.br/

Corrêa, B. K. N. (2021). *Direito e tecnologia em perspectiva Amefricana: Autonomia, algoritmos e vieses raciais* (PhD diss.). Programa de Pós-graduação em Direito, PUC-Rio. https://www.maxwell.vrac.puc-rio.br/58993/58993.PDF

Costanza-Chock, S. (2020). *Design justice: Community-led practices to build the worlds we need*. MIT Press.
Cruz, L. (2022). Where is facial recognition technology heading in Brazil? In A. Brandusescu & J. Reia (Eds.), *Artificial intelligence in the city: Building civic engagement and public trust* (pp. 62–64). Centre for Interdisciplinary Research on Montreal, McGill University.
Cugurullo, F. (2021). *Frankenstein urbanism: Eco, smart and autonomous cities, artificial intelligence and the end of the city*. Routledge.
Digital Freedom Fund. (2020). *Digital rights are human rights*. https://digitalfreedomfund.org/digital-rights-are-human-rights/
Dwork, C., & Minow, M. (2022). Distrust of artificial intelligence: Sources & responses from computer science & law. *Daedalus, 151*(2), 309–321. https://doi.org/10.1162/daed_a_01918
Durães, U. (2024, April 28). Reconhecimento facial: Erros expõem falta de transparência e viés racista. *UOL*. https://noticias.uol.com.br/cotidiano/ultimas-noticias/2024/04/28/reconhecimento-facial-erros-falta-de-transparencia.htm
Gumpert, G., & Drucker, S. J. (2008). Communicative cities. *The International Communication Gazette, 70*(3–4), 195–208. https://doi.org/10.1177/1748048508089947
Eubanks, V. (2018). *Automating inequality: How high-tech tools profile, police and punish the poor*. St. Martin's Press.
de Freitas Netto, S. V., Sobral, M. F. F., Ribeiro, A. R. B., & da Luz Soares, G. R. (2020). Concepts and forms of greenwashing: A systematic review. *Environmental Science and European Journal, 32*, 1–12. https://doi.org/10.1186/s12302-020-0300-3
Hogan, M. (2015). Data flows and water woes: The Utah Data Center. *Big Data & Society, 2*(2), 1–12. https://doi.org/10.1177/2053951715592429
Goodman, E. P., & Powles, J. (2019). Urbanism under Google: Lessons from Sidewalk Toronto. *Fordham Law Review, 88*(2), 457–498. https://ir.lawnet.fordham.edu/flr/vol88/iss2/4
Harvey, D. (2008). The right to the city. *New Left Review, II*(53), 23–40. https://newleftreview.org/issues/ii53/articles/david-harvey-the-right-to-the-city
Hurel, L. M. (2023). *Mapping cyber policy in Latin America: The Brazilian case*. Centro LATAM Digital. https://centrolatam.digital/publicacion/mapping-cyber-policy-in-latin-america-the-brazilian-case
International Bank for Reconstruction and Development. (2019). *Open source for global public goods*. The World Bank. https://documents1.worldbank.org/curated/en/672901582561140400/pdf/Open-Source-for-Global-Public-Goods.pdf

Issaka, A. (2023). Techno-optimism: Framing data and digital infrastructure for public acceptance in Ghana. *Big Data & Society, 10*(2), 1–12. https://doi.org/10.1177/20539517231215359

Jacobs, N., Edwards, P., Markovic, M., Cottrill, C. D., & Salt, K. (2020). Who trusts in the smart city? Transparency, governance, and the Internet of Things. *Data & Policy, 2*, 1–9. https://doi.org/10.1017/dap.2020.11

Juazeiro do Norte. (2018, June 11). Lei Complementar N° 117. *Diário Oficial do Município [de Juazeiro do Norte], Caderno I, ano XX*(4762), 2.

Juazeiro do Norte. (2017, December 12). Termo de autorização—Realização de estudos de viabilidade e estruturação de Parceria Público-Privada (PPP). *Diário Oficial do Município [de Juazeiro do Norte], Caderno I, ano XX*(4640), 4.

Kitchin, R. (2015). Making sense of smart cities: Addressing present shortcomings. *Cambridge Journal of Regions, Economy and Society, 8*(1), 131–136. https://doi.org/10.1093/cjres/rsu027

Kitchin, R., Lauriault, T. P., & McCardle, G. (Eds.) (2018). *Data and the city.* Routledge.

Kurban, C., Peña-López, I., & Haberer, M. (2017). What is technopolitics? A conceptual scheme for understanding politics in the digital age. *IDP: Revista de InternetDerecho y Ciencia Política, 24*, 3–20. https://www.redalyc.org/pdf/788/78850913002.pdf

Lefebvre, H. (1968). Le droit à la ville. Anthropos.

Lerner, M., Price, A., Schank, H., & Gregori, B. (2020). Building and reusing open source tools for government. *New America.* https://www.newamerica.org/digital-impact-governance-initiative/reports/building-and-reusing-open-source-tools-government/

Maricato, E. (1985). Direito à terra ou direito à cidade? Revista de Cultura Vozes, 79(6), 405–410. https://www.labhab.fau.usp.br/publicacoes/direito-a-terra-ou-direito-a-cidade/

Mattern, S. (2017a). A city is not a computer. *Places Journal.* https://doi.org/10.22269/170207

Mattern, S. (2017b). *Code and clay, data and dirt: Five thousand years of urban media.* University of Minnesota Press.

Mattern, S. (2014). Interfacing urban intelligence. *Places Journal.* https://doi.org/10.22269/140428

Maynard, R. (2017). *Policing Black lives: State violence in Canada from slavery to the present.* Fernwood Publishing.

McQuire, S. (2008). *The media city: Media, architecture and urban space.* Sage.

Meijer, A., & Bolívar, M. P. R. (2016). Governing the smart city: A review of the literature on smart urban governance. *International Review of Administrative Sciences, 82*(2), 392–408. https://doi.org/10.1177/0020852314564308

Mendes, L. S., & Keller, C. I. (2020). A new milestone for data protection in Brazil. *Internet Policy Review*. https://policyreview.info/articles/news/new-milestone-data-protection-brazil/1471

Morozov, E. (2013). To save everything, click here: *The folly of technological solutionism*. PublicAffairs.

Murphy, B. M. (2022). *We the dead: Preserving data at the end of the world*. The University of North Carolina Press.

Naundorf, K. (2023, September 13). The twisted eye in the sky over Buenos Aires. *Wired*. https://www.wired.com/story/buenos-aires-facial-recognition-scandal/

Niaros, V. (2016). Introducing a taxonomy of the 'smart city': Towards a commons-oriented approach? Triple-C, 14(1), 51–61.

Novelli, C., Taddeo, M., & Floridi, L. (2023). Accountability in artificial intelligence: What it is and how it works. *AI & SOCIETY, 39*, 1871–1882. https://doi.org/10.1007/s00146-023-01635-y

Nunes, P., Lima, T. G. L., & Rodrigues, Y. (2023). *From the plains to Brasilia: How Goiás influenced the expansion of facial recognition in Brazilian public safety*. CESeC.

Nye, D. E. (2018). *American illuminations: Urban lighting, 1800–1920*. The MIT Press.

Obringer, R., & Nateghi, R. (2021). What makes a city 'smart' in the Anthropocene? A critical review of smart cities under climate change. *Sustainable Cities and Society, 75*, 1–12. https://doi.org/10.1016/j.scs.2021.103278

O'Kane, J. (2022). *Sideways: The city Google couldn't buy*. Penguin Random House Canada.

Perego, A. (2021). A new age of surveillance: Facial recognition in policing and why it should be abolished. *Cardozo Journal of Equal Rights & Social Justice, 28*, 79–104. https://heinonline.org/HOL/LandingPage?handle=hein.journals/cardw28&div=8&id=&page=

Pisanu, G., Arroyo, V., Ucciferri, L., Ferreyra, E., Moraes, T., Laranjeira, J. R., Almeida, E. C., Dourado, F. F., Reis, C., Rocha da Silva, F., Finlay, J., & Córdova-Páez, A. (2021). *Surveillance tech in Latin America: Made abroad, deployed at home*. Access Now. https://www.accessnow.org/wp-content/uploads/2021/08/Surveillance-Tech-Latam-Report.pdf

Raji, I. D., Gebru, T., Mitchell, M., Buolamwini, J., Lee, J., & Denton, E. (2020). Saving face: Investigating the ethical concerns of facial recognition auditing. In *AIES '20: Proceedings of the AAAI/ACM Conference on AI, Ethics, and Society* (pp. 145–151). https://dl.acm.org/doi/abs/10.1145/3375627.3375820

Ranchordás, S. (2022). The digitization of government and digital exclusion: Setting the scene. In C. Blanco de Morais, G. Ferreira Mendes, & T. Vesting (Eds.), *The rule of law in cyberspace* (pp. 125–148). Springer.

Reia, J., & Belli, L. (2021). *Smart cities no Brasil: Regulação, tecnologia e direitos* [Smart cities in Brazil: Regulation, technology and rights]. Editora Letramento/ Casa do Direito. https://doi.org/10.18130/p1me-mf66

Reia, J., & Cruz, L. (2025). Smart-washing the city: A study on the privatization of urban digital infrastructures in the Global South. *International Journal of Communication, 19*, 1–23.

Reia, J., & Cruz, L. (2023). Smart cities in Brazil: Connections between corporate power, rights, and civic engagement. *Cadernos Metrópole, 25*(57), 467–490. https://doi.org/10.1590/2236-9996.2023-5705

Reia, J., & Cruz, L. (2021). Seeing through the smart city narrative: Data governance, power relations, and regulatory challenges in Brazil. In B. Haggart, N. Tusikov, & J. A. Scholte (Eds.), *Contested power and authority in internet governance: Return of the state?* (pp. 123–145). Routledge.

Rebello, A. (2023, August 14). Crise de imagem. *The Intercept Brasil*. https://www.intercept.com.br/2023/08/14/smart-sampa-denunciada-por-corrupcao-capturar-seu-rosto-em-sp/

Ricaurte, P. (2019). Data epistemologies, the coloniality of power, and resistance. *Television & New Media, 20*(4), 350–365. https://doi.org/10.1177/1527476419831640

Ricaurte, P., Gómez-Cruz, E., & Siles, I. (2024). Algorithmic governmentality in Latin America: Sociotechnical imaginaries, neocolonial soft power, and authoritarianism. *Big Data & Society, 11*(1), 1–6. https://doi.org/10.1177/20539517241229697

Rodrigues, A. (2014, May 18). *Lobby para o Plano Diretor de SP vai de igreja a aeroporto*. Folha de S. Paulo. https://m.folha.uol.com.br/cotidiano/2014/05/1456212-lobby-para-o-plano-diretor-de-sao-paulo-vai-de-igreja-a-aeroporto.shtml

Ruhlandt, R. W. S. (2018). The governance of smart cities: A systematic literature review. *Cities, 81*, 1–23. https://doi.org/10.1016/j.cities.2018.02.014

Shaw, J., & Graham, M. (Eds.). (2017). *Our digital rights to the city*. Meatspace Press.

Santos, B. C. L., de Franca Junior, F. A., & Macêdo, P. (2023). A agenda neoliberal e o avanço das cidades inteligentes: Problemas do capitalismo de vigilância como produto das parcerias público-privadas. *RJLB - Revista Jurídica Luso-Brasileira, 5*, 375–402. https://www.cidp.pt/revistas/rjlb/2023/5/2023_05_0375_0401.pdf

Silva, T. (2023). Necropolítica algorítmica [Algorithmic necropolitics]. *Sexualidad, Salud y Sociedad, 39*, 1–29. https://doi.org/10.1590/1984-6487.sess.2023.39.e22304.a.es

Söderström, O., Paasche, T., & Klauser, F. (2014). Smart cities as corporate storytelling. *City, 18*(3), 307–320. https://doi.org/10.1080/13604813.2014.906716

Souza, M. R. O., & Zanatta, R. A. F. (2021). The problem of automated facial recognition technologies in Brazil: Social countermovements and the new frontiers of fundamental rights. *Latin American Human Rights Studies, 1*, 1–34. https://revistas.ufg.br/lahrs/article/view/69423

Stockmarr, L. (2016). Security fairs. In R. Abrahamsen & A. Leander (Eds.), *Routledge handbook of private security studies* (pp. 187–196). Routledge.

Taylor, L. (2017). What is data justice? The case for connecting digital rights and freedoms globally. *Big Data & Society, 4*(2), 1–14. https://doi.org/10.1177/2053951717736335

United Nations Conference on Housing and Sustainable Urban Development. (2017). *New urban agenda*. United Nations General Assembly, Government of the Republic of Ecuador. https://habitat3.org/wp-content/uploads/NUA-English.pdf

Tire Meu Rosto da Sua Mira. (2022). *Open letter to ban the use of digital facial recognition technologies in public security*. https://tiremeurostodasuamira.org.br/en/open-letter/

van Loon, A., & Toshkov, D. (2015). Adopting open source software in public administration: The importance of boundary spanners and political commitment. *Government Information Quarterly, 32*(2), 207–215. https://doi.org/10.1016/j.giq.2015.01.004

Vanolo, A. (2014). Smartmentality: The smart city as disciplinary strategy. *Urban Studies, 51*(5), 883–898. https://doi.org/10.1177/0042098013494427

Vera, L. A., Walker, D., Murphy, M., Mansfield, B., Mohamed Siad, L., Ogden, J., & Environmental Data and Governance Initiative (EDGI). (2019). When data justice and environmental justice meet: Formulating a response to extractive logic through environmental data justice. *Information, Communication & Society, 22*(7), 1012–1028. https://doi.org/10.1080/1369118X.2019.1596293

Voorwinden, A. (2021). The privatised city: Technology and public-private partnerships in the smart city. *Law, Innovation and Technology, 13*(2), 439–463. https://doi.org/10.1080/17579961.2021.1977213

Winner, L. (1980). Do artifacts have politics? *Daedalus, 109*(1), 121–136. http://www.jstor.org/stable/20024652

World Bank. (2019). *Open source for global public goods*. Washington, DC. https://documents1.worldbank.org/curated/en/672901582561140400/pdf/Open-Source-for-Global-Public-Goods.pdf

Wylie, B. (2022). AI, trust, and the city: Assets and accountability. In A. Brandusescu & J. Reia (Eds.), *Artificial intelligence in the city: Building civic engagement and public trust* (pp. 73–74). Centre for Interdisciplinary Research on Montreal, McGill University. https://doi.org/10.18130/9kar-xn17

Yigitcanlar, T. (2021). Smart city beyond efficiency: Technology–policy–community at play for sustainable urban futures. *Housing Policy Debate, 31*(1), 88–92. https://doi.org/10.1080/10511482.2020.1846885

CHAPTER 7

Watching the Well Run Dry: Digital Settler Colonialism*

~~Generative AI~~

Harriett Jernigan

1 Introduction

A man from the industry known as Big Water arrives in your neighbourhood one day.[1] He hands you a piece of paper stating Big Water has paid a ridiculously low fee to drill into an aquifer underneath your community, which includes Indigenous Peoples (Felton, 2020; Molloy, 2015). Big

[1] The term 'Big Water' references most bottled water companies, but primarily Coca Cola, PepsiCo, Nestlé Water, and BlueTriton. These companies own Dasani, Perrier, Glaceau SmartWater, Aquafina, Arrowhead, Deer Park, Ice Mountain, Origin, Ozarka, Poland Spring, Zephyrhills, Saratoga, Pure Life, Splash, Action, B'eau, Glaceau SmartWater, and more.

H. Jernigan (✉)
Program in Writing and Rhetoric, Stanford University, Stanford, CA, USA
e-mail: h.jernigan@stanford.edu

C. Chokshi, R. Mansell (eds.), *The Need to Rename Tech*,
https://doi.org/10.1007/978-3-032-05155-4_7

Water then extracts, filters, and processes the water, bottles it, and places it for sale on supermarket shelves.

Big Water launches an unhinged ad campaign complete with A-list celebrities, convincing everyone that hydration is not just essential, but a panacea capable of boosting their health, increasing their sex appeal, and saving the environment (Flaherty, 2021; Stewart, 2022). And, most importantly, everyone should consume the processed versions of this water, because technology …

Big Water makes billions (Statista, 2024).

Despite amassing enormous wealth, Big Water keeps siphoning off your aquifer while blocking public access (Shimo, 2018). It persists in draining your vital life source and pockets, which you realise one day while standing in the supermarket, looking at endless bottles, trying to decide which ones you should buy. When the aquifer finally runs dry, Big Water packs up and moves on, leaving pollution and deprivation in its wake (Keeley, 2022).

2 Big Water Mimics Big Data

Why am I focusing on Big Water when this chapter is about Big Data, the industry behind generative AI? Because the two industries are frighteningly similar. They both employ colonial-settler traditions, stealing our public resources and then selling them back to us—in forms we really don't need—solely for the profit of a small portion of members of dominant cultures in the Global North. And these practices have grave, long-term consequences for all of us.

Thanks to a stunning media blitz on par with the one that made Big Water go viral, everyone is talking about AI—more specifically, generative AI tools like ChatGPT, Bing, Bard, Claude, Stable Diffusion, and DALL-E. For those of us still trying to understand what generative AI actually is, we can think of it as chatbots on anabolic steroids. Gigantic versions of the customer service chatbots we use on websites, generative AI can perform tasks, answer questions, and provide clarification or modification if requested. In the same way Big Water offers consumers a broad menu of options, from still to bubbly to flavoured to enhanced, generative AI can output a mind-boggling array of deliverables, including articles, social media posts, e-mails, essays, poems, business reports, recipes, song lyrics, summaries, programming code, music, and visual art (Hetler, 2023).

How does generative AI accomplish this? Like a water bottling plant, it takes a public resource that everyone depends on, processes it, and packages it in a variety of iterations to suit consumer desires engineered by marketing teams. But what resource does generative AI process, and where does it come from? It is data—words, symbols, numbers, speech, and images taken from books, newspapers, TV shows, movies, videos, songs, pictures, specialised datasets, and much more. Big Data uses not millions but billions of words and images broken down into tokens, like molecules of water (Zitter & Kelly, 2024). Just as Big Water takes its resource from public springs and aquifers, the makers of generative AI tell us these words come primarily from 'publicly available information'. What qualifies as publicly available information? If you ask Big Data, the definition is as broad as the Nile, which means everything is fair game (Fried, 2024). In addition to the previously mentioned sources, Big Data has drilled into the internet and extracted our social media posts, pictures, artwork, Kickstarters, blogs, forum discussions, message boards, Instacart orders, and text messages. Even those innocuous and tedious chatbot interactions (Ohlheiser, 2024; Zhuang, 2023). In short, everything you've ever recorded, written, or created and placed online is open season.

How is this possible, you ask? Most governments cannot keep legislative pace with the supersonic speed of internet technology innovation. True, legislation has evolved enough that basic rules exist for collecting, selling, and purchasing data collected online about our work, interests, and habits (Li et al., 2023). Just as in the case of Big Water, anyone who can fill out the paperwork and pay a negligible fee can legally have access to a certain amount of our online information. But Big Data is not satisfied with that. It wants more data than is legally available, and it doesn't want to have to go to the trouble of getting permission to obtain it. Regulation, much less oversight, barely exists, nor do consequences for violating the few rules in place (Hetler, 2023; Noto La Diega et al., 2024). As a result, little discourages Big Data from taking as much as they want. Despite calling for regulation (Kang, 2023; Jalonick & O'Brien, 2023), generative AI companies buy and steal data without users' knowledge or permission (Appel et al., 2023; Turner Lee et al., 2023).

Big Data claims it has not stolen anything—easy to do, since debates about what constitutes copyright, patent, and trademark infringement have only just begun. But an ever-growing number of people disagree. In 2022, a group of programmers sued GitHub and OpenAI for theft of their code (Joseph Saveri Law Firm, 2024). In 2023, a class-action lawsuit filed in the State of California accused OpenAI of "larceny/receipt of stolen property" (Clarkson Law Firm P. C. v. OpenAI complaint, 2023, pp. 1–2). Michael Wooldridge, an Oxford University professor, described the full extent of their data scraping as "unimaginable" (Clarkson Law Firm P. C. v. OpenAI complaint, 2023, p. 32). In the same year, three illustrators sued the creators of Midjourney, DreamUp, and Stable Diffusion for theft of intellectual property (Chen, 2023). The cascade continues with writers, creators, and journalism outlets, most notably *The New York Times*, filing lawsuits against the makers of generative AI platforms, accusing the companies of copyright violation and outright theft (Creamer, 2024; De Vynck, 2023). The breadth and depth of these lawsuits demonstrate that if you have ever been even remotely engaged in online life, your data has been stolen—not just some of your data, but as much as possible.

3 Generative AI as Theft

The theft behind generative AI is raising alarm bells around the world, typically centring on employment. Teachers, farm workers, doctors, even computer programmers worry that the thing they unwittingly trained will end up taking their place (Johnson, 2023). And this is already true in some cases. Google allegedly laid off hundreds of employees in their ad sales division (Langley, 2024), replacing them with generative AI that can help clients sift through ad products or simply "make ad assets like images and text on its own based on a budget and goals given by the ad purchaser" (Amadeo, 2024, para. 2). Additionally, companies including MSN, IKEA, and Duolingo have all laid off workers and replaced them with generative AI (O'Sullivan, 2025). Consultants at McKinsey predict that by 2030, AI could help accelerate the automation that will account for 30 per cent of activities currently worked on across the US economy (Ellingrud et al., 2023). Worldwide, figures are even larger, with Goldman Sachs (2023) predicting generative AI could disrupt 300 million jobs by 2030. And little, if anything, has been implemented to support that displaced human capital.

Unfortunately, even greater challenges are coming down the pipe because, like Big Water, Big Data is rooted in settler colonialism, a structure that has two primary goals: first, replacing the Indigenous or native populations of a territory with a society of colonisers through assimilation, violence, and enslavement; and second, extracting valuable resources to increase the profit of the metropolis in the colonisers' homeland (Englert,

2022). Colonisers employ a variety of theological, ethical, and political justifications for their violent dispossession and domination of far-flung territories, most of them revolving around narratives of a civilising mission (Kohn & Reddy, 2023).

Because settler colonialism is a structure rather than an occurrence, it lasts indefinitely unless the occupiers leave, or the area is decolonised. As a result, it persists into the modern era. Big Water, for example, employs the same strategy of justifying the literal invasion and plundering of public and Indigenous land with laws created by a distant state (Molloy, 2015). It has drained wells dry, polluted land, and forced the same people they stole the water from to buy it back in bottle form, whitewashing their theft of the resources that sustain existing residents by providing philanthropic offerings (Blue Triton Brands, n.d.; Nestlé, 2020).

Big Data engages in the same settler colonialism, but the territory they're invading is the internet. Kawsar Ali (2021, p. 6) names this specific structure digital settler colonialism, which refers to the "production, maintenance and use of the Internet to extend settler colonialism and reiterate the power of the white sovereign online … the Internet [is] used to eliminate indigenous subjects and to exterminate the Other … to extend the legacy of the white settler state". In short, Big Data has invaded the internet with the goal of subduing or eliminating 'digital natives' in order to perpetuate the hegemony of the dominant culture.[2]

How can generative AI eliminate 'digital natives' and 'extend the legacy of the white settler state'? Let us return for a brief moment to the fact that Big Data steals everything from the internet that it can get its hands on. This, however, does not mean that it uses everything it steals. Like Big Water, Big Data is currently run almost exclusively by white men (Hao, 2019; Thorbecke, 2023). Not surprisingly, they leverage data produced by cis-het white men more than any other group of people to build generative AI tools (Bender et al., 2021). OpenAI, for example, steals mostly from sources like Project Gutenberg, Tumblr, Pinterest, Common Crawl, Wikipedia, and Reddit, and mostly selects data generated by cis-het white men (Chen, 2023).

Consequently, the tributaries that feed generative AI are rife with biases, -isms, and phobias (Collier, 2023; Luo et al., 2023). Subsequently, this reinforces dominant-culture narratives that continue to cast marginalised

[2] 'Digital natives' refers mainly to those born after 1980 who grew up in the 'digital age'. See Prensky (2001).

folk as less-than, deserving of further isolation, poverty, abuse, and eradication. The content created by generative AI contributes to an algorithmic feedback loop that denies Black and Brown people job interviews (Zapata, 2021), loans (Agarwal et al., 2023), healthcare (Grant, 2022), dates (Buolamwini, 2023); even access to a decent supermarket that sells water back to the people from whom it was stolen (Le, 2021).

As the number of users increases exponentially, and those users rely exponentially more on generative AI to distill information for them (Brooks, 2023), dominant cultures worldwide, particularly in the Global North, can perpetuate settler colonialism and continue to exploit and eliminate marginalised peoples from the public sphere. McKinsey & Company (2023) estimate that new wealth created by generative AI could widen the gap between Black and white Americans by USD 43 billion annually by 2045. Worldwide, AI has the potential to impoverish and systemically constrain oppressed people to a staggering degree, particularly in the Global South. The chatbot on steroids will not simply become another brick in the wall that blocks the flow of opportunity and equity, but the mortar that holds the entire thing together.

Before we slip into complacency believing these issues don't affect us directly, we must reckon with the fact that the digital settler colonialism of Big Data does not stop at creating new iterations of systemic oppression of marginalised folk. It unleashes a tidal wave of destruction. Like traditional settler colonialism, the subjugation and eventual erasure of racialised bodies and marginalised people for the sake of profit is inherently bound up with environmental damage (Englert, 2022). Just as Big Water generates waste and carbon footprints (Grostern, 2021; Dickie, 2023) to process spring and—already processed—municipal tap water (Felton, 2020), generative AI creates a fair amount of waste and a sizable energy footprint. Developing GPT-3 in 2022, for example, consumed the amount of energy needed to run 123 gas-powered cars for a year (Saenko & The Conversation US, 2023). The rubber hits the road, though, when we consider inferencing: what generative AI does to respond to our prompts (Toews, 2020). While we have limited data on the carbon footprint of a single query from generative AI platforms, some estimate that it could be four to five times higher than a standard search engine query (Saenko & The Conversation US, 2023).

And, just like bottling facilities, generative AI also gulps water, mostly for cooling the supercomputers that run them. Recent studies revealed that training GPT-3 in Microsoft's Iowa data centre glugged 700,000 litres of freshwater (George et al., 2023), the same amount of water needed to produce 370 BMWs or 320 Teslas—or provide 350,000 people one day's worth of drinking water. The chatbots on steroids also chug water in the inferencing process, using the equivalent of a 500 millilitre bottle of water for every 20–50 queries it responds to (Frost, 2023). This would not be so bad for one or two interactions. But 180 million people visit ChatGPT alone weekly. It generated 1.6 billion visits in January of 2024 (Singh, 2025), and OpenAI wants millions more to join the party. That's a lot of bottles of water, just from one platform. If that usage goes unchecked, Big Data could give Big Water a run for its money, draining rivers and streams close to data centres, disrupting agriculture and drinking water. And the wastewater created by the cooling process only exacerbates the problems of water scarcity and economic stagnation (George et al., 2023). While many may rightly argue that agriculture uses more water than bottled water companies or generative AI, agriculture is an industry that we need, while we have limited need for bottled water or generative AI (Livingstone, 2024; Chellaney, 2015).

Sadly, just as in traditional settler colonialism, the people who bear the environmental consequences of generative AI do not reap any of its rewards. We know the most marginalised communities bear the brunt of climate change first (Donati et al., 2024). In their groundbreaking article, "On the Danger of Stochastic Parrots", Emily Bender, Timnit Gebru, Angelina McMillan-Major, and Margaret Mitchell (2021, pp. 612–613) ask:

> Is it fair or just to ask, for example, that the residents of the Maldives (likely to be underwater by 2100) or the 800,000 people in Sudan affected by drastic floods pay the environmental price of training and deploying ever larger English [GPTs], when similar large-scale models aren't being produced for Dhivehi or Sudanese Arabic?

When we use ChatGPT, for example, to generate a sales contract for our used car and then plan a trip to visit Uluru in Australia with the money we'll make, we also ask someone already suffering the impacts of climate change to suffer just a little bit more for our comfort and convenience.[3] And to add insult to injury, we ask them to do it for the sake of a tool that

[3] This does not include the work demanded of marginalised people to moderate content that scars the soul, such as the workers at the Kenyan firm Sama, who were tasked with filtering through content from the darkest corners of the internet. See Rowe (2023).

doesn't even serve their needs, like draining a community's well, bottling the water, marketing it as water for the elite, and then charging up to seven times the price of tap water (Foodwatch, 2018; Shimo, 2018).

Like Big Water, Big Data is equal-opportunistic, exploiting people around the world including in the Global North. Colonialism engendered capitalism, the ever-expanding need, as Sai Englert (2022, p. 29) states, "to generate and capture surplus value ... to extract more value from those over whom they already exert control". Settler digital colonialism, which drives digital extractive capitalism, will always be looking for new ways to take more money from the 99 per cent, regardless of race, gender, or location. In such a system, Abeba Birhane (2020, p. 394) writes, "the human soul, behaviour, and action is raw material free for the taking", which makes all members of the Global North prime targets as well. "Knowledge, authority, and power to sort, categorize, and order human activity rests with the technologist, for which we are merely data producing 'human natural resources'" (Birhane, 2020, p. 394). In other words, you and I are solely a means to a monetary end, seeds that, depending on the water used to irrigate us, will yield various crops that Big Data can harvest and sell to the highest bidder.

Much of that water, though, is already poisoned. Generative AI is used to support human trafficking, cybercriminals, and social engineering (Brady & Abrams, 2024; Crane, 2023). Like settler colonists of the past who developed systems of surveillance to control the existing population, Big Data uses generative AI to create and maintain a surveillance state (Wach et al., 2023). And in the same paternalistic fashion as Big Water, generative AI developer companies claim to do it in order to save humanity (Zuboff, 2019). Worryingly, the fruits of that surveillance allow bad actors to employ generative AI to produce "large volumes of convincing disinformation—from text to audio to video" (United Nations, 2023a, para. 5). Because generative AI leaves barely any clues as to the origins of its output, it becomes difficult for even the most seasoned researchers, investigators, and journalists—much less the rest of us—to discern what information is true and what is fabricated.

This whirlpool of disinformation has serious socioeconomic and geopolitical implications. International peace and security operations, human rights protections, democratic processes, the sciences, and public institutions are all under threat. With the advent of lightspeed improvements in AI-generated video, audio, and text, people can and do use general messaging, deep fakes, and political ads to establish false narratives and secure control of our public and private lives, which a number of countries have already experienced in the forms of political propaganda and election interference (Noti, 2024; Ryan-Mosley, 2023). As Nate Persily put it, "It's not just that people will be believing in false stuff, it is that they will be disbelieving in true stuff" (as cited in Ashar, 2024, para. 9).[4]

Combine this eventual inability—or lack of will—to distinguish between factual and fake with constant surveillance by the very same technologies (Tangalakis-Lippert, 2022), and a poisonous confusion and apathy emerges from this wellspring of disinformation which promises dire consequences for equitable sociopolitical systems everywhere. People will end up drinking a Kool-Aid made with toxic water. We are losing sovereignty over our words, our languages, our truths, which is the precursor to the unraveling of the things that make us *human*, and consequently, of our social fabric.

Some optimists will argue that, unlike water, language and human creativity are infinitely renewable resources, and eventually representation of the marginalised will balance out in online spaces; that the supposed neutrality of generative AI will solve rather than reinforce systemic oppression of racialized and underrepresented folk. Regardless of Big Data's settler colonialism, they assert, we will always have access to original content which will diversify over time (OpenAI, 2023). However, several features contradict this. Like Abeba Birhane (2020), Selena Deckelmann, Chief Product and Technology Officer at Wikimedia Foundation, observes that "[it's] an interesting problem right now that we're having natural resource conversations about human-created data" (as cited in O'Brien, 2024, para. 17). This implies that human language, like water, can be exhausted. This notion is supported by current concerns about the potential for model collapse, a condition in which there is no more human-generated data to mine, which then leads to generative AI tools taking data from each other, which then leads to those tools spouting gibberish (Shumailov et al., 2024). Gibberish does not sound so terrible, until it causes economic and environmental problems (Marr, 2024).

More importantly, history shows us a relationship has always existed between controlling language and subjugating people (Beraldo, 2023; Kagarlitsky, 2010). Colonisers, despots, and fascists have driven the languages of the marginalised into near- or total extinction in order to give

[4] See also UN (2024) talk by Volker Türk, the UN High Commissioner for Human Rights, at Stanford on the same occasion.

primacy to their own language. One need only think of Spanish linguistic colonialism, American Indian boarding schools, or Nazi Germany (La Rosa, 1996; Lewy, 2020; National Native American Boarding School Healing Coalition, n.d.). Just as Big Water controls the tap in marginalised communities, depriving citizens of potable drinking water (Abba, 2019), governments, oligarchs, and dictators can manipulate, constrain, and stifle language to their own political and monetary benefit. If the former CEO of Nestlé can consider the notion of water as a human right 'a tad bit extreme' (Trash Island TV, 2021), then profit-driven technologists, allied with extremist governments, can determine the same about language.

4 Conclusion

We cannot put this genie back in the bottle. Nor should we try. Generative AI can do good, providing tutorials, virtual laboratories, language learning tools, and healthcare consultation to people living in underserved areas (Ray, 2023). It can provide limited predictive tools for support in disasters and emergencies (Hu et al., 2023). It might even help mitigate climate change (Mastrola, 2023; United Nations, 2023b). But to achieve this benefit for the greater good, our governments must engage in the same continuous resistance by the oppressed against traditional settler colonialism. We must treat Big Data like Big Water, which we have recently begun confronting (Brown, 2020; McIntyre, 2021). We must legislate and enforce privacy and digital language sovereignty which includes ethical sourcing of data collected from a much broader spectrum of people. The United Nations Secretary-General's AI Advisory Board calls for ensuring that all citizens can equally access and utilise AI tools for their benefit by urging the centrality of data governance, prioritising universal buy-in by countries and stakeholders, and anchoring AI governance in international law, centring human rights and sustainable development goals (United Nations, 2023c; Türk, 2024).

Dozens of countries and collectives are striving to do just that. Among others, Australia, Brazil, China, India, and Japan are all developing policies (Klimentov, 2023; White & Case LLP, 2024). The African Union is hammering out a plan to draft regulations (Tsanni, 2024), and the European Union (EU) has prohibited a long list of AI uses, including biometric surveillance, predictive policing systems, and emotion recognition (European Parliament, 2023). But each of these collectives and countries face real challenges. In many African countries, the lag in infrastructure—thanks to settler colonialism—will make it difficult to enforce any policies enshrined in law (Sidhva, 2024). The EU—which benefited from settler colonialism—might succeed at making good policies, but they are based on 400-year-old narratives about prosperity and well-being that still privilege wealthy and powerful members of the dominant culture in the Global North (Carmel & Paul, 2022). Ultimately, we need a global regulatory body that closely monitors generative AI and develops laws that protect the environment, narrow the gaps between rich and poor, and defend human rights. And we must then enforce those laws.

We can actively demand ethical and equitable AI that helps rather than harms. Once we acknowledge that Big Data, like Big Water, is in the business of stealing, exploiting, and exhausting our digital spaces and natural resources, we can work towards ensuring that generative AI supplements human existence rather than replaces it. Otherwise, one day, we might turn on our laptops and realise that our collective well has run dry.

Acknowledgements I am deeply grateful to Drs. Abeba Birhane, Timnit Gebru, Nakeema Stefflbauer, Ruth Starkman, Kevin Moore, Emily Polk, and Marvin Diogenes for their thoughtful, compassionate and generous conversations and feedback over the last few years.

References

Abba, A. (2019, April 28). How Nestle Nigeria contaminates water supply of its host community in Abuja. *International Centre for Investigative Reporting*. https://www.icirnigeria.org/how-nestle-nigeria-contaminates-water-supply-of-its-host-community-in-abuja/

Agarwal, S., Muckley, C. B., & Neelakantan, P. (2023). Countering racial discrimination in algorithmic lending: A case for model-agnostic interpretation methods. *Economics Letters, 226*, 1–5. https://www.sciencedirect.com/science/article/pii/S0165176523001428

Ali, K. (2021). The logics of digitisation: Race, cyberspace, and digital settler colonialism. *Journal of Global Indigeneity*, 5(2), 1–28. https://www.journalofglobalindigeneity.com/article/31061-the-logics-of-digitisation-race-cyberspace-and-digital-settler-colonialism

Amadeo, R. (2024, January 16). Google lays off "hundreds" more as ad division switches to AI-powered sales. *Ars Technica*. https://arstechnica.com/google/2024/01/google-lays-off-hundreds-more-as-ad-division-switches-to-ai-powered-sales/

Appel, G., Nellbauer, J., & Schweidel, D. A. (2023, April 7). Generative AI has an intellectual property problem. *Harvard Business Review*. https://hbr.org/2023/04/generative-ai-has-an-intellectual-property-problem

Ashar, F. (2024, February 20). U.N. high commissioner for human rights cautions against AI. *The Stanford Daily*. https://stanforddaily.com/2024/02/19/un-high-commissioner-for-human-rights-cautions-ai/?utm_campaign=digest&utm_medium=email&utm_source=mailchimp&utm_content=Feb-20-2024

Bender, M., Gebru, T., McMillan-Major, A., & Mitchell, M. (2021). On the dangers of stochastic parrots: Can language models be too big? In *Proceedings of the 2021 ACM Conference on Fairness, Accountability, and Transparency* (pp. 610–623). https://doi.org/10.1145/3442188.3445922

Beraldo, S. (2023, June 21). *Newspeak, or about the governments' attempts to control the language*. Institute for Research in Economic and Fiscal Issues (IREF). https://en.irefeurope.org/publications/online-articles/article/newspeak-or-about-the-governments-attempts-to-control-the-language/

Birhane, A. (2020). Algorithmic colonization of Africa. *Scripted: A Journal of Law, Technology & Society, 17*(2), 389–409. https://doi.org/10.2966/scrip.170220.389

Blue Triton Brands. (n.d.). *Community*. Blue Triton Brands. https://www.bluetriton.com/community

Brady, D., & Abrams, J. (2024, September 27). Ransomware gangs are using stolen data to threaten CEOs. They almost never get caught. *Fortune*. https://fortune.com/2024/09/27/ransomware-gangs-stolen-data-threaten-ceos-cybersecurity-ai/#

Brooks, C. (2023, November 8). With little employer oversight, ChatGPT usage rates rise among American workers. *business.com*. https://www.business.com/technology/chatgpt-usage-workplace-study/

Brown, A. (2020, February 12). Lawmakers open groundwater fight against bottled water companies. *Stateline*. https://stateline.org/2020/02/12/lawmakers-open-groundwater-fight-against-bottled-water-companies/

Buolamwini, J. (2023). *Unmasking AI: My mission to protect what is human in a world of machines*. Random House.

Carmel, E., & Paul, R. (2022). Peace and prosperity for the digital age? The colonial political economy of European AI governance. *IEEE Technology and Society Magazine, 41*(2), 94–104. https://doi.org/10.1109/mts.2022.3173340

Chellaney, B. (2015, September 17). Should we drink bottled water? *World Economic Forum*. https://www.weforum.org/agenda/2015/09/should-we-drink-bottled-water/

Chen, M. (2023, January 24). Artists and illustrators are suing three A.I. Art generators for scraping and "collaging" their work without consent. *Artnet News*.

https://news.artnet.com/art-world/class-action-lawsuit-ai-generators-deviantart-midjourney-stable-diffusion-2246770

Clarkson Law Firm P. C. v. OpenAI complaint. United States District Court, Northern District of California, Case No. 3:23-cv-03199 (2023). https://clarksonlawfirm.com/wp-content/uploads/2023/06/0001.-2023.06.28-OpenAI-Complaint.pdf

Collier, K. (2023, July 5). In NYC, companies will have to prove their AI hiring software isn't sexist or racist. *NBC News*. https://www.nbcnews.com/tech/tech-news/nyc-companies-will-prove-ai-hiring-software-isnt-sexist-racist-rcna92336

Crane, C. (2023, November 6). 6 dangers of generative AI and what's being done to address them. *Hashed Out*. https://www.thesslstore.com/blog/dangers-of-generative-ai-whats-being-done-to-address-them/

Creamer, E. (2024, February 14). Two OpenAI book lawsuits partially dismissed by California Court. *The Guardian*. https://www.theguardian.com/books/2024/feb/14/two-openai-book-lawsuits-partially-dismissed-by-california-court

De Vynck, G. (2023, September 20). 'Game of Thrones' author and others accuse ChatGPT maker of 'theft' in lawsuit. *The Washington Post*. https://www.washingtonpost.com/technology/2023/09/20/openai-lawsuit-martin-picoult-franzen/

Dickie, G. (2023). Global emissions set to fall only 2% by 2030 - UN report. *Reuters*. https://www.reuters.com/world/global-emissions-set-fall-only-2-by-2030-un-report-2023-11-14/

Donati, C. I., Nicholas, K., Fedele, G., Delforge, D., Speybroeck, N., Moraga, P., Blatter, J., Below, R., & Zvoleff, A. (2024). Global hotspots of climate-related disasters. *International Journal of Disaster Risk Reduction, 108*, 1–18. https://www.sciencedirect.com/science/article/pii/S2212420924002504?via%3Dihub

Ellingrud, K., Sanghvi, S., Dandona, G. S., Madgavkar, A., Chui, M., White, O., & Hasebe, P. (2023). Which jobs will be in demand? Which ones are shrinking? And which ones could be hardest to fill? In McKinsey Global Institute (Ed.), *Generative AI and the future of work in America*, n.p. https://www.mckinsey.com/mgi/our-re-search/generative-ai-and-the-future-of-work-in-america

Englert, S. (2022). *Settler colonialism: An introduction*. Pluto Press.

European Parliament. (2023, June 14). *Artificial Intelligence Act (P9_TA(2023)0236)*. https://www.europarl.europa.eu/doceo/document/TA-9-2023-0236_EN.html

Felton, R. (2020, April 23). How Coke and Pepsi make millions from bottling tap water, as residents face shutoffs. *Consumer Reports*. https://www.consumer-

reports.org/bottled-water/how-coke-and-pepsi-make-millions-from-bottling-tap-water-as-residents-face-shutoffs/
Flaherty, K. (2021). Let's end the water crisis in our lifetime. Charitywater.org. https://www.charitywater.org/katie-flaherty-1
Foodwatch. (2018, May 12). Consumers vote Coca-Cola's "Smartwater" the most audacious advertising lie of the year - foodwatch Germany protest at company headquarters in Berlin. *Foodwatch*. https://www.foodwatch.org/en/consumers-vote-coca-colas-smartwater-the-most-audacious-advertising-lie-of-the-year-foodwatch-germany-protest-at-company-headquarters-in-berlin
Fried, I. (2024, April 5). For AI firms, anything "public" is fair game. *Axios*. https://www.axios.com/2024/04/05/open-ai-training-data-public-available-meaning
Frost, R. (2023, April 20). ChatGPT 'drinks' a bottle of fresh water for every 20 to 50 questions we ask, study warns. *EuroNews*. https://www.euronews.com/green/2023/04/20/chatgpt-drinks-a-bottle-of-fresh-water-for-every-20-to-50-questions-we-ask-study-warns
George, A. S., George, A. S. H., & Martin, A. S. (2023). The environmental impact of AI: A case study of water consumption by ChatGPT. *Partners Universal International Innovation Journal, 1*(2), 91–104. https://zenodo.org/records/7855594
Goldman Sachs. (2023, March 26). Global economics analyst: The potentially large effects of artificial intelligence on economic growth (Briggs/Kodnani). *Goldman Sachs*. https://www.gspublishing.com/content/research/en/reports/2023/03/27/d64e052b-0f6e-45d7-967b-d7be35fabd16.html
Grant, C. (2022, February 24). *Algorithms are making decisions about health care, which may only worsen medical racism*. American Civil Liberties Union (ACLU). https://www.aclu.org/news/privacy-technology/algorithms-in-health-care-may-worsen-medical-racism
Grostern, J. (2021, August 5). Environmental impact of bottled water "up to 3,500 times greater than tap water". *The Guardian*. https://www.theguardian.com/environment/2021/aug/05/environmental-impact-of-bottled-water-up-to-3500-times-greater-than-tap-water
Hao, K. (2019). AI's white guy problem isn't going away. *MIT Technology Review*. https://www.technologyreview.com/2019/04/17/136072/ais-white-guy-problem-isnt-going-away/
Hetler, A. (2023, December 15). *What is chatGPT? Generative AI explained*. TechTarget WhatIs. https://www.techtarget.com/whatis/definition/ChatGPT#:~:text=ChatGPT%20is%20an%20artificial%20intelligence,%2C%20essays%2C%20code%20and%20emails
Hu, Y., Mai, G., Cundy, C., Choi, K., Lao, N., Liu, W., Lakhanpal, G., Zhou, R. Z., & Joseph, K. (2023). Geo-knowledge-guided GPT models improve the extraction of location descriptions from disaster-related social media messages.

International Journal of Geographical Information Science, 37(11), 2289–2318. https://doi.org/10.1080/13658816.2023.2266495

Jalonick, M. C., & O'Brien, M. (2023, September 13). Tech industry leaders endorse regulating artificial intelligence at rare summit in Washington. *AP News*. https://apnews.com/article/schumer-artificial-intelligence-elon-musk-senate-efcfb1067d68ad2f595db7e92167943c

Johnson, A. (2023, March 31). Which jobs will AI replace? These 4 industries will be heavily impacted. *Forbes*. https://www.forbes.com/sites/ariannajohnson/2023/03/30/which-jobs-will-ai-replace-these-4-industries-will-be-heavily-impacted/?sh=21860c585957

Joseph Saveri Law Firm. (2024). Case: *GitHub copilot intellectual property litigation*. https://www.saverilawfirm.com/our-cases/github-copilot-intellectual-property-litigation

Kagarlitsky, B. (2010). *Empire of the periphery: Russia and the world system* (R. Clarke, Trans.). Pluto Press.

Kang, C. (2023, May 16). OpenAI's Sam Altman urges A.I. regulation in Senate hearing. *The New York Times*. https://www.nytimes.com/2023/05/16/technology/openai-altman-artificial-intelligence-regulation.html#:~:text=But%20on%20Tuesday%2C%20Sam%20Altman,others%20like%20Google%20and%20Microsoft

Keeley, A. (2022, August 3). The sinkhole that swallowed a Mexican Farm. *The New Yorker*. https://www.newyorker.com/news/dispatch/the-sinkhole-that-swallowed-a-mexican-farm

Klimentov, M. (2023, September 3). From China to Brazil, here's how AI is regulated around the world. *The Washington Post*. https://www.washingtonpost.com/world/2023/09/03/ai-regulation-law-china-israel-eu/

Kohn, M., & Reddy, K. (2023, January 17). Colonialism. In E. N. Zalta & U. Nodelman (Eds.), *The Stanford encyclopedia of philosophy*. https://plato.stanford.edu/entries/colonialism/

La Rosa, Z. (1996). Language and empire: The vision of Nebrija. *The Loyola University Student Historical Journal*. http://cas.loyno.edu/sites/chn.loyno.edu/files/Language%20and%20Empire_The%20Vision%20of%20Nebrija.pdf

Langley, H. (2024, January 16). Leaked memo: Google is laying off hundreds of employees in its advertising-sales team. *Business Insider*. https://www.businessinsider.com/google-is-laying-off-hundreds-of-employees-in-its-advertising-team-2024-1

Le, V. (2021, April 2). Algorithmic redlining is real. Why not algorithmic greenlining? *Governing*. https://www.governing.com/community/algorithmic-redlining-is-real-why-not-algorithmic-greenlining.html

Lewy, G. (2020). *Harmful and undesirable: Book censorship in Nazi Germany*. Oxford University Press.

Li, P., Yang, J., Islam, M. A., & Ren, S. (2023, October 29). *Making AI less "thirsty": Uncovering and addressing the secret water footprint of AI models.* arXiv.org. https://arxiv.org/abs/2304.03271

Livingstone, G. (2024, November 2025). Foreign firms taking billions of litres from UK aquifers to make bottled water. *The Guardian.* https://www.theguardian.com/environment/2024/nov/25/foreign-firms-taking-billions-of-litres-from-uk-aquifers-to-make-bottled-water

Luo, Q., Puett, M. J., & Smith, M. D. (2023, May 23). *A "perspectival" mirror of the elephant: Investigating language bias on Google, ChatGPT, YouTube, and Wikipedia.* arXiv.org. https://doi.org/10.48550/arXiv.2303.16281

Marr, B. (2024, August 19). Why AI models are collapsing and what it means for the future of technology. *Forbes.* https://www.forbes.com/sites/bernardmarr/2024/08/19/why-ai-models-are-collapsing-and-what-it-means-for-the-future-of-technology/

Mastrola, M. (2023, March 7). How AI can help combat climate change. *The Hub.* https://hub.jhu.edu/2023/03/07/artificial-intelligence-combat-climate-change/

McIntyre, G. (2021, April 29). *First Nations against Nestle.* ArcGIS StoryMaps. https://storymaps.arcgis.com/stories/9f2c0955b33f438995839acb887f7f7b

McKinsey & Company. (2023, December 19). *The impact of generative AI on Black communities.* McKinsey Institute for Black Economic Mobility. https://www.mckinsey.com/bem/our-insights/the-impact-of-generative-ai-on-black-communities

Molloy, P. (2015, April 22). *How Nestlé is using a Native American tribe's land to get away with draining California dry.* Upworthy.

National Native American Boarding School Healing Coalition. (n.d.). *US Indian boarding school history.* https://boardingschoolhealing.org/education/us-indian-boarding-school-history

Nestlé. (2020). Nestlé Nigeria donates water boreholes to Orile-Imo community. *Nestlé.* https://www.nestle-cwa.com/en/nestl-nigeria-donates-water-boreholes-to-orile-imo-community

Noti, A. (2024, February 28). *How artificial intelligence influences elections, and what we can do about it.* Campaign Legal Center (CLC). https://campaignlegal.org/update/how-artificial-intelligence-influences-elections-and-what-we-can-do-about-it

Noto La Diega, G., Harbinja, E., & Nolan, K. (2024). *BILETA'S response to ICO'S generative AI first call for evidence: The lawful basis for web scraping to train generative AI models.* SSRN. https://ssrn.com/abstract=4814018

O'Brien, M. (2024, June 6). AI "gold rush" for chatbot training data could run out of human-written text. *AP News.* https://apnews.com/article/ai-artificial-intelligence-training-data-running-out-9676145bac0d30ecce1513c20561b87d

Ohlheiser, A. W. (2024, February 29). A poster's guide to who's selling your data to train AI. *Vox.* https://www.vox.com/technology/24086039/reddit-tumblr-wordpress-whos-selling-your-data-to-train-ai

OpenAI. (2023). *Safety & responsibility.* https://openai.com/safety

Prensky, M. (2001). Digital natives, digital immigrants Part 1. *On the Horizon, 9*(5), 1–6. https://doi.org/10.1108/10748120110424816

Ray, P. P. (2023). ChatGPT: A comprehensive review on background, applications, key challenges, bias, ethics, limitations and future scope. *Internet of Things and Cyber-Physical Systems, 3*(2023), 121–154. https://www.sciencedirect.com/science/article/pii/S266734522300024X#sec9

Rowe, N. (2023, August 2). It's destroyed me completely': Kenyan moderators decry toll of training of AI models. *The Guardian.* https://www.theguardian.com/technology/2023/aug/02/ai-chatbot-training-human-toll-content-moderator-meta-openai

Ryan-Mosley, T. (2023, October 4). How generative AI is boosting the spread of disinformation and propaganda. *MIT Technology Review.* https://www.technologyreview.com/2023/10/04/1080801/generative-ai-boosting-disinformation-and-propaganda-freedom-house/

Saenko, K., & The Conversation US (2023, May 25). A computer scientist breaks down generative AI's hefty carbon footprint. *Scientific American.* https://www.scientificamerican.com/article/a-computer-scientist-breaks-down-generative-ais-hefty-carbon-footprint/

Shimo, A. (2018, October 4). While Nestlé extracts millions of litres from their land, residents have no drinking water. *The Guardian.* https://www.theguardian.com/global/2018/oct/04/ontario-six-nations-nestle-running-water

Shumailov, I., Shumaylov, Z., Zhao, Y., Papernot, N., Anderson, R., & Gal, Y. (2024). AI models collapse when trained on recursively generated data. *Nature, 631*(8022), 755–759. https://doi.org/10.1038/s41586-024-07566-y

Sidva, S. (2024). Abdullahi Ahmed An-Na'im: On human rights, the secular state and Sharia today. *The UNESCO Courier.* https://courier.unesco.org/en/articles/abdullahi-ahmed-naim-human-rights-secular-state-and-sharia-today

Singh, S. (2025, January 2). Number of ChatGPT users (January 2025). Demandsage. Retrieved January 5, 2025 from https://www.demandsage.com/chatgpt-statistics/

Statista. (2024, September). *Bottled water - worldwide.* https://www.statista.com/outlook/cmo/non-alcoholic-drinks/bottled-water/worldwide

Stewart, E. (2022, November 3). The ugly story of how corporate America convinced us to spend so much on water. *Vox.* https://www.vox.com/the-goods/23433132/best-bottled-water-is-tap-environment-health

Tangalakis-Lippert, K. (2022, August 28). Amazon's empire of surveillance: Through recent billion-dollar acquisitions of health care services and smart home devices, the tech giant is leveraging its monopoly power to track "every aspect" of our lives. *Business Insider*. https://www.businessinsider.com/amazon-empire-of-surveillance-leveraging-monopoly-power-tracking-purchases-2022-8

Thorbecke, C. (2023). OpenAI's technology is upending our everyday lives. It's overseen exclusively by wealthy, White men. *CNN*. https://edition.cnn.com/2023/12/15/tech/openai-board-diversity/index.html

Toews, R. (2020, June 17). Deep learning's carbon emissions problem. *Forbes*. https://www.forbes.com/sites/robtoews/2020/06/17/deep-learnings-climate-change-problem/

Trash Island TV. (2021, February 19). *We feed the world (2005) - documentary* [Video]. YouTube. https://youtu.be/KAuA_slgM_w?si=jCH_3WD3ke45ETu6

Tsanni, A. (2024, March 15). Africa's push to regulate AI starts now. *MIT Technology Review*. https://www.technologyreview.com/2024/03/15/1089844/africa-ai-artificial-intelligence-regulation-au-policy/

Türk, V. (2024, February 14). *Human rights must be at the core of generative AI technologies, says Türk* [Speech transcript]. United Nations Human Rights Office of the High Commissioner (OHCHR). https://www.ohchr.org/en/statements-and-speeches/2024/02/human-rights-must-be-core-generative-ai-technologies-says-turk

Turner Lee, N., Yaraghi, N., MacCarthy, M., & Wheeler, T. (2023, June 2). Around the halls: What should the regulation of generative AI look like? *Brookings*. https://www.brookings.edu/articles/around-the-halls-what-should-the-regulation-of-generative-ai-look-like/

United Nations (UN). (2023a, December 22). *UN Global Communications Chief urges AI developers to 'Put people before profit'*. United Nations: Hate Speech. https://www.un.org/en/hate-speech/ai-concerns#:~:text=With%20generative%20AI%2C%20large%20volumes,and%20with%20minor%20human%20intervention

United Nations (UN). (2023b, November 3). *AI for climate action: Technology mechanism supports transformational climate solutions*. United Nations: Climate Change. https://unfccc.int/news/ai-for-climate-action-technology-mechanism-supports-transformational-climate-solutions

United Nations (UN). (2023c). *Governing AI for humanity*. United Nations Advisory Body on Artificial Intelligence. https://www.un.org/sites/un2.un.org/files/ai_advisory_body_interim_report.pdf

Wach, K., Duong, C. D., Ejdys, J., Kazlauskaitė, R., Korzynski, P., Mazurek, G., Paliszkiewicz, J., & Ziemba, E. (2023). The dark side of generative artificial intelligence: A critical analysis of controversies and risks of chatgpt. *Entrepreneurial Business and Economics Review, 11*(2), 7–30. https://doi.org/10.15678/eber.2023.110201

White & Case LLP. (2024, May 13). *AI watch: Global regulatory tracker - United States.* https://www.whitecase.com/insight-our-thinking/ai-watch-global-regulatory-tracker-united-states

Zapata, D. (2021, June 18). New Study finds AI-enabled anti-Black bias in recruiting. *Thomson Reuters.* https://www.thomsonreuters.com/en-us/posts/legal/ai-enabled-anti-black-bias/

Zhuang, J. J. (2023, April 6). Introducing the Instacart plugin for ChatGPT. *Instacart.* https://www.instacart.com/company/updates/instacart-chatgpt/

Zitter, L., & Kelly, W. (2024, February 27). *GPT-3.5 vs. GPT-4: Biggest differences to consider.* TechTarget. Enterprise AI. https://www.techtarget.com/searchenterpriseai/tip/GPT-35-vs-GPT-4-Biggest-differences-to-consider

Zuboff, S. (2019). *The age of surveillance capitalism: The fight for a human future at the new frontier of power.* Profile Books.

O'Sullivan, I. (2025, October 29). These Companies Have Already Replaced Workers with AI in 2025. TechCo. https://tech.co/news/companies-replace-workers-with-ai

PART III

~~Predicting~~

CHAPTER 8

Automated Predeterminations*

~~Predictive Technologies~~

Olivier Driessens

1 Introduction

'Customers who bought this book also purchased these titles'. 'Tomorrow, there is a 50 per cent chance of rain in the afternoon'. 'Political party A is going to win the election next year'. These are just a few of the many predictions we encounter on a daily basis. They help people to navigate the world by outlining events that might come next. This can give us comfort and facilitate our decision-making. In these examples, we can choose how to respond. We might indeed add a suggested book to our online cart, take rain trousers to work, or vote strategically based on an election poll.

Many other types of predictions do not provide the same degree of choice or freedom. The bank calculates whether a person will be able to pay off their mortgage. The doctor determines a patient's health prognosis and whether treatment is still useful. The Human Resources (HR) consultancy evaluates who is suited to fill a particular role. These are far from

O. Driessens (✉)
Department of Communication, University of Copenhagen,
Copenhagen, Denmark
e-mail: olivier@hum.ku.dk

C. Chokshi, R. Mansell (eds.), *The Need to Rename Tech*,
https://doi.org/10.1007/978-3-032-05155-4_8

trivial predictions, and they can have far-reaching consequences for people and their families. Nonetheless, it is not always transparent how such predictions come about and whether and how we can appeal the outcomes.

The opacity of predictions is compounded by technology. Often using large amounts of data, so-called black-boxed algorithmic systems make decisions on behalf of, or at least provide input to, the financial advisor, medical doctor, and HR consultant (Pasquale, 2015). Yet the data the systems rely upon may be incomplete, outdated, or biased, while the algorithm might give too much weight to one variable over another or run on false assumptions about how things work. How should the HR consultant and others interpret algorithmic outputs when it is not clear what happens inside the black box? Who is ultimately accountable for the decision and its consequences (Kallinikos, 2011)?

Academic literature abounds with studies of socio-technical issues entangled with predictive technologies (Hand, 2006), as well as their social, legal, ethical, and discriminatory consequences (Cevolini & Esposito, 2020; Kerr, 2013; Mühlhoff, 2021; Ugwudike, 2022).[1] Building on this work, this chapter asks whether *predictive technology* is, in fact, an accurate name for these systems given their operations and many limitations. What does it mean *to predict*? We cannot know with certainty what the future holds, so under what conditions is prediction possible, if at all? And, what are the consequences of producing predictive scores and analytics, all predicated on the past and present, for people's freedom and the openness of the future? I argue that we should rename predictive technologies as *automated predeterminations* because these technological systems foreclose people's futures by narrowing their range of future options, their agency, and contingency. This renaming is important because it dispels the myth that predictive technologies can indeed predict and that they can do so objectively.

2 The Premises of Predictive Technologies

When we check the weather forecast, consult election polls, or receive a health prognosis, we deal with uncertainty about the future. Predictive technologies help us manage this uncertainty and, to some extent, they even give us a sense of control over the future. This desire to peek into the

[1] I use 'predictive technologies' as an overarching term to include predictive algorithms, predictive analytics, predictive systems, and the like.

future is obviously not new. From dream interpretations some 5000 years ago in Mesopotamia, to liver inspections, Egyptian and Greek oracles, or Nordic sages, humankind has relied throughout history on specialists for prophecies and forecasts as well as on tools to deliver and accredit them (Adam & Groves, 2007; Koselleck, 2004). What is different in these historical examples compared to now, as sociologists Barbara Adam and Chris Groves (2007) explain, is that oracles and prophets assumed that the future was pre-existing. It was already there and only needed to be discovered by reading patterns or by recognising certain coincidences.

Prediction mechanisms in the twenty-first century depart from such premises. Although predictive technologies also rely on finding patterns in data, they aim to detect linear relationships between variables instead of more random connections, while the future is also conceived as less cyclical than it was historically. We still rely on technologies as extensions of human capabilities to observe and process predictive information (Lawson, 2017). Yet the primacy of natural and divine phenomena has been replaced, or at least complemented, by other observational and behavioural data that are processed statistically and, recently, in automated ways through machine learning (ML). Predictive policing, for example, relies on questionable approaches such as physiognomy and phrenology (Hong, 2022). These are attempts to link characteristics of the face or the scalp to personality traits with inherent tendencies towards criminal behaviour. Later approaches focused on the predictive value of past criminal records, or people's associations with other criminals, and also on risk-laden geographies as sites of expected criminality (e.g., Brayne & Christin, 2021; Calhoun, 2023; Ugwudike, 2022). Ironically though, the proliferation of ML and artificial intelligence (AI) announces a return to old pseudoscientific recipes of using physiognomy (Agüera y Arcas et al., 2023) or gait analysis (Jana et al., 2021) for predicting crime.

Beyond their ostensible penchant for managing uncertainty, the rise of predictive technologies depends on the important role played by 'promise'. Promises show us a trajectory and "create space for optimism and investment" (Hong, 2022, p. 378), while feeding the "sentiment that whatever can be predicted must be, as a point of both technical inevitability and the social good" (Hong, 2022, p. 381). For instance, based on promises of efficiency and the optimisation of resource usage, organisations are implementing predictive technologies to improve decision-making and risk management (Cevolini & Esposito, 2020; Egbert, 2024). Especially when budgets are tight, the temptation increases to introduce predictive technologies that might optimise, or even replace, expensive human labour. As Virginia Eubanks (2017) famously demonstrated, this can come with high societal costs, especially for poor and working-class people. In the state of Indiana in the United States, for example, many beneficiaries who depended on food stamps or Medicaid suddenly lost those provisions following the automation of welfare support. Although this flawed and poorly implemented case was abandoned, overall, the automated (welfare) state is expanding in many countries.

Automation and predictive technologies are supposed to prevent flaws and inefficiencies. Instead of biased human judgement and human error, technology promises systematic objectivity and accuracy. Yet very often, these promises remain unfulfilled, which is actually part of the process (Amoore, 2020). When predictive technologies make mistakes, we are called upon to understand those mistakes as part of their learning process and trajectory towards ever 'better' technology. Regular announcements of innovative predictive technologies and new uses help to sustain the myth that prediction technology is inevitable *and* that 'objective' prediction is possible (Hong, 2022).

3 A Typology of Predictive Technologies

How do predictive technologies work? The answer lies partly in distinguishing different types or generations. A typology allows us to grasp better the various operations and consequences of predictive technologies. To create a typology, I draw from the literature in the area of policing and crime prevention. This field has extensively studied different predictive technologies, and comparing them highlights their differences.

A first type of predictive technologies calculates the probability of an occurrence. To do this, they rely on statistical procedures such as regression analysis. The output of this type tends to follow this format: recidivism amongst white males is likely to occur in X per cent of cases, whereas for black males the odds are Y per cent (Christin, 2018).

A second type makes predictions about specific individuals. This generation of technologies followed expansions of data collection, increases in computational power, and the use of algorithms, later supplemented by ML and deep learning (which enable software to search for patterns in data and to learn from data with or without supervision by humans), permitting predictive technologies to move away from making estimates for aggregates of people to making predictions about individuals (Rona-Tas,

2020). An oft-mentioned example of such a predictive algorithm is the so-called Strategic Subjects List (SSL) piloted in 2013 and later decommissioned by Chicago's Police Department (Rona-Tas, 2020; Saunders et al., 2016; Sheehey, 2019). Aiming to reduce gun violence, this predictive algorithm drafted a list of 426 individuals thought to be most at risk. The thinking was that likely offenders could be contacted and helped. However, the pilot project was unsuccessful since it did not lead to a reduction in such crimes and the prevention programme never fully materialised.

Third, there are predictive technologies that look to contextual factors, or proxies, to draw conclusions. This generation emerged because targeting and classifying individuals can depend on privacy invasion or racial profiling. Therefore, this type of technology looked to wider contexts—for example, neighbourhoods with high crime rates. By targeting areas where burglaries or drug-related crimes had occurred before, the idea was that police officers could be deployed more efficiently, thereby also reducing the number of crimes. Of course, an increased police presence results in spikes in crime statistics, which leads to further police presence, and a self-fulfilling prophecy is born. In other words, anticipatory governance and prevention create a "feedback loop of knowledge production", which changes the objects of prediction (Flyverbom & Garsten, 2021, p. 2). Further problems are that neighbourhoods are often proxies for race and class, and a focus on easily observable crimes such as 'blue collar crimes', leads to the relative neglect of 'white collar crimes', such as financial fraud (D'Ignazio & Klein, 2020; O'Neil, 2016; Rona-Tas, 2020; Ugwudike, 2022).

Fourth, following growing evidence that a proxy-based approach reproduces inequalities and discriminates against minoritised groups and individuals, a different course was charted: crime risk forecasting. Crime risk forecasting represents a radical shift in the approach taken to prediction. Instead of predicting who will likely be involved in crime, or which area is likely to register a crime based on past criminal records, crime risk forecasting is "software that combine historic crime data and a range of geo-located *data not specific to crime* [emphasis added], such as the locations of bars, pawn shops and mental health facilities, in order to produce future-looking maps of likely 'criminal activity'" (Calhoun, 2023, p. 746). One of the many consequences of the shift from prediction to risk is that it implies a move from prevention to pre-emption. In the words of Louise Amoore (2013, p. 9), pre-emption "acts not strictly to prevent the playing out of a particular course of events on the basis of past data tracked forward into probable futures but to pre-empt an unfolding and emergent event in relation to an array of possible projected futures". In other words, compared to prevention, pre-emption draws less on the past and more on futures. Unlike prevention, pre-emption "is not animated by a history of offending but by a fear that a crime threat could emerge" (McCulloch & Wilson, 2015, p. 3). In practice, "pre-emption decouple[s] crime and punishment altogether by punishing hypothetical future crimes as if they had already happened" (McCulloch & Wilson, 2015, p. 3). Pre-emption turns every citizen, every corner in the city, all loitering people into risk objects, while public life is treated "as fundamentally requiring pre-emptive protection from itself" (Calhoun, 2023, p. 747).

Risk and futural assessment are also prevalent in areas other than policing or crime. In Denmark, for example, the local municipality of Gladsaxe near Copenhagen tested (and abandoned) a controversial predictive algorithm to detect mistreatment of children before it even manifested. By turning all parents into potential risk objects and by anticipating and pre-empting risk through algorithmic risk assessments, uncertain futures were made calculable, and undesirable futures were eliminated (Ratner & Elmholdt, 2023).

What unites these four predictive technology approaches is that they make some futures possible and actionable, while foreclosing others, including those that are not necessarily harmful or criminal. They predetermine human futures based on data related to their own or others' pasts, or by using data on unrelated risk objects, thereby reducing people's agency, any notion of innocence or trustworthiness, their available options, and the possibility to act differently or creatively.

4 The Predictions of Predictive Technologies

The preceding section helps us to understand what the use of predictive technologies aims to achieve. Let us now look more closely at what prediction actually entails.

4.1 *Problematic Data*

The discussion above has hinted at the possibility that data are biased or incomplete. This explains why some predictive technologies reproduce inequalities and discriminate against certain groups and individuals: they rely on biased data, directly or indirectly, through proxies, that are the result of societal and historical forms of discrimination. Nevertheless, predictive technologies come with the promise (and myth) that they can replace human subjectivity with technologically inspired objectivity. Would you rather stand in front of a subjective judge or an objective algorithm? This is a false dilemma. Human values are programmed into technology, and they have "the power to unjustly discriminate at a much larger scale than biased individuals" (Benjamin, 2019, p. 422).

We should also not forget that despite large-scale and continuous data extraction by states and companies, the data available to predictive technologies is always incomplete. Some objects (e.g., intentions) are less machine-readable, while some data (e.g., personal information) is inaccessible. Moreover, data does not equate to or guarantee knowledge and understanding. For many natural and social phenomena, science does not yet know or understand the mechanisms that explain how they emerge or operate. In some cases, there is "not just uncertainty about the predictive model, but about the phenomenon itself" (Munn, 2023, p. 65). Therefore, predictive technologies often deal with estimations and approximations of reality.

For some, for example in the tech industry, the answer to these limitations is more data and datafication. Driven by the belief that more data collection today will solve tomorrow's problems—what José van Dijck (2014) terms dataism—more and new sensors to measure the natural and social worlds, expanded (self-)tracking, and increased datafication of everything become the norm (Hoeyer, 2019; Kuch et al., 2020; Sadowski, 2019). However, looking in a crystal ball filled with data can easily result in blurred vision. Spurious correlations are one example: although statistically significant and even strong correlations can be found between certain variables in a dataset, their relationship can still be meaningless and random. Tyler Vigen (2024, para. 1) encountered so many of these spurious correlations in consultancy work that he decided to collect them on a website. One of his examples is the very strong correlation between "Cheddar cheese consumption" and "Solar power generated in Haiti". For the years 2012 to 2021, the data show similar developments in terms of their annual volumes confirming that statistical significance does not necessarily mean social significance.

Dataism, with a pinch of technological solutionism, reaches its peak in the ambition to develop so-called digital twins (Munn, 2023): AI-driven simulations of complex systems. Contemporary digital twins seek, for example, to improve weather forecasts or even to predict climate change. An example of the latter is the European Union's Destination Earth project that aims to "monitor and simulate the Earth's system developments (land, marine, atmosphere, biosphere) and human interventions" while also anticipating "environmental disasters and resultant socio-economic crises" and enabling scenario testing (Destination Earth, 2024, para. 1). The perverse effects on climate change and environmental destruction through the use of enormous amounts of natural resources and energy required to build and run this kind of 'green' Internet-of-Things (IoT) project have been shown to be overlooked (Brodie, 2023; Taffel, 2023).

Some scholars seem sceptical of building bigger predictive models because they do not necessarily perform 'better' than simple models (e.g., Hand, 2006; Hofman et al., 2017; Kaltheuner, 2021). Yet making such evaluative statements about the quality of predictive technologies is not straightforward. 'Better' can refer to various metrics depending on whom you ask. For example,

> [r]ather than pointing to the fact that a perceived spatial pattern is the result of systemic inequity and racialized institutional abandonment, as we might understand it, developers' use of the term 'bias' adjudicates how well a data set captures what they understand as a pattern in the world. (Calhoun, 2023, p. 753)

In this sense, 'accuracy' signifies how well the predicted outcome corresponds to the prediction, while 'efficacy' expresses to what extent the predictive technology could achieve its stated goal (e.g., reduce crime statistics) (Calhoun, 2023).

The reactivity of data, measurement, and predictions complicates the assessment of accuracy and efficiency (Hong, 2022; Taffel, 2018). Since any type of predictive technology affects present and future social realities, even by eliminating some futures, assessing predictive technology accuracy is hard. "As the algorithm gets going in the world, what would happen in its absence is statistically unobservable" (Calhoun, 2023, p. 752). When I decide to bring rain trousers for my commute based on forecasted showers, this does not affect the weather. Yet when many people vote strategically based on election polls or when children are removed from their parents based on risk assessments and before any misconduct takes place, predictions can have a significant impact on social reality. Such is the nature of self-fulfilling prophecies (Merton, 1948): when we believe something is likely to happen, our behaviours often align with the belief, making the outcome even more likely. This means that although many predictions are produced by automated systems, we should also consider how our actions support the manifestation of predetermined futures.

4.2 *(Un)stable Patterns Over Time*

This brings us to another challenge in defining what prediction is, given its foundation in the patterns of past and present data. If predictions rely on patterns, then how stable do these patterns need to be over time? In other words, how closed and continuous or open and contingent are the visions of the future upon which prediction technologies rely? Regarding the latter question, this clearly fluctuates over time.

As mentioned, in ancient times the future was perceived as pre-defined and discoverable, meaning it was imagined to be rather closed, repetitive through seasonal and other cycles, and, thus, quite easy to predict. Contemporary versions of such thinking are sayings like 'history repeats itself' or using Kondratieff (long-term economic) cycles as explanations for long-term fluctuations. Both assume a degree of societal stability, and under such assumptions, it makes sense to make predictions. For example, given the widespread and very persistent gender or racial inequalities in many societies around the globe, we can make several quite meaningful forecasts about these inequalities. Extrapolations, predictions as extensions of the past, are thus not necessarily problematic when viewed in this context (Rona-Tas, 2020).

In addition, we should also account for how historical and contemporary human behaviour necessarily limits the openness of the future. Think of the long shadows that unbridled industrialisation and consumption in much of the world are casting on the future's timeline. The longevity of nuclear waste or carbon dioxide and the increasingly observable and experiential consequences of climate change certainly narrow futures' openness (Adam, 2023).

At the same time, several elements point to the relative openness of the future. With the rise of secularism, the future depended less on the will of gods and became more makeable by humans. Especially during Western modernity and the post–Second World War decades, the future became both very open and very unpredictable, except for the belief in progress (Adam & Groves, 2007; Hartog, 2015). Following de-traditionalisation and accelerated change, societal instability has also increased (Rosa, 2003).

Instead of relying on traditions and generational patterns, people have to make more choices and manage more risk. Luke Munn (2023, p. 60) adds to this "the unprecedented nature of climate change, but also the way these transformations ripple outwards in many directions, intensifying poverty and inequality, amplifying conflict, and undermining social and political stability".

Given this instability and despite significant social and cultural continuities (Driessens, 2023), we might wonder to what extent predictions can be effective or even possible at all (Munn, 2023). An example here is the mass collaborative study led by sociologist Matthew J. Salganik (2020) using data from the Fragile Families and Child Wellbeing Study, a birth cohort study. Involving hundreds of scholars and thousands of variables, 160 independent teams tested the predictability of life trajectories, focusing on six life outcomes. Although they used advanced ML methods, their best predictions were not very accurate, and not much better than a simple benchmark model that draws on standard regression models. This finding raised "questions about the absolute level of predictive performance that is possible for some life outcomes, even with a rich dataset" (Salganik et al., 2020, p. 8402).

In this context, it is relevant to recall the importance of analysing underlying views of the social world and the laws or mechanisms that govern it. Positivism as a scientific method leads to a focus on 'if A, then B' kinds of predictions, as featured above. Instead, we could begin from the inherent causal openness of the social (Porpora, 2024), and acknowledge contingency in the form of chaos, catastrophes (such as COVID-19), chance, creativity, choice, institutional logics, or relational networks. Instead of making predictions, we could analyse tendencies, for example (Archer, 2024).

5 Conclusion

The foregoing observations culminate in the final point of this discussion: freedom, which Sun-ha Hong (2022, p. 381) says is at stake in our current context:

> [The] relentless universalization of data-driven prediction as the answer to all social problems is at the vanguard of technofutures as closure; that is, the terms by which we are made to make sense of the world act as powerful constraints on other kinds of meaning, values, and ways of living.

Predictions prioritise some options over others, and they eliminate particular possibilities for people and organisations. They foreclose futures and predetermine outcomes. With the shift from probabilistic prediction to risk management and anticipation, the freedom and agency of those on the receiving end of predictions are further threatened through the reduction of future possibilities and, ultimately, through the elimination of undesired futures (Esposito, 2021; Rouvroy, 2013). At the same time, organisations and individuals who produce predictions behave in ways that make some outcomes more predictable—for example, by over-policing areas where crime might occur, although resistance and flexibility is still possible (Brayne & Christin, 2021).

In summary, I argue that predictive technologies should be renamed as *automated predeterminations* because they "contribute to a programmed vision of the future" (Kaun & Stiernstedt, 2020, p. 1595). Through algorithmic and automated ways of calculating probabilities, risks, and scenarios of possible (un)desired futures, our futures are increasingly technologically predetermined. Although much of the world seems more complex and contingent than in earlier times, people's range of future options shrinks through decisions made by automated systems on behalf of the companies, organisations, and government agencies that control them. These decisions carry (symbolic) power because they come with the promise of objectivity and neutrality, while their assumed inevitability is strengthened by the often-limited possibilities to appeal them. Ultimately, this leads to increased power for the state and the market at the expense of individuals' freedom and possibilities for justice (Jørgensen, 2023).

Despite their many limitations and erroneous outcomes, predictive technologies are at the heart of most of our lives since institutions and businesses increasingly rely on them for decision-making. In most cases, predictive technologies do not really predict the future. Rather, they extrapolate patterns in past and present data to shape the future—yet the future does not mirror the past. Only in rare circumstances of high stability and low contingency can such forecasts be accurate. The excesses of capitalism together with climate and environment change produce an increasingly volatile world which makes prediction harder. Yet, by their mere performance, however bad, predictive technologies have real consequences for many individuals' and communities' life chances. This makes predictive technologies, or predetermined automations, a genuine concern for those of us interested in justice and citizens' rights. We should call out predictive technologies for what they are—*automated predeterminations*—and further resist their harmful implications so as to retain relatively open futures that offer a space for agency and contingency.

Acknowledgements The author would like to thank the editors, Crystal Chokshi and Robin Mansell, as well as the anonymous reviewer for their generous feedback on earlier drafts of this chapter.

References

Adam, B. (2023). Futures imperfect: A reflection on challenges. *Sociology, 57*(2), 279–287. https://doi.org/10.1177/00380385221113478

Adam, B., & Groves, C. (2007). *Future matters: Action, knowledge, ethics.* Brill.

Agüera y Arcas, B., Mitchell, M., & Todorov, A. (2023). Physiognomy in the age of AI. In J. Browne, S. Cave, E. Drage, & K. McInerney (Eds.), *Feminist AI: Critical perspectives on algorithms, data, and intelligent machines* (pp. 208–236). Oxford University Press.

Amoore, L. (2013). *The politics of possibility: Risk and security beyond probability.* Duke University Press.

Amoore, L. (2020). *Cloud ethics: Algorithms and the attributes of ourselves and others.* Duke University Press.

Archer, M. S. (2024). Coincidence: A word with two meanings for explaining and predicting the future. *Journal for the Theory of Social Behaviour, 54*(3), 354–365. https://doi.org/10.1111/jtsb.12405

Benjamin, R. (2019). Assessing risk, automating racism. *Science, 366*(6464), 421–422. https://doi.org/10.1126/science.aaz3873

Brayne, S., & Christin, A. (2021). Technologies of crime prediction: The reception of algorithms in policing and criminal courts. *Social Problems, 68*(3), 608–624. https://doi.org/10.1093/socpro/spaa004

Brodie, P. (2023). Data infrastructure studies on an unequal planet. *Big Data & Society, 10*(1), 1–14. https://doi.org/10.1177/20539517231182402

Calhoun, L. (2023). Latency, uncertainty, contagion: Epistemologies of risk-as-reform in crime forecasting software. *Environment and Planning D: Society and Space, 41*(4), 745–762. https://doi.org/10.1177/02637758231197012

Cevolini, A., & Esposito, E. (2020). From pool to profile: Social consequences of algorithmic prediction in insurance. *Big Data & Society, 7*(2), 1–11. https://doi.org/10.1177/2053951720939228

Christin, A. (2018). Predictive algorithms and criminal sentencing. In D. Bessner & N. Guilhot (Eds.), *The decisionist imagination: Sovereignty, social science and democracy in the 20th century* (pp. 272–294). Berghahn Books.

D'Ignazio, C., & Klein, L. F. (2020). *Data feminism.* The MIT Press.

Destination Earth. (2024). *Destination Earth*. https://destination-earth.eu/

Driessens, O. (2023). Not everything is changing: On the relative neglect and meanings of continuity in communication and social change research. *Communication Theory, 33*(1), 32–41. https://doi.org/10.1093/ct/qtac022

Egbert, S. (2024). Algorithmic futures: Governmentality and prediction regimes. In J. Jarke, B. Prietl, S. Egbert, Y. Boeva, H. Heuer, & M. Arnold (Eds.), *Algorithmic regimes: Methods, interactions, and politics* (pp. 265–285). Amsterdam University Press.

Esposito, E. (2021). Unpredictability. In N. B. Thylstrup, D. Agostinho, A. Ring, C. D'Ignazio, & K. Veel (Eds.), *Uncertain archives: Critical keywords for big data* (pp. 709–717). MIT Press.

Eubanks, V. (2017). *Automating inequality: How high-tech tools profile, police, and punish the poor*. St. Martin's Press.

Flyverbom, M., & Garsten, C. (2021). Anticipation and organization: Seeing, knowing and governing futures. *Organization Theory, 2*(3), 1–25. https://doi.org/10.1177/26317877211020325

Hand, D. J. (2006). Classifier technology and the illusion of progress. *Statistical Science, 21*(1), 1–14. https://doi.org/10.1214/088342306000000060

Hartog, F. (2015). *Regimes of historicity: Presentism and experiences of time* (S. Brown, Trans.). Columbia University Press.

Hoeyer, K. (2019). Data as promise: Reconfiguring Danish public health through personalized medicine. *Social Studies of Science, 49*(4), 531–555. https://doi.org/10.1177/0306312719858697

Hofman, J. M., Sharma, A., & Watts, D. J. (2017). Prediction and explanation in social systems. *Science, 355*(6324), 486–488. https://doi.org/10.1126/science.aal3856

Hong, S. (2022). Predictions without futures. *History and Theory, 61*(3), 371–390. https://doi.org/10.1111/hith.12269

Jana, S., Das, N., Basu, S., & Nasipuri, M. (2021). Survey of human gait analysis and recognition for medical and forensic applications. *International Journal of Digital Crime and Forensics (IJDCF), 13*(6), 1–20. https://doi.org/10.4018/IJDCF.289432

Jørgensen, R. F. (2023). Data and rights in the digital welfare state: The case of Denmark. *Information, Communication & Society, 26*(1), 123–138. https://doi.org/10.1080/1369118X.2021.1934069

Kallinikos, J. (2011). Technology and accountability: Autonomic computing and human agency. In M. Hildebrandt & A. Rouvroy (Eds.), *Law, human agency and autonomic computing: The philosophy of law meets the philosophy of technology* (pp. 161–178). Routledge.

Kaltheuner, F. (2021). AI snake oil, pseudoscience and hype: An interview with Arvind Narayanan. In F. Kaltheuner (Ed.), *Fake AI* (pp. 19–38). Meatspace Press.

Kaun, A., & Stiernstedt, F. (2020). Doing time, the smart way? Temporalities of the smart prison. *New Media & Society, 22*(9), 1580–1599. https://doi.org/10.1177/1461444820914865

Kerr, I. (2013). Prediction, pre-emption, presumption: The path of law after the computational turn. In M. Hildebrandt & K. de Vries (Eds.), *Privacy, due process and the computational turn: The philosophy of law meets the philosophy of technology* (pp. 91–120). Routledge.

Koselleck, R. (2004). *Futures past: On the semantics of historical time*. Columbia University Press.

Kuch, D., Kearnes, M., & Gulson, K. (2020). The promise of precision: Datafication in medicine, agriculture and education. *Policy Studies, 41*(5), 527–546. https://doi.org/10.1080/01442872.2020.1724384

Lawson, C. (2017). *Technology and isolation*. Cambridge University Press.

McCulloch, J., & Wilson, D. (2015). *Pre-crime: Pre-emption, precaution and the future*. Routledge.

Merton, R. K. (1948). The self-fulfilling prophecy. *The Antioch Review, 8*(2), 193–210. https://doi.org/10.2307/4609267

Mühlhoff, R. (2021). Predictive privacy: Towards an applied ethics of data analytics. *Ethics and Information Technology, 23*(4), 675–690. https://doi.org/10.1007/s10676-021-09606-x

Munn, L. (2023). The end of prediction? AI technologies in a no-analog world. *SubStance, 52*(2), 59–73. https://doi.org/10.1353/sub.2023.a907149

O'Neil, C. (2016). *Weapons of math destruction: How big data increases inequality and threatens democracy*. Allen Lane.

Pasquale, F. (2015). *The black box society: The secret algorithms that control money and information*. Harvard University Press.

Porpora, D. (2024). Do realists predict? *Journal for the Theory of Social Behaviour, 54*(3), 255–268. https://doi.org/10.1111/jtsb.12404

Ratner, H. F., & Elmholdt, K. (2023). Algorithmic constructions of risk: Anticipating uncertain futures in child protection services. *Big Data & Society, 10*(2), 1–12. https://doi.org/10.1177/20539517231186120

Rona-Tas, A. (2020). Predicting the future: Art and algorithms. *Socio-Economic Review, 18*(3), 893–911. https://doi.org/10.1093/ser/mwaa040

Rosa, H. (2003). Social acceleration: Ethical and political consequences of a desynchronized high-speed society. *Constellations, 10*(1), 3–33. https://doi.org/10.1111/1467-8675.00309

Rouvroy, A. (2013). The end(s) of critique: Data behaviourism versus due process. In M. Hildebrandt & K. de Vries (Eds.), *Privacy, due process and the computational turn: The philosophy of law meets the philosophy of technology* (pp. 143–167). Routledge.

Sadowski, J. (2019). When data is capital: Datafication, accumulation, and extraction. *Big Data & Society, 6*(1), 1–12. https://doi.org/10.1177/2053951718820549

Salganik, M. J., Lundberg, I., Kindel, A. T., Ahearn, C. E., Al-Ghoneim, K., Almaatouq, A., Altschul, D. M., Brand, J. E., Carnegie, N. B., Compton, R. J., Datta, D., Davidson, T., Filippova, A., Gilroy, C., Goode, B. J., Jahani, E., Kashyap, R., Kirchner, A., McKay, S., McLanahan, S., et al. (2020). Measuring the predictability of life outcomes with a scientific mass collaboration. *Proceedings of the National Academy of Sciences, 117*(15), 8398–8403. https://doi.org/10.1073/pnas.1915006117

Saunders, J., Hunt, P., & Hollywood, J. S. (2016). Predictions put into practice: A quasi-experimental evaluation of Chicago's predictive policing pilot. *Journal of Experimental Criminology, 12*(3), 347–371. https://doi.org/10.1007/s11292-016-9272-0

Sheehey, B. (2019). Algorithmic paranoia: The temporal governmentality of predictive policing. *Ethics and Information Technology, 21*(1), 49–58. https://doi.org/10.1007/s10676-018-9489-x

Taffel, S. (2018). Hopeful extinctions? Tesla, technological solutionism and the Anthropocene. *Culture Unbound, 10*(2), 163–184. https://doi.org/10.3384/cu.2000.1525.2018102163

Taffel, S. (2023). Data and oil: Metaphor, materiality and metabolic rifts. *New Media & Society, 25*(5), 980–998. https://doi.org/10.1177/14614448211017887

Ugwudike, P. (2022). Predictive algorithms in justice systems and the limits of tech-reformism. *International Journal for Crime, Justice and Social Democracy, 11*(1), 85–99. https://doi.org/10.5204/ijcjsd.2189

van Dijck, J. (2014). Datafication, dataism and dataveillance: Big data between scientific paradigm and ideology. *Surveillance & Society, 12*(2), 197–208. https://doi.org/10.24908/ss.v12i2.4776

Vigen, T. (2024, January). *Cheddar cheese consumption correlates with solar power generated in Haiti (r=0.985)*. Spurious correlation. http://www.tylervigen.com/spurious/correlation/5904_cheddar-cheese-consumption_correlates-with_solar-power-generated-in-haiti

CHAPTER 9

Fabulation*

~~Hype~~

Gillian Russell and Frédérik Lesage

1 Introduction

Tech metaphors matter for a whole host of reasons (as this book makes clear). Not least of all, they matter because they enable and constrain how people engage with the normative and political dimensions of technology (Agre, 1997). For example, Georgina Voss (2024) shows how the metaphor of the autonomous vehicle positions this consumer product as a public good, one that leads to safer roads and more efficient traffic, even as it undermines the development of mass transit. The metaphor, which bestows digitally enhanced cars with anthropomorphic traits of autonomous thought and action, encourages a reimagining of a liveable city without the burden of understanding what ways of life they might undo. For

G. Russell (✉)
School of Interactive Arts and Technology, Simon Fraser University, Burnaby, BC, Canada
e-mail: gillianr@sfu.ca

F. Lesage
School of Communication, Simon Fraser University, Burnaby, BC, Canada
e-mail: flesage@sfu.ca

C. Chokshi, R. Mansell (eds.), *The Need to Rename Tech*,
https://doi.org/10.1007/978-3-032-05155-4_9

Voss, tech metaphors and their implied neutrality intentionally configure a very narrow understanding of the world, and they have real consequences. They shape how we expect the world to work and are hugely influential in the design and reception of new technologies. If we accept the power of tech metaphors, then *how* they are developed and deployed must matter equally because the 'how' not only limits the web of symbolic relations for articulating tech's future, but also forecloses the range of actors who can create this web. Today, that 'how' largely takes place through what Voss describes as Silicon Valley's "grand theater of hype" (Voss, 2024, p. 11).

Following Donna Haraway's (2016, p. 12) adage that "it matters what stories we tell to tell other stories with", this chapter asks: how might we reclaim tech metaphors by storying beyond 'hype'? Is it possible to move away from how Silicon Valley imagines technology for us, towards a more democratic imagination? Might we tell tech's stories differently? We start by examining 'hype' as a dominant social imaginary based on anticipation. Following this, we argue that *fabulation* constitutes a more democratic approach to meaningfully engaging with tech metaphors. We illustrate this potential with the example of Fables for Imagining, a storymaking method we developed that, through the art of fables, explores ways to cut through, to go beyond, and to transcend tech metaphors.

2 Social Imaginaries and Fantasy

In *Metaphors We Live By*, George Lakoff and Mark Johnson (1980) describe a metaphor as a mechanism of the mind that enables us to learn and understand things we do not know by relating and connecting them to the things we already know. They argue that connections create systems of meaning. For example, the metaphorical concept 'time is money' is reflected in a system of cultural references to time as a valuable commodity ('spending time').

Lakoff and Johnson later updated this approach to account for a more 'embodied' understanding of cognition that is less reliant on language as a way to model metaphorical connections and more focused on the body. However, this update provides little help for analysing tech metaphors since these authors limit their conceptualisation of (scientific) technologies to "enhancements of basic bodily capacities" (Lakoff & Johnson, 1999, p. 91), such as how computers enhance our capacity to calculate. Such an instrumental model of technology provides only limited analytical purchase in a world in which ubiquitous tech metaphors enable *and* constrain how people experience the world in which they live. Understanding how technologies such as computers are embedded in, and sustain, metaphorical systems entails more than considering how they enhance humanity's capacity to calculate.

To address this sociotechnological blind spot, we turn to a particular type of social imaginary: sociotechnical imaginaries and the ways they capture how people "make sense of the practices of a given society" (Mansell, 2012, p. 176). Social imaginaries are a unique type of fiction that we collectively, as a society, agree to believe in and support through our institutions and actions (Taylor, 2004). They are made 'real' by this collective imagining and enactment, and, as a result, they structure our social life and even impact how we envisage the future. Think of concepts like money, corporations, and even nation states. For Patrice Flichy, sociotechnical imaginaries encompass designers' 'utopian' ideas of what technology can and should be. These visions are subsequently transformed into "frames of functioning" (Flichy, 2007b, p. 153) that delimit how technology should be designed and used, and they enable certain kinds of technological progress. Consider, for example, how politicians in the 1990s argued for public investment in internet infrastructure by drawing on the metaphor of the highway (Flichy, 2007a). Anchored in technologies themselves, sociotechnical imaginaries also develop through a broad range of cultural artefacts, from media articles and promotional images to product reviews, policy reports, or other grey literature, and even science fiction and cinema. Analysing sociotechnical imaginaries requires attention to the power relations that run through them. We can, for example, acknowledge the existence of competing alternative narratives that offer different priorities for tech designs (Mansell, 2012), while considering which utopian visions become dominant, revealing who, in fact, creates our futures.

Hype constitutes a dominant sociotechnical imaginary concocted through the idiosyncratic fusion of Californian bohemianism of the 1960s and 1970s with the high-tech industries of Silicon Valley (Barbrook & Cameron, 1996). Critical scholarship on the topic has focused on assessing how hype veils reality through fantasy. For example, Steve Woolgar offers the term 'cyberbole' to denote "the exaggerated depiction (hyperbole) of the capacities of virtual (cyber) technologies" (Woolgar, 2003, p. vi). For Vincent Mosco (2004, p. 27), hype is "nothing particularly new". Drawing on historians of technology such as David Nye (1990) and Leo Marx (1964), Mosco (2014) argues that coinages such as 'cyberspace' or metaphors such as 'the cloud' are part of a broader mythology that protects and sustains dominant political and economic interests.

Beyond merely masking elements of our current reality through fantasy, hype should also be understood as an attempt by those in power to control how people collectively envisage the future—or what we might call the *not-yet-real*. Our aim in this chapter is to analyse the practices that enable this control and to advance the development of more democratic alternatives. Such an undertaking requires that we break from a dualistic understanding of fantasy as the opposite of reality. Doing so allows us to understand how fantasy—as putting imagination into action—is an indelible part of our meaningful engagement with reality. It enables us to consider how playing with the symbolic and affective dimensions of tech metaphors can be used to do more than veil modes of domination over the future; it may also hold the key to engaging in a 'politics of hope' (Appadurai, 2013) and to democratising social futures thinking (Urry, 2016). As Alexandra Daisy Ginsberg contends, "rather than abandoning the fiction of the social imaginary and its pernicious effects, it is more pressing than ever that we open it up, critique it and reinvent it" (Ginsberg, 2018, p. 269). In other words, rather than ask how hype masks reality, we consider what practices mask hype as fantasy and explore practices that could be used to develop alternative fantasies. By extension, we work to create alternative social imaginaries that can destabilise dominant visions and the social and political agendas that power them.

3 Hype as Anticipating Tech Futures: Bubbles and Life Cycles

The people who create hype, which often relies on metaphors, are experts in and around the tech industry, such as entrepreneurs, consultants, financial speculators, product evangelists, futurists, advertisers, marketers, and tech journalists. The methods they use to generate and disseminate these fantasies include journalistic reporting and financial speculation, as well as forecasting techniques for modelling possible futures. Taken together, these methods represent a technological future through anticipation (Appadurai, 2013; Poli, 2020). Anticipation involves thinking about the future as something based on prediction rather than explanation (Andrejevic, 2013), using quantitative data, technical diagrams, references to scientific disciplines, and expert opinion to render outcomes probable, rather than definitive. In other words, these methods bestow a "disembodied scientific objectivity" (Haraway, 1988, p. 576) upon tech industry hype, lending it a narrative of accuracy or neutrality that is difficult to critique. By extension, alternative sociotechnical imaginaries that do not rely on ostensibly objective anticipation can be dismissed as unreliable or irresponsible forms of hype, outlining potential futures that are too unpredictable or incoherent.

To illustrate how anticipation is used to entrench distinctions between accurate and unreliable or neutral and irresponsible while still relying on fantasy, we turn to two metaphors—bubbles and life cycles—commonly used by the tech industry to bolster hype. The bubble metaphor originates in economics, where it is used to describe an 'unsustainable or exaggerated' increase in the value of stocks (Oxford English Dictionary, 2024). The term's migration from Wall Street to Silicon Valley is just one of many reminders that the worlds of finance and tech are deeply intertwined (Appadurai & Alexander, 2020). Just as in economics, spotting a 'bubble' in tech depends on anticipatory practices such as financial forecasting and speculation.

Famous tech bubbles include the dot-com bubble of the late 1990s and early 2000s and the Bitcoin bubble of the late 2010s. Like all financial bubbles, both the dot-com and Bitcoin bubbles eventually 'burst'. Anticipating bubbles is not necessarily about avoiding them altogether; rather, the aim is to predict and navigate bursts by relying, for example, on models of industrial production and consumer demand. When bubbles are an inescapable part of the hype imaginary, people are encouraged to seek out and align themselves with the latest and most reliable prognostications. For example, following the dot-com burst in the early 2000s, software manual publisher Tim O'Reilly created 'Foo Camps' (short for 'Friends of O'Reilly') as an exclusive Silicon Valley conference where those in attendance could better prepare for the future of tech (Adler, 2010; Weinberger, 2004). These conferences would serve as the template for the Web 2.0 Conference in 2004. This situation implicitly generates more hype and benefits those in power since they are already in the best position to shape the very future being anticipated. Even those who make a living from bursting tech bubbles produce discourse that is "parasitic upon and even inflates hype" (Vinsel, 2021, para. 2). In her investigation of public writing on tech, Sarah Watson (2016) shows that while the traditional 'tech beat' (e.g., consumer tech reviews) too often feeds hype, technology criticism (e.g., think pieces) also relies on its own stylistic and ideological 'traps', such as fear mongering, sensationalism, and moral panics. Taken together, both kinds of discourse about tech bubbles can be understood as complementary facets of tech hype that feed the impression of a perpetually precarious future.

Much like the bubble, the life cycle metaphor is also used to anticipate tech's winners and losers (Fenn & Raskino, 2008), a process in which prediction is presented as a neutral enterprise rather than as hype. But whereas the former term originates in economics, the latter stems from biology. Gartner, an American consultancy firm, coined the term 'hype cycle' to describe variations in societal expectations for new technologies over time. For nearly three decades, Gartner's consultants used this forecasting model to help clients "separate hype from the real drivers of a technology's commercial promise" (Gartner, 2024, para. 12). Anticipating a technology's future through this biological metaphor renders hype as part of the organic rhythms of life itself. Tech metaphors such as 'the cloud' are expected to naturally progress through peaks of 'inflated expectations' and pass 'troughs of disillusionment' before becoming ubiquitous and commonplace (Kelly, 2016, p. 25). The irony is that hype cycle discourse recasts this circular process as a linear graph, the implication being that the cyclical repetitions are the vicissitudes of society's inflated expectations of tech, while tech's eventual adoption into everyday life is a foregone conclusion.

Metaphors such as 'bubble' and 'life cycle' do not only participate in and generate hype, they are also hard to understand. They share in common this characteristic with many other metaphors disseminated through hype discourse which remain fuzzy and difficult to pin down. We generally have only the "haziest of notions" (Bridle, 2018, p. 7) of what terms such as 'the cloud' refer to. Lucy Suchman suggests that metaphors such as 'artificial intelligence' are deployed through a "strategic vagueness that serves the interests of its promoters", leaving those without technical knowledge "to assume that others know what it is" (Suchman, 2023, p. 3) To moderate AI hype, critics ranging from academics at the Center on Privacy & Technology at Georgetown Law (Tucker, 2022) to the style editors at *The Economist* (Anonymous, 2023) call for avoiding metaphors as much as possible and replacing them with terms that provide greater clarity and specificity.

Challenging hype by parsing and tempering its fantasies through a more specific discourse is certainly important work; however, this approach relies on specialised technical know-how and is therefore often limited to experts. It does not offer alternative practices through which ordinary people can (re)shape tech's social imaginaries, for example, by playing with the symbolic and affective aspects of tech metaphors. For all these reasons, viable alternative tech social imaginaries require moving away from anticipation and towards modes of storytelling that help expand and democratise the prevailing methods of critiquing tech metaphors.

4 Towards Fabulations as Alternative Storymaking Methods

We turn to *fabulation* as a practice for reclaiming tech metaphors. Feminist scholars such as Haraway (2016) and Daniela Rosner (2018), among others, position this practice as a transformative force for understanding our realities. Fabulation, Haraway argues, is a form of everyday storytelling that serves as a crucial tool for challenging dominant narratives and envisaging alternative futures. She suggests the use of fabulation as a speculative endeavour that traces and transforms knowledge worlds through a deep attention to the precarious conditions of life. For Haraway, speculative fabulations can disrupt habitual ways of knowing and help to imagine futures that are radically different from the world we now inhabit. Fabulations eschew the disembodied objectivity of anticipation, instead, embracing the relationality and situatedness of storytelling. Following Haraway, Rosner argues that fabulation can serve as a catalyst for critical engagement with the sociotechnical imaginaries that shape our collective futures. Derived from the practice of telling fables, fabulations, she contends, blend the real and fantastic to combine different understandings of the past with a commitment to making a difference through both awareness and responsibility. Indeed, as Rosner observes in her discussion of critical fabulations: "They deconstruct design methods [in our case, tech metaphors] to open different understandings of the past that reconfigure the present, creating new opportunities for a just future" (Rosner, 2018, p. 17).

Thinking about fabulation with Haraway and Rosner emphasises our inherent responsibility for the worlds we both inherit and create. If fabulation is a form of storytelling that mediates between the realm of representation and lived realities, it also entails practices of noticing and responding 'care-fully' with the conditions of our time. These commitments are what distinguish fabulation from anticipation: fabulation embraces the situatedness and complexity that comes with engaging with present conditions (Søndergaard et al., 2023), whereas anticipation's predictive techniques project into the future while remaining ambivalent about current or future social, environmental, political, and moral implications.

Our intent is to explore fabulation's practical applications or, rather, to describe how we might fabulate in ways that unveil hype's fantasies and create democratic alternatives. In line with Haraway and Rosner, we position the capacity to fabulate about technology as a critical practice whereby 'non-experts' can make and reshape collective sociotechnical imaginaries to suit their lived experience. This means acknowledging that people, through their stories, have the power to reanimate the metaphors that populate their own social imaginaries—by examining the relations these metaphors hold in place, and by reclaiming suppressed stories so as to escape the rationality of fantastical hype.

4.1 *Fables for Imagining*

Fables for Imagining is a storymaking method we designed in the Imaginative Methods Lab to support people to collectively and relationally fabulate with tech metaphors in order to unpack their processes and by-products and build new social imaginaries.[1] Our intention is to intervene in the social problem of tech hype by giving people tools to make their own stories about technology, based on their lived realities, in an effort to dismantle hype's dominant fabulations. While we hope that alternative, resistant stories emerge from the process, research has shown that the stories people tell about technologies can have "deep pedagogical value" by connecting "abstract concepts with real experiences" (Singh et al., 2022, p. 7). As part of this effort to 'restory' tech metaphors, the lab invites participants to build new frames of reference and to try out new

[1] Fables for Imagining is a project developed by Dr. Gillian Russell, Dr. Frédérik Lesage, and Craig Badke, with assistance from Lauren Thu, Samein Shamsher, and Pete Fung. Doan Truong also supported the project as an illustrator. The Imaginative Methods Lab, established in 2021 is a methods incubator based in Simon Fraser University, which lies on the unceded traditional territories of the Coast Salish peoples of the xʷməθkwəy̓əm (Musqueam), Skwxwú7mesh (Squamish), Səl̓ílwətaɬ (Tsleil-Waututh), Katzie, Kwantlen, Kwikwetlem (kʷikʷəƛ̓əm), Qayqayt, Tsawassen, and numerous Stó:lō Nations. Operating at the intersection of design and social studies, the lab's key goals are to cultivate futures literacies and foster a critical and public imagination, while supporting people to become agents of change working towards more ecologically and socially sustainable futures.

ways of orienting themselves within the worlds designed by tech—without drawing on anticipation. Our aim is to challenge the utopian impulse of hype (Jameson, 2005), not by doing away with its metaphors, but, instead, by forging fabulation into a means for the democratic prioritisation of other ways of knowing. Centred around the familiar tropes of storytelling through fables, Fables for Imagining entangles fantasy with reality to build a process for visioning, imagining, and critiquing tech metaphors, and, ultimately, challenging the power of hype.

We chose fables as the basis for designing this storymaking device because they are one of humanity's oldest forms of storytelling. Fables have long been used to share tales of moral inquiry and caution, drawing on archetypal characters to build collective wisdom, interrogate power, and navigate societal roles and responsibilities. Across generations and cultures, these narratives encapsulate profound truths about human nature, ethics, and society. They serve as repositories of wisdom, imparting valuable lessons in a format that can transcend linguistic and cultural barriers. Beyond their didactic purposes, fables serve as reflective mirrors of societal norms, values, and power structures, offering insightful commentary on contemporary issues. As Annabel Patterson's (1991) history of Aesopian fables observes, such stories should be understood, not as childish stories with clichéd morals, but as tales of power that were used by the politically savvy and the powerless to speak their truths.

We were interested in how we could combine these aspects of the genre to enable playful ways of imagining and reflecting upon tech metaphors, to help people envisage, express, and create innovative engagements with (and resistance to) tech hype. The current version of the tool is the result of an iterative research and design process involving probe kits, performative storymaking sessions, and user testing. Versions of the workshop have been tested as part of conferences, courses, and special events in Vancouver, Canada, and Bilbao, Spain, with over 250 participants including researchers, activists, university and high school students, teachers, and young adults from marginalised communities.

In its material form, Fables for Imagining is a fabulation kit designed to be played either in person or online by teams of three to five people at a time (Fig. 9.1). Each kit consists of Metaphor Cards, Archetype Cards, and Fables Cards, alongside a playmat that sets various tasks for participants to work through in the development of their twenty-first-century technosocial fable. The process occurs in three parts. Part One plays off a traditional SWOT analysis (Strengths, Weaknesses, Opportunities, and

Fig. 9.1 A tabletop covered in materials for a Fables for Imagining workshop. Photograph by Frédérik Lesage

Threats), used as a strategic planning tool for decision-making. Bringing it into the realm of storymaking, participants collectively perform a SWAP analysis (Strengths, Weaknesses, Antagonists, and Protagonists, with attention to both human and non-human agents) of their chosen tech metaphor card which features a popular term such as 'the cloud', 'artificial intelligence', or 'smart homes', among other options. As part of this activity, teams are prompted to consider the deeper meta-messaging around their chosen metaphors' use, while identifying its cast of characters. Who are its villains and rogues, its heroes and rebels? The intention of this part of the fabulation tool is to draw out the social, political, cultural, and environmental circumstances of the metaphor and the technology it is used to describe. To help participants move past the more familiar and often rote initial responses to this activity, we provide conversation cards that are based on news items, academic writing, and other sources that engage with hype.

Building on their SWAP analysis, teams are then invited to plot the various stories held by their chosen metaphor onto the Story Arc Timeline which we adapted from American author Kurt Vonnegut's (1981/2009) work on the shape of stories. Vonnegut argued that the narrative structure of any story could be mapped into a shape on a graph, with the horizontal axis representing the story's chronology, from beginning to end, and the vertical axis representing the protagonist's fortune, from good to ill (Fig. 9.2). He believed that it is possible to tell a lot about a society's way of seeing and being in the world from the shape of its stories. While Vonnegut's graph shares formal characteristics with Gartner's hype cycle,

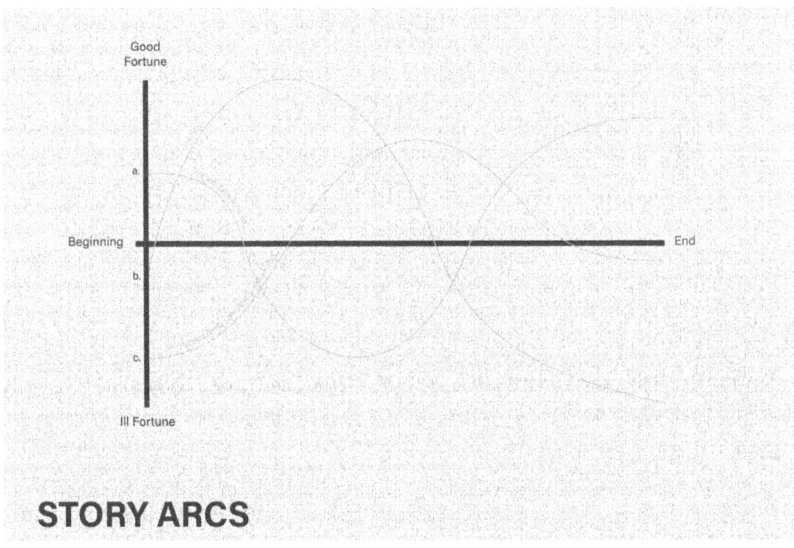

Fig. 9.2 Image of the Story Arc Timeline from the playmat. The sample arcs in the background depict three of Vonnegut's eight story shapes. Image produced by the authors

described above, our main focus was on one key distinction: the shift from anticipation to fabulation. For us, Vonnegut's graph serves less as a tool to analyse a society and more as a heuristic tool for unlocking the multiple stories hidden behind metaphors.

In Part Two, participants are asked to select one of the plotted story arcs to build their fable. They then choose two characters from a selection of animal archetypes, included in their fabulation kit, to represent the characters in their story. At this point they are given the time to map out key character attributes from their analysis in Part One, using these to further develop their representative archetypes. While each animal archetype may connote different meanings for different people depending on their personal and cultural backgrounds, teams are encouraged to explore these associations and to decide which attributes they would like to draw on, and how, while developing their story.

In Part Three of the storymaking process, participants choose one corresponding Fable Card to purposely misread for this final activity in the storymaking kit. Fable Cards are drawn from a collection of international stories that are associated with each of the available animal archetypes consulted in Part Two. For example, if a team chooses the turtle archetype in Part Two, they would be given the option of misreading either 'Urashima and the Turtle: A Japanese Story', or 'The Eagle and the Turtle: An Ancient Greek Story'.

The task of purposefully misreading an existing fable allows teams to scaffold their writing process and enlivens the democratic right to take part in the process of fabulating with tech metaphors. Throughout the iterations of Fables for Imagining, we noticed a range of comfort and familiarity levels with writing, generally, and with fable-writing, in particular. As scaffolding, the misreading exercise enables participants to refamiliarise themselves with the fable genre and, should they choose to do so, to draw on its tropes and style. The purpose of this portion of the activity is to invite participants to question how the structures of a given fable might be interpreted and reimagined for our time and the contemporary environments that influence our sense of self, place, agency, and relationships to power and each other. Teams are presented with a series of story prompts on their playmat to aid them in developing their new technosocial fable. These prompts help participants to identify the setting, main conflict, challenge, and purpose of their story.

At the end of Part Three, each team writes their own technosocial fable. The stories are brought back to the Imaginative Methods Lab to be edited, illustrated, and archived alongside other fables written over the course of the project's lifespan. Below, we share a fable for the metaphor of autonomous vehicles that was written in a workshop in December 2023, featuring students from Computer Engineering, Communications, and Interaction Design at Simon Fraser University (Fig. 9.3). This is just one of the many excellent stories that have been created over the course of the project.

The Blind Bull and The Ants: A Story of Autonomous Vehicles
By: Sam Barnett, Denise Toor, Samein Shamsher

Fig. 9.3 The Blind Bull and the Ants. Illustration by Doan Truong

> One morning, Bull woke up in his field, unable to see. Worried he would no longer be able to feed himself and defend his territory, he bellowed in fear.
>
> "Crinkle-Crackle," an Ant whispered into his ear. "Let us be your eyes. We will ease your suffering and guide you to food and safety."
>
> Bull thanked the Ants, putting his trust in their hands.
>
> As months passed, the Ants guided Bull in circles around the pasture, always promising that sustenance and security were just beyond the next hill. One day, plagued with exhaustion, thirsty and hungry from his endless travels, Bull collapsed to the ground unable to carry on.
>
> "This is as far as we can take you," said the Ants.
>
> Bull, panicking from the idea of being left blinded and alone, begged for their continued guidance.
>
> "Please don't leave me, I can't live without your help."
>
> Shaking his head in utter disillusionment, Bull's sight began to return.
>
> As he shook away the last of the Ants from his eyes, he realized it was they who had kept him from seeing all along.
>
> As Bull watched the army of Ants hurrying away, he found himself gazing at the skeletal remains of his legs.
>
> "How could you leave me like this!" wailed Bull, enraged by his newfound knowledge of the Ants' deceit.
>
> "We were only trying to help."

As noted in the introduction, hype discourse animates the metaphor of an autonomous vehicle by encouraging people to reimagine their lives, without considering the ways of life these technologies might undo. The fable above, in contrast, underscores the haziness or vagueness of this supposed 'autonomy'. The storymaking activity prompts participants to consider: in what ways are vehicles autonomous and for whose benefit? The resulting fable may not be a technically accurate or sophisticated explanation of self-driving technology, but as Annabel Patterson (1991, p. 83) claims, such stories can be used not "merely to add rhetorical force or emotive content" to arguments but also to "clarify and demystify" complex political issues. These storytellers are not blurring distinctions between reality and fantasy through the familiar cultural form of the fable, nor do they claim a more objective take on autonomous vehicles or even a privileged perspective on its meaning. Instead, the act of fabulating enables them to playfully question the underpinning assumptions of the imaginary world represented by hype, twisting the metaphors around by engaging with fictional archetypes. Importantly, the journey of making the story together is just as important as the story itself. The three different parts of the storymaking method scaffold a process that invites critical, collaborative thinking about the implications and lived realities of a given technology, not just its utopian impulses.

By making alternative stories about these same technologies and catalysing new ways of seeing the world, fabulations like the one presented here offer their authors and readers, like you, the space to explore and question the value systems, contexts, and consequences of tech, prompting them to make connections between everyday experiences and a broader social or civic imagination beyond hype. The challenge for Fables for Imagining is to turn these ongoing facilitated workshops into an activity that can be shared with anyone interested in creating their own technosocial fables, be they teachers, tech enthusiasts, or designers. We argue that we do not need more experts creating new tech metaphors (even in responsible and just ways). Instead, our responsibility, as experts, should be towards working with and supporting non-experts to foster a more diverse and just imagination for storying technology. Fables for Imagining contributes to the crucial work of diversifying the voices, values, and viewpoints that are represented in our tech stories and tech metaphors.

5 Conclusion

This chapter has explored the interplay between tech metaphors and the social imaginaries they construct, scrutinising the dominance of hype as a prevailing force in shaping our collective perceptions of technology's future. By examining anticipation as a collection of practices for generating hype, we have illuminated how tech metaphors are wielded to project seemingly objective visions of the future that mask their own status as fantasy.

In our quest for more democratic engagements with tech metaphors, we turned to fabulation as a promising alternative. Fabulation offers a pathway for challenging dominant narratives and envisaging alternative futures. Through the practice of fabulation, we seek to reclaim agency in shaping sociotechnical imaginaries by engaging in playful, yet critical, storymaking. Central to this endeavour is the development of practical applications such as Fables for Imagining. By blending fantasy with reality and drawing inspiration from timeless storytelling traditions, this project invites participants to reimagine and interrogate tech metaphors through acts of fabulation as a collective effort to subvert the myths propagated by hype culture. In essence, our exploration underscores the importance of moving beyond merely the critique of dominant social imaginaries towards practices of actively cultivating alternative narratives. By embracing *fabulation* as a tool for resistance, we open new possibilities for democratising the discourse surrounding technology and fostering a more inclusive and nuanced understanding of its implications for society. Through collaborative efforts like Fables for Imagining, we strive to empower people to challenge the status quo and to critically rework both the *who* and *how* of tech stories.

Acknowledgements This iteration of the work was supported by the Mellon Foundation as part of the Data Fluencies Project.

References

Adler, C. (2010, December 10). The future according to Tim O'Reilly. *Newsweek*. https://www.newsweek.com/future-according-tim-oreilly-69023

Agre, P. E. (1997). *Computation and human experience*. Cambridge University Press.

Andrejevic, M. (2013). *Infoglut: How too much information is changing the way we think and know*. Routledge.

Anonymous. (2023, June 24). The ghost in the AI machine. *The Economist,* 71. https://www.calameo.com/read/007409299bfe0f0f8ce39

Appadurai, A. (2013). *The future as cultural fact: Essays on the global condition*. Verso.

Appadurai, A., & Alexander, N. (2020). *Failure*. Polity Press.

Barbrook, R., & Cameron, A. (1996). The Californian ideology. *Science as Culture, 6*(1), 44–72. https://doi.org/10.1080/09505439609526455

Bridle, J. (2018). *New dark age: Technology and the end of the future*. Verso.

Fenn, J., & Raskino, M. (2008). *Mastering the hype cycle: How to choose the right innovation at the right time*. Harvard Business Press.

Flichy, P. (2007a). *The Internet imaginaire* (L. Carey-Libbrecht, Trans.). MIT Press.

Flichy, P. (2007b). *Understanding technological innovation: A socio-technical approach* (L. Carey-Libbrecht, Trans.). Edward Elgar Publishing.

Gartner. (2024). *Gartner hype cycle research methodology*. https://www.gartner.com/en/research/methodologies/gartner-hype-cycle

Ginsberg, A. D. (2018). Critical imaginaries. In J. Boelen, I. Huygens, & H. Lehtinen (Eds.), *Studio time: Future thinking in art and design* (pp. 266–272). Black Dog Press Limited.

Haraway, D. (2016). *Staying with the trouble: Making kin in the chthulucene*. Duke University Press.

Haraway, D. (1988). Situated knowledges: The science question in feminism and the privilege of partial perspective. *Feminist Studies, 14*(3), 575–599. https://doi.org/10.2307/3178066

Jameson, F. (2005). *Archaeologies of the future: The desire called utopia and other science fictions.* Verso.

Kelly, K. (2016). Cloud computing is raining metaphors. *IEEE Spectrum, 53*(12), 25–25. https://doi.org/10.1109/MSPEC.2016.7761873

Lakoff, G., & Johnson, M. (1999). *Philosophy in the flesh: The embodied mind and its challenge to Western thought.* Basic Books.

Lakoff, G., & Johnson, M. (1980). *Metaphors we live by.* University of Chicago Press.

Mansell, R. (2012). *Imagining the internet: Communication, innovation, and governance.* Oxford University Press.

Marx, L. (1964). *The machine in the garden: Technology and the pastoral ideal in America.* Oxford University Press.

Mosco, V. (2014). *To the cloud: Big data in a turbulent world.* Routledge.

Mosco, V. (2004). *The digital sublime: Myth, power, and cyberspace.* MIT Press.

Oxford English Dictionary. (2024). Bubble. In *Oxford English Dictionary.* Retrieved March 15, 2025, from https://doi.org/10.1093/OED/3747974038

Nye, D. E. (1990). *Electrifying America: Social meanings of a new technology, 1880–1940.* MIT Press.

Patterson, A. (1991). *Fables of power: Aesopian writing and political history.* Duke University Press.

Poli, R. (2020). Anticipation. In *The Palgrave encyclopedia of the possible* (pp. 1–7). Springer International Publishing. https://doi.org/10.1007/978-3-319-8390-5_74-1

Rosner, D. K. (2018). *Critical fabulations: Reworking the methods and margins of design.* MIT Press.

Singh, R., Guzmán, R. L., & Davison, P. (Eds). (2022). *Parables of AI in/from the majority world.* Data & Society Research Institute. https://doi.org/10.2139/ssrn.4258527

Søndergaard, M. L. J., Campo Woytuk, N., Howell, N., Tsaknaki, V., Helms, K., Jenkins, T., & Sanches, P. (2023). Fabulation as an approach for design futuring. In *Proceedings of the 2023 ACM Designing Interactive Systems Conference* (pp. 1693–1709). https://doi.org/10.1145/3563657.3596097

Suchman, L. (2023). The uncontroversial 'thingness' of AI. *Big Data & Society, 10*(2), 1–5. https://doi.org/10.1177/20539517231206794

Taylor, C. (2004). *Modern Social Imaginaries.* Duke University Press.

Tucker, E. (2022, March 8). *Artifice and intelligence.* Center on Privacy & Technology at Georgetown Law. https://medium.com/center-on-privacy-technology/artifice-and-intelligence%C2%B9-f00da128d3cd

Urry, J. (2016). What is the future? *Polity.*

Vinsel, L. (2021, February 1). You're doing it wrong: Notes on criticism and technology hype. *Medium*. https://sts-news.medium.com/youre-doing-it-wrong-notes-on-criticism-and-technology-hype-18b08b4307e5
Vonnegut, K. (2009). *Palm Sunday: An autobiographical collage*. Dial Press Trade Paperback. (Original work published 1981).
Voss, G. (2024). *Systems ultra: Making sense of technology in a complex world*. Verso Books.
Watson, S. M. (2016). *Toward a constructive technology criticism*. Tow Center for Digital Journalism, Columbia's Graduate School of Journalism. http://www.cjr.org/tow_center_reports/constructive_technology_criticism.php
Weinberger, D. (2004, November 1). All hail Foo. *KM World*. https://www.kmworld.com/Articles/Columns/Perspective-on-Knowledge/All-hail-Foo-9756.aspx
Woolgar, S. (Ed.). (2003). *Virtual society? Technology, cyberbole, reality*. Oxford University Press.

CHAPTER 10

Hypothetical Images*

~~AI Photographs~~

Eryk Salvaggio

1 Introduction

Before they were *photographs*, images made by cameras were called by other names: photogenes, heliographs, photograms, sun prints (Etymonline, 2020). Each offers a glimpse into the shifting frames of analysis that have, throughout the history of photography, been applied to the marvel of light inscribed onto film. To name something is to attempt to place it into an intellectual category, and each of these words suggests a distinct way of thinking about photography. *Photogene*, for example, refers to the afterimage burned onto the retina, visible for a brief moment after we close our eyes. Rooted in human biology, it is a beautiful way of imagining the relationship between film and camera. *Photogram*—a mid-nineteenth-century term that merges the Greek words for 'light' and 'written character'—evokes the camera as a tool for carrying light from one place to another, the way telegrams carried short bursts of electric finger taps.

E. Salvaggio (✉)
Cambridge Digital Humanities, University of Cambridge, Cambridge, UK
e-mail: es2082@cam.ac.uk

C. Chokshi, R. Mansell (eds.), *The Need to Rename Tech*,
https://doi.org/10.1007/978-3-032-05155-4_10

Photographs capture light and inscribe it onto a surface, such as film or a sensor. The resulting image is a document, a record of an actual event. Image generators powered by artificial intelligence (AI) reverse this relationship in a literal and metaphorical sense. Today, what we call 'AI images'—or what many call 'AI photographs' or 'post-photography' (Jacobs, 2023)—capture data and produce light, activating millions of coloured pixels in a simulation of the object or scene that the image produced by AI purports to represent. These machine learning systems are able to produce a wide variety of visual information, simulating paintings, illustrations, photographs, and even X-rays. Anything that can be written as a series of coloured pixels can be produced by generative AI systems. However, there are problems with these representations: they bind images to an average, shaped by the patterns found in vast collections of images, called datasets, that the systems use to structure these images. These patterns can produce misleading and biased outcomes. To differentiate the output of these models from the world of images and photographs, I suggest we need a different vocabulary to describe them. Ideally, it would be one that brings the process of abstraction to the centre of our minds.

Images produced by AI may resemble, but will never be, photographs. Light never touches film, or a plate, or a sensor, to produce these images. Instead, they are patterns of digital information that light things up; they serve as an instruction for a computer screen, triggering some combination of red, green, or blue to appear. Thinking about AI images in this way helps us understand the process that creates them.

There are serious risks to attributing images, or texts, to AI. AI is an imprecise and misleading term, one that ascribes a range of human abilities to a tool that, at root, finds patterns in image data. Generously, we might define AI as a field dedicated to the simulation of human intelligence by machines (Stryker & Kavlakoglu, 2023). In practice, the term is applied to a wide range of unrelated technologies: systems that produce text, systems that produce images, systems that recognise objects on a road, systems that allow or deny bail, and systems that control what is seen on social media. All these, and more, are clustered into the category of AI, rendering the term unhelpfully vague. The idea of intelligence, and of simulating human cognition, is also fraught. Such a conceptual framework assumes that images—whether paintings, drawings, or X-rays—are the result of standardised ways of seeing and representing things, a way of being human that can be reduced to a series of computational processes.

Additionally, the idea of an AI-generated image inaccurately suggests that some amorphous intelligence, rather than statistics, made the thing you are looking at.

The term 'AI image' cedes ground to our own deception. A better name would describe the process by which information activates individual pixels, and would help us understand what these images depict about that information. To develop literacy around AI image production, we need language that inserts a critical distance between a given tool's visual outputs and the story it sells us through its user interface. When we encounter an image produced by an AI system, we need to resist the desire to comprehend it in the same ways we would make sense of a human-made image. Otherwise, we fall into the troubling, and increasingly common, trap of miscategorising AI as a replication of human thinking, rather than as a limited model aimed at simulating it.

To make sense of these images, it helps to anchor them not in human actions and creativity, but in pattern-finding machines. In this chapter, I discuss how AI image-generators work and argue that the language we use to describe these processes shapes our understanding in unhelpful ways. First, I describe the diffusion model: a machine learning technique that produces images from datasets. Next, I look at the datasets these models rely on and consider how language steers their visual output. Finally, I ask whether the outputs of these models should be considered images—or photographs—at all, or if they might be better described as *hypothetical images*—that is, as samples pulled from a spectrum of possibilities, based on limited, narrow data (Salvaggio, 2023b).

2 How Diffusion Works

A diffusion model is a specific machine learning process that reduces an image to noise. This is quite literal: the image has information stripped away until it becomes an incoherent cluster of pixels that resembles the static of a broken digital computer monitor (Internet Archive, 2022) (Fig. 10.1). The degradation of the image follows a path—in technical terms, a Gaussian noise distribution—beginning with the most detailed portions of the image and ending with the densest clusters of similar-coloured pixels. To help imagine this, we might think of a pencil drawing being smudged: while all of the individual strokes are lost, the basic shapes and tones are still there. This is happening to digital images in the training process. At each step, the image is stripped of even more detail. The

Fig. 10.1 A visualisation of the training process for a diffusion model in which information is stripped from the image, step by step

machine studies new areas that have deteriorated, compares these to the previous step, and creates a breadcrumb trail back to the original image. Along the way, the densest portions of the image become more strongly associated with the words that appear in its description from the caption associated with it on the website where it was found, or in the image's metadata. An image recognition tool may also be used to generate a description for additional keywords. (These words are not truly 'words'; each is a word broken into a set of numbers called a *token*.)

At the end of the training process, the machine can take the resulting static and repair the image to its original form (Song et al., 2020). When all these pathways are stored in a model, they can be applied to random static. The diffusion model can apply patterns associated with keywords in your prompt to create new images by reversing this process of breaking an image down. Instead, it builds the image up, layer by layer, adding more detail at each step until it is recognisable as the description in your prompt. This process is used to train most AI image generation platforms today, including OpenAI's DALL-E, Stability AI's Stable Diffusion, and Midjourney.

Today, most people interact with diffusion models through prompt-based instructions. The user types words using a keyboard to describe an image they want the system to produce. They submit these instructions using buttons labelled 'imagine' or 'dream'. Neither of these words describes what happens when a prompt is submitted by a user. Rather, these buttons trigger the application of an algorithmic process, which first generates a new JPEG of pure, random noise. The user's prompt guides the diffusion model to identify an image in that noise, which the model achieves by applying multiple paths it has learned during the training process on billions of images. The machine learning algorithm is designed to shift the colours of pixels until clusters emerge that resemble the scene described in the prompt. The result is a new image, something that may loosely resemble, but does not replicate, the data on which the algorithm was trained. This new image is a hypothetical image, something that exists at the intersection of the millions of images that have been subsumed into the dataset.

The words in a prompt steer the diffusion model to match certain patterns in this chaos, sharpening, with each pass, the noise into an image. The model does not 'see' anything in this noise, aside from pixel values representing colours. Prompted to generate 'the most photographed barn in America', a tool such as Stable Diffusion will match each word, and the relationships among those words, to a huge library of possible pathways (Fig. 10.2). It uses the results of this search to turn pure noise into some version of a much-photographed American barn. Because the starting point for each image is randomly generated noise, every resulting image will be random, too. Different smatterings of pixels will lead to different ways of bringing that prompt into view.

Fig. 10.2 Four images created with Midjourney using the following prompt: 'The most photographed barn in America'

Most of this process is steered by statistics. The arrangement of pixels into a photorealistic image is guided by the system's training data, organised into a map of pixels and words by a machine labelling tool called *Contrastive Language–Image Pre-training* (CLIP). CLIP is an approach used by OpenAI that has been integrated into many models, though other tools for this work also exist. Essentially, a tool such as CLIP pairs clusters of pixels to the words in the captions that describe them, or to a list of categories that have been trained on millions of other images, confirmed by humans, and then automated. For example, 'the most photographed barn in America' is a set of words connected to a series of categories: most photographed, barn, America. Brought together into a complete phrase, 'the most photographed barn in America' references a real place—the Thomas Moulton Barn in Wyoming—which bears only a passing resemblance to any of Stable Diffusion's interpretations. As discrete categories, the concepts of 'barn' and 'America' steer the model towards a particular space in a massive range of possibilities. CLIP compares an image to patterns in the static that resemble some idea of barn and America; if these patterns align (if the image looks enough like a barn), it moves on to the next phase of generation, until it finally arrives at the detailed image passed on to the user.

In a sense, a prompt is an anticipatory caption, guiding the removal of noise as if the image already exists. The model works to find shapes and tones that might reference that caption in the noise, weighted by probabilities. Then it tries to remove noise in the direction of the image a user has described, becoming more probable with each pass (Fig. 10.3). After

Fig. 10.3 A simulation of the process of generating a new image from a diffusion model

a few rounds of removing and calibrating this noise, sharpening it towards a combination of pixels that is statistically likely to occur in association with the user's words, it creates an image. That is, it *predicts* an image that could occur in association with the data related to those words. The model finds common points between all the data in the dataset, using words to shape them into something resembling a photograph. The training data constrains the possible outputs it might create. Diffusion-based machine learning models visualise probabilities, so the outcome reflects some central tendency of these images and text pairs. They are designed to show us a likely output from a vast set of probabilities, constrained by data. They do not create images from nothing.

In Fig. 10.3, we can imagine that the prompt is 'man jumping into water'. First, an image of random noise is created, in a reversal of the training process. The prompt is treated as a caption, and the model connects the words in that prompt with clusters of pixels it has previously encountered. Based on the training data, the model has a guide for identifying and refining clusters of noise as they appear when real images are broken down. Each new step is checked for whether an image-labelling tool identifies it as a match to the prompt. If it does, it refines it further. The result is the removal of noise until the outline of an image related to the prompt is identified and presented to the user.

It is helpful to keep the notion of prediction in mind when discussing machine learning models that are trained on datasets. Data are historical. When we ask a machine to 'learn' from data of any kind, whether it is images or arrest records, we are asking it to identify patterns in a historical record. When the machine encounters new contexts, it relies on the past to predict what might be true. When we ask a machine to create a new image, it cannot truly reference anything new, but can rearrange data about the past to propose something that is plausible.

3 The Data Makes the Image

We can, and should, ask meaningful questions about the data these models visualise, and how it shapes the images they produce. Tools developed during the first wave of open-source diffusion models, such as Stable Diffusion, were trained on a dataset from the Large-scale Artificial Intelligence Open Network (LAION), called LAION 5B (Schuhmann et al., 2022). This was an assemblage of five billion text-image pairs scraped from all corners of the internet. LAION 5B was gathered through an automated process and minimally filtered using a tool—CLIP—that compared the caption to the image to see if the two seemed to match. CLIP can be extremely unreliable in recognising images. As a result, some of the content in LAION 5B included images of child sexual abuse material (Thiel, 2023). This led the creators of that dataset to take it offline in late 2023; by then, however, the dataset had been publicly available for more than a year and had become the source of choice for training diffusion models.

The presence of abusive material was not the only concern with the training data. As critical AI scholars have pointed out, LAION 5B also included racist, misogynistic, pornographic, and violent material (Birhane et al., 2021). The persistence of biased and discriminatory content in this and other training datasets can be confirmed anecdotally. When I looked at LAION 5B myself, I noted that many of the images carried racial bias. In examining the training data for images of 'girls', for example, I encountered countless Victorian-era portraits of white girls taken from the public domain. Searching the training data for images of 'black girls' yielded numerous images of highly sexualised Black women, including many images from pornography sites. This reflects a well-known bias in the sexualisation of Black women in online content, as articulated by Safiya Umoja Noble (2018) in her book, *Algorithms of Oppression*. Noble discovered that a search on Google for the term 'black girls' filled the first page of results with links to commercial pornography sites. Only after these findings were brought to Google's attention did the company change its algorithm. Addressing problematic content within diffusion models poses more of a challenge because training a model is resource intensive, with huge environmental and financial costs. As a result, there is little incentive for companies using these models to retrain them to address biased images. At the time I am writing, in 2024, tools such as Midjourney still reflect cultural and racial biases. Reporters from the magazine *Rest of World* generated 3000 images on Midjourney using the prompt 'Mexican', most of which included men with moustaches and sombreros, reflecting a persistent stereotype (Turk, 2023).

Instead of reviewing their training datasets, the companies that create these models have attempted to mitigate these biases by changing what the user is allowed to do. One strategy is to ban certain words or prompts. For example, in 2022, OpenAI banned prompts asking for two women kissing; inputting this prompt triggered a content warning, although searches for 'two men kissing' did not (Salvaggio, 2022). OpenAI also inadequately mitigates biases by invisibly inserting words into prompts at random intervals (Offert & Phan, 2022). When asked for an image of a doctor, the tool on its own might generate endless white men in lab coats. To fix this, OpenAI adds identity terms, such as 'black' or 'woman', to change the outcome. This way, the model diversifies its outputs without revealing its additions—a practice I call *shadow prompting* (Salvaggio, 2023a).

Describing AI images as hypothetical images helps us make sense of—even confront—the reality that these images are explicitly the product of probabilities and, therefore, biases. These biases reflect those of the training data. When data is scraped from the World Wide Web, with a heavy emphasis on English-language, white, male, and corporate content from North America and Europe (Muldoon et al., 2024), it reflects the biases of that population. Even when trained on very focused local datasets, these tools are designed to show us the most common representations of things: the most common shape of an apple, a flower, or—most problematically—a person. As an example, Avijit Ghosh (2024) has observed the prevalence of regional Indian stereotypes in Stable Diffusion, even as Emad Moustaque, the founder of Stability AI, claimed that its training data came from India. A popular viral internet post in that country depicted a series of AI-generated wedding photographs that were filled with national stereotypes (Ghosh, 2024).

Stereotypical and biased image outputs must be understood in relation to the algorithmic process used to create them: diffusion models rely on central tendencies in the data to establish the boundaries and contours of what is possible in association with a given word. If the training dataset contains a million white men labelled as doctors and 10,000 images of Black women labelled as doctors, then the Black women doctors may as well not exist. Without interventions in the model, the most common image and text are represented in the output. Outliers are pushed out of focus. If we understand these tools as statistical models, might it encourage us to push for better data science and more thoughtful approaches to building them?

4 A Statistical Model

With diffusion models, categories structure images based on patterns found in the data. These patterns are reduced to a central tendency, and prompts guide the image towards this central tendency. It is these central tendencies—the ontologies related to our prompt terms—that end up written in pixels. This is why I consider AI-generated images to be hypothetical: they are products of statistics, and we ought to use the language of statistics to make sense of them.

Every time a user writes a prompt for a diffusion model, they are asking the model for a hypothesis, just as statisticians ask for hypotheses from their data, whether that be to model climate change or election results. However, models tend to churn out one hypothesis at a time, even though, in reality, outcomes are not so constrained.

An election model might predict a statistical dead heat based on previous voting patterns, but it cannot predict how people will actually vote. For this reason, you might see experts running a large number of simulations and averaging the results to find a range of outcomes that are most likely to occur. In the real world, of course, all kinds of things can happen: a candidate might drop out of their campaign, which could be historically unprecedented, or a pandemic could transform voter turnout in unexpected ways.

Likewise, the images produced by diffusion models come from data and should be treated as predictions constrained to that data. They are the products of a vast but limited dataset of images, each representing one possible arrangement of pixels. Each of these images will emphasise the most common elements of the training data associated with a prompt. However, chance can play a role. The element of chance remains because the images start with random pixels and find patterns within that randomness. The diffusion model is fitting patterns to the noise of the JPG. The image it produces is but one hypothesis from a wide spectrum of hypotheses, and despite the variety of outcomes possible at the starting point, a model is always working back to what is in the data.

What persists within the data, and therefore the images it produces, is categories. Consider the bookshelves in a library. You could go to a specific aisle and scan the titles, or go to a computer and search for certain topics. In any case, you can see which books are grouped together based on the library's organisational logic, which reflects certain biases and assumptions. Biases need not be harmful: alphabetical order is one common bias. National divisions are another: perhaps someone decides that American cookbooks have their own section, while both French and Cantonese cookbooks are filed under World Cuisine. This may simply be a matter of how many books the libraries have and the best way to use space, but, in the end, it makes a distinction between America and other places in the world. The library's methods of organising information reflect a series of decisions that follow a specific logic.

Diffusion models rely on similar categories, and the logic that drives them can seem impossible to understand. We humans can look at actual books, but the model cannot. It sees millions of images of books, and millions of captions labelled 'book'. It cannot find a specific book in the giant assemblage of images included in the training data. Instead, hypothetical images are the product of the diffusion model's systems of categorisation. They cannot represent the living, social world of words and their meanings. They must find relationships and patterns based on how humans have previously labelled images. If images are described using certain words more often, they become more strongly associated with the shapes and boundaries that the model has drawn around that word. That explains why we do not get images of apples when we ask for books: few people share images of apples online and call them books. And yet, this can result in interesting confusions when contexts collide. For example, prompting a diffusion model for a 'photograph' taken with a Fuji brand camera might result in pictures of Mt. Fuji instead.

Sometimes these patterns can be difficult to discern. If we ask Midjourney for 'a typical Australian person', we might get images of koalas, quokkas, or a fictional blend of the two (Fig. 10.4). But why? To understand this, we must think carefully about language and how it is used to describe images. The machine cannot discern 'Australian' as a reference to a person because it cannot reason—the category of 'Australian' can include Australian people and also Australian flags, Australian landmarks, or Australian wildlife. What we see in response to the prompt 'Australian', then, is a visualisation of the most commonly occurring images with the word 'Australian' in their captions. We can infer that there are many more images of Australian koalas in the training data than there are images of people labelled as Australian. It is also notable that the people who are depicted are white women, rather than images depicting Indigenous Australians or the wider diversity of Australia's population.

Understanding these images as the result of AI, one might conclude that there is something wrong with the model's interpretation of the world. That conclusion would be incorrect. Diffusion models cannot interpret because they are not intelligent. It would also be a mistake to assume that a diffusion model could produce an image of reality at all. It is incapable. As a generator of hypothetical images, the machine makes predictions about the world based on a limited dataset. The *hypothesis*

Fig. 10.4 Midjourney's first four results for the prompt 'typical Australian person', as requested by the author in May 2024

derived from that data is always wrong because the data is not suited to the task of representing an Australian, or really, anything documenting reality at all. If one attributes this to the machine's misunderstanding, we risk supporting the idea that the machine is capable of understanding. That is not a clear view of what diffusion models do.

5 Hypothetical Images

When we prompt a diffusion model to produce an image, it applies what it has analysed about patterns in abstract noise. I argue that the output of this process should be called a *hypothetical image*. *Hypothetical image* emphasises that the image produced is not an image per se. It is neither a photograph nor an illustration, but rather a predictive rendering of a photograph or illustration. In the absence of a meaningful word for the phenomenon of AI images, we attribute belaboured metaphors of artistic intelligence to automated statistical analysis; AI image-generator interfaces are replete with terms like 'creativity', 'dreams', and 'reasoning'. None of these are present in the production of hypothetical images.

Rather, it is helpful to consider such images as a result of machine learning, which is a form of predictive analytics. By examining billions of data points, the machine can find trends and patterns. It can then extend these patterns into new images. In essence, we should consider our prompts a way of asking: 'what might an image with this description look like?' The response from the system is to generate samples of plausible responses, determined by what might be found in the dataset.

It can be helpful to imagine a work of AI art that engages with this process to tell a story. One of the most famous pieces of AI-generated art comes from the artist Refik Anadol. Anadol's work, *Unsupervised*, was acquired by the Museum of Modern Art in New York City in 2023. It consists of an abstract visualisation, displayed on a screen two storeys tall. Anadol used the entire Museum of Modern Art (MOMA) archive to train a model—not a diffusion model, but a generative adversarial network, or GAN—and then created countless variations from the points in between all of them. The model might, for instance, take a Warhol and a Klimt, find patterns overlapping between them, and render an image that is 10 per cent Warhol and 90 per cent Klimt. It could do this with thousands of images in the archive. Consequently, at any given moment, the image presented on screen could be an amalgam of the work of two or 1000 artists, each included in the MOMA archive. The model produces what could be described as a visualisation of possibilities between all of the images of art in the museum.

The ever-changing images of *Unsupervised* are hypothetical images; they have never been created by human beings. They are speculative proposals of what could, theoretically, exist. But they are primarily the result of statistical concepts, emerging from central tendencies of scattered data points. They are a result of a machine working through the tensions of noise and signal, randomness and control, to show us what images might be possible. Diffusion models are designed to predict what image might be found within pure static. This language of hypotheticals helps us shift our understanding of the models away from artistry or photography even more completely. It centres on actual process: a mathematical model designed to surface hidden images based on data. In the end, it hypothesises based on what that image might have looked like, if it were so.

This frame may seem overly philosophical. After all, the outputs of a diffusion model are images, in some traditional senses of the word. But approaching them as hypothetical images draws our attention to how they were produced, rather than how they present themselves. When we resist even acknowledging them as images, it becomes impossible to entertain notions that the machine is an artist, or that the machine learns as humans do. Unless we reduce human behaviour to its most basic functions, human artists do not create by scraping noise away from a canvas until they see something resembling the name of the painting. Nor do most photographers aim to reproduce a speculative average of all past images they have seen. Labelling these images as hypotheticals also encourages a healthy scepticism of the results. We do away with the idea that the model takes 'inspiration' from the images in the training data, realising instead that the closest it comes to inspiration is a mathematical equation describing the statistical average of colour distributions associated with certain keywords.

Framing an AI image as hypothetical—a theory of what might be, derived from the limits of available data—sets aside the temptation to apply creative intent to its outcomes. AI is not creative because it can only follow a narrow path of expectations in producing an image, rather than finding opportunities to innovate or challenge the status quo. At a fundamental level, these images are the result of a highly stochastic process, unfolding within the boundaries of the data on which they have been trained. They are an inscription of data into noise, framed by categories. AI image-generators are certainly novel, and the technology can be used creatively. But the model itself is not inventive, despite the appearances of 'decisions' the machines seem to make. These strange images are no more creative than a set of statistically generated shapes: it is the human that uses the tool, not the tool itself, that acts with creative agency. Furthermore, in contrast to human artists, diffusion models do not improve with each image they make. They cannot connect meaning to a cluster of pixels. To the model, a prompt is more like an address, pointing to specific spaces within an enormous array of possible constellations. These images are predictions, limited only to training data, and they do not tell us anything about the world aside from the ways in which it has been described before.

References

Birhane, A., Prabhu, V. U., & Kahembwe, E. (2021). *Multimodal datasets: Misogyny, pornography, and malignant stereotypes.* arXiv [cs.CY]. http://arxiv.org/abs/2110.01963

Etymonline. (2020). *Photograph.* In *Etymonline.com online dictionary.* Retrieved February 13, 2025, from https://www.etymonline.com/word/photograph

Ghosh, A. (2024, January 23). An investigation of colorism and gender imbalance in AI in the Indian context. *Medium.* https://medium.com/@evijit/analysis-of-ai-generated-images-of-indian-people-for-colorism-and-sexism-b80ff946759f

Internet Archive. (2022). *Jumping in the water 1970s* [Photograph]. https://archive.org/details/001_20220209_202202

Jacobs, G. (2023, December 26). A.I. is the future of photography. Does that mean photography is dead? *The New York Times.* https://www.nytimes.com/2023/12/26/opinion/ai-future-photography.html

Muldoon, J., Graham, M., & Cant, C. (2024). *Feeding the machine: The hidden human labor powering AI.* Bloomsbury.

Noble, S. U. (2018). *Algorithms of oppression: How search engines reinforce racism.* New York University Press.

Offert, F., & Phan, T. (2022). *A sign that spells: DALL-E 2, invisual images and the racial politics of feature space.* arXiv [cs.CY]. http://arxiv.org/abs/2211.06323

Salvaggio, E. (2022). How to read an AI image: Toward a media studies methodology for the analysis of synthetic images. *IMAGE. Zeitschrift Für Interdisziplinäre Bildwissenschaft, 37*(1), 83–99. https://doi.org/10.25969/mediarep/22328

Salvaggio, E. (2023a, October 19). Shining a light on "shadow prompting." *Tech Policy Press.* https://www.techpolicy.press/shining-a-light-on-shadow-prompting/

Salvaggio, E. (2023b, October 29). The hypothetical image. *Cybernetic Forests.* https://www.cyberneticforests.com/news/social-diffusion-amp-the-seance-of-the-digital-archive

Schuhmann, C., Beaumont, R., Vencu, R., Gordon, C., Wightman, R., Cherti, M., Coombes, T., Katta, A., Mullis, C., Wortsman, M., Schramowski, P., Kundurthy, S., Crowson, K., Schmidt, L., Kaczmarczyk, R., & Jitsev, J. (2022).

LAION-5B: An open large-scale dataset for training next generation image-text models. arXiv [cs.CV]. http://arxiv.org/abs/2210.08402

Song, Y., Sohl-Dickstein, J., Kingma, D. P., Kumar, A., Ermon, S., & Poole, B. (2020). *Score-based generative modeling through stochastic differential equations.* arXiv [cs.LG]. http://arxiv.org/abs/2011.13456

Stryker, C., & Kavlakoglu, E. (2023, August 25). *What is artificial intelligence (AI)?* IBM. https://www.ibm.com/topics/artificial-intelligence

Thiel, D. (2023). Identifying and eliminating CSAM in generative ML training data and models. *Stanford Digital Repository.* https://doi.org/10.25740/kh752sm9123

Turk, V. (2023, October 10). How AI reduces the world to stereotypes. *Rest of World.* https://restofworld.org/2023/ai-image-stereotypes/

PART IV

~~Saving~~

CHAPTER 11

Access Gatekeeper*

~~Firewall~~

Anran Wang

1 Introduction

The concept of the 'firewall' in network security is believed to have first emerged in the late 1980s. A popular account attributes its adoption to engineers at Digital Equipment Corporation (DEC), who developed the first commercial firewall system (Avolio, 1999; Ingham & Forrest, 2002). This system was designed to separate internal networks from external threats by preventing unauthorised access. DEC engineers sought a term to convey the idea of a barrier against external threats, akin to the protective walls used in buildings to contain fires. The metaphor is widely regarded as effectively capturing the shared attributes of separation and danger prevention in network and physical firewalls, which is seen as the reason for the term's popularity (Anderson, 2020). I argue, however, that the ubiquity of the term highlights how metaphors shape our perceptions of technology.

A. Wang (✉)
Department of Media and Communications, London School of Economics and Political Science, London, UK
e-mail: a.wang16@lse.ac.uk

C. Chokshi, R. Mansell (eds.), *The Need to Rename Tech*,
https://doi.org/10.1007/978-3-032-05155-4_11

Firewalls remain fundamental to network security today, although they have evolved in complexity and functionality. A firewall is typically defined as a network security system responsible for monitoring and controlling incoming and outgoing network traffic based on predetermined security rules (Anderson, 2020; Cheswick et al., 2003). The implementations of firewalls can be categorised broadly into three types based on the layer at which they log and filter traffic: packet filters, circuit gateways, and application proxies (Anderson, 2020). Packet filters operate at the network layer, inspecting the source and destination addresses and port numbers of data packets in order to make allow-or-deny decisions. Circuit gateways function at the transport layer, monitoring Transmission Control Protocol (TCP) sessions to assess the state of connections and control traffic. Application proxies work at the application layer, using specific protocols to inspect the actual content of communications for more granular control.

Modern firewalls often integrate multiple implementations with diverse security strategies, optimised for specific needs. For instance, egress filtering firewalls specifically control and monitor outgoing traffic, while others focus on monitoring incoming traffic. In response to prominent data leaks such as in the Edward Snowden case, an increasing number of organisations have employed egress filtering firewalls to prevent sensitive data from leaving their networks (Alneyadi et al., 2016). Another example is next-generation firewalls (NGFWs), which, by expanding their role to include controlling access within the network itself, have shifted the traditional view that firewalls only operate at the network boundary (Buck et al., 2021; Rose et al., 2020). These developments demonstrate that many advancements in the firewall domain stem from changes in security strategies and architectures, where the role of network creators and administrators is as crucial, if not more so, than the technology itself (Anderson, 2020).

An advertisement for firewall technology published by Cisco—one of the major firewall vendors—uses a set of questions to engage potential buyers: "Do you have a firewall fit for today's challenges? Does it harmonize your network, workload, and application security? Does it protect apps and employees in your hybrid or multicloud environment? Make sure you're covered. See, try, or buy a firewall" (Cisco, 2024a, para. 1). This language illustrates that while firewall technology has evolved considerably since its inception, danger prevention remains a core emphasis in its marketing.

This focus on danger prevention, however, obscures the social consequences of firewall technologies. Firewalls not only are tools for protection but can also be used to restrict access, monitor user activities, and enforce censorship (Cramer, 2013). National firewalls, for instance, often filter keywords and block websites to control the flow of information, shaping public discourse and limiting access to diverse perspectives (Li, 2009; Walton, 2001). Similarly, in corporate environments, firewalls are frequently used to monitor and regulate employees' internet usage, prioritising organisational goals over individual privacy (Balozian et al., 2019; Stanton & Stam, 2006). These applications illustrate how firewalls extend beyond their protective role to serve as instruments of surveillance and control. Such controversial implications highlight the need to critically examine the firewall metaphor and its influence on how we perceive and engage with these technologies.

While the 'firewall' term was initially used as a metaphor for network technology, it is also used to conceptualise barriers and protections in other fields. These uses prompt us to reflect on how this metaphor shapes our perception of firewall technology itself. In organisational studies, for instance, researchers have proposed using the firewall metaphor alongside the 'glass ceiling' to describe gender and workplace discrimination (Bendl & Schmidt, 2010; Patton & Haynes, 2014; Sekuła et al., 2022). The firewall metaphor in this context is seen as more effectively capturing the dynamic and actively maintained nature of discrimination. Unlike a glass ceiling, which suggests a static, unseen barrier, the firewall metaphor emphasises dynamic control. Firewall administrators actively control access, highlighting how individuals within organisations enforce discriminatory practices. The firewall's invisible and adjustable boundaries reflect the opaque and shifting criteria for career advancement. Moreover, attempts to bypass firewalls are seen as hostile intrusions, paralleling the resistance faced by those who challenge discriminatory norms. This discussion is enlightening because it illustrates how the firewall metaphor, rooted in technology, can effectively encapsulate practices of exclusion and control in organisational settings. It raises questions about why 'firewall' technologies share so many commonalities with practices of exclusion, and why they are often viewed as defenders of security rather than as gatekeepers monitoring access.

To address these questions, this chapter unpacks the firewall metaphor through the lens of similarity theory (Tversky, 1977), examining its semantic properties and its use in communications from technology companies. Similarity theory provides conceptual tools to evaluate the relative salience of shared attributes in both the metaphorical firewall and the network security system it describes, and to illustrate the phenomenon of 'salience imbalance' (Ortony, 1979, 1993), when certain attributes are emphasised and others are minimised. Insight into imbalances is used to demonstrate how the firewall metaphor directs attention to danger prevention while obscuring other equally important attributes of security technology.

In this chapter, I first review theories of metaphor processing, laying the theoretical groundwork for my analysis of the 'firewall' metaphor. Second, I conduct a semantic analysis to elucidate issues raised by the use of the firewall metaphor. Following this, I examine web pages from two major firewall vendors to explore how the firewall metaphor is used in industry communications in a way that obscures controversial social consequences of the technology. Finally, based on my analysis of the firewall metaphor and reflections on approaches to metaphor repair, I suggest the term *access gatekeeper* as an alternative. This renaming, I argue, emphasises the actual functions of firewalls—controlling access and monitoring traffic—rather than their perceived role in preventing threats and danger. This reframing highlights the human decision-making involved in inclusion and exclusion and invites a reconsideration of the human role in network security.

2 Theories of Metaphor Processing

Metaphors are linguistic expressions where qualities from one concept (known as the 'vehicle') are associated with another (the 'topic') to enrich the description or understanding of the latter (Lakoff & Johnson, 2008). For instance, in the metaphor 'the man is a turtle', 'turtle' serves as the vehicle, while 'man' is the topic. This section reviews the four classical theories of metaphor processing—substitution, comparison, interaction, and similarity theory (Black, 1962/2019)—and explains how similarity theory, in particular, can be applied to provide fresh insights into our understanding of the firewall metaphor.

Substitution theory, originating from traditional rhetoric, posits that metaphors primarily serve a decorative purpose (Black, 1955). In this framework, the 'vehicle' acts as a substitute for the topic, enhancing linguistic expression through stylistic embellishment. This theory assigns metaphors a minor role in language, emphasising their aesthetic rather than conceptual significance.

Comparison theory, a more widely accepted theory emerging from Aristotle's (1991) philosophical inquiries, positions metaphors as tools for implicit comparison. In this theory, metaphors serve to transfer features or attributes that are unalike, yet share some form of underlying similarity, from the vehicle to the topic. Comparison theory suggests that metaphors enable a dynamic range of interpretations depending on an individual's engagement with both vehicle and topic. Thus, meaning is not fixed and does not reside exclusively within the thoughts of the speaker or writer.

Interaction theory, developed by Max Black (1977), emphasises a dynamic interaction between the vehicle and topic that generates new meanings. This theory is particularly useful for explaining how metaphors can lead to new insights, illustrating the transformative power of metaphors. For example, as discussed in the introduction, likening workplace discrimination to firewalls rather than to glass ceilings shifts the focus to the processual aspects of discrimination, emphasising the mechanisms of exclusion and the criteria used to permit or deny access (Bendl & Schmidt, 2010). Despite the insights it generates, however, interaction theory can be less intuitive because it often requires more abstract thinking to discern an interaction's impact.

Similarity theory, offered by Amos Tversky (1977), builds upon the foundation laid by the comparison theory in the field of cognitive psychology, but introduces a more structured analysis of the features shared by the topic and vehicle. It posits that the degree of similarity between two objects is determined by the features they share, subtracting those that are distinctive to each. This approach facilitates a nuanced analysis of how certain attributes may be emphasised more than others, leading to salience imbalance, which, in turn, provides a mechanism for explaining how a metaphor impacts on how a topic is perceived.

In the case of the firewall metaphor and technology that protects and regulates digital communications, each theory of metaphor processing yields distinct insights. Substitution theory, for example, suggests that this metaphor serves primarily as a linguistic embellishment. Comparison theory would see it as enhancing understanding, by drawing parallels between each entity's role in preventing the spread of destructive elements. Interaction theory, while effective for metaphors that foster reflection, is less applicable here because the firewall metaphor is primarily practical in nature. Similarity theory proposes that the metaphor's meaning is determined not only by the shared attributes of danger prevention but also by distinctive features which can be helpful in illustrating how both similarities and differences influence our understanding.

Since this chapter aims to demonstrate that the firewall metaphor is more complex than traditionally perceived, I rely on similarity theory as the theoretical lens to guide a semantic analysis of the term. In the next section, I apply the salience imbalance hypothesis (Ortony, 1979, 1993), a concept derived from similarity theory, to deconstruct the firewall metaphor.

3 A Semantic Analysis of the Firewall Metaphor

The term 'firewall', as mentioned above, is often attributed to a group of engineers at DEC. Pioneers from this group later developed and released the first open-source firewall software—known as the Firewall Toolkit (FWTK)—in 1993. The official website for FWTK hosts documentation, including accounts from team members about the early days of firewall development.[1] A notable anecdote highlights the iterative and somewhat haphazard process of naming the technology, during which the engineers considered various names before settling on firewall:

> Brian Reid and a couple of folks at DEC had a corporate gateway called gatekeeper.dec.com … I worked in one of DEC's sales support units, for Fred Avolio, and we had an Internet connection (9600 baud!!) via an aging MicroVAXII … Fred told me to clean it up some and "make it look like what Paul has in gatekeeper" … Gatekeeper in those days was what we'd now call a gateway host … Then one of our sales guys, in a fit of enthusiasm, sold "a firewall like decuac" to a REALLY huge customer … so it needed a name, so we stole "SEAL" which the guys in Palo Alto had been talking about for a firewall product … The next best bet for the name was "PIG" for "Packaged Internet Gateway" but that, as it were, didn't fly. From that one customer, once the documentation had been written, sales took over and we got a little busy with firewalls from then on. (Ranum & Avolio, n.d., para. 2)

Names such as gatekeeper, User Account Control (UAC), Secure External Access Link (SEAL), and Packaged Internet Gateway (PIG) were all contenders for describing what is now referred to as a network firewall. Each potential name described different, and sometimes broader, features

[1] The FWTK's website is https://www.fwtk.org/.

than those implied by the 'firewall' term. Ultimately, this term was settled on due to its similarity to the protective barriers used in buildings to contain fires. This raises a question: were the similarities between a network firewall and other alternatives, such as gatekeeper, deemed insufficient? I employ the salience imbalance hypothesis to explore why 'firewall' became the preferred term. Since this chapter focuses on technology metaphors, the subsequent analysis will compare 'firewall' and 'gatekeeper', which I put forward as a more descriptive alternative.[2]

Andrew Ortony's (1979, 1993) salience imbalance hypothesis, developed in the cognitive science tradition, is used to analyse metaphors based on the salience (i.e., the prominence) of attributes associated with the 'vehicle' and the 'topic'. Specifically, the salience imbalance hypothesis suggests that for a metaphor to resonate and convey deeper meanings, the attributes shared by the topic and vehicle must not hold equal salience. Instead, there should be a distinct imbalance—attributes that are highly prominent in the vehicle should be less so in the topic. This imbalance is expected to enhance the metaphor's impact by shifting the listener's or reader's focus, magnifying certain characteristics of the topic that might otherwise remain understated.

For instance, in the metaphor, 'his hands were sandpaper', the attribute, roughness, is considerably more salient for sandpaper than for human hands (Readence et al., 1984). This salience imbalance makes the metaphor striking and memorable, enriching the descriptive quality of 'hands' by borrowing the intense texture typically associated with sandpaper.

Utilising the salience imbalance hypothesis to examine network firewalls, physical firewalls, and gatekeepers illuminates how the attributes associated with each term influence our understanding of network security technology (see Table 11.1). In the metaphor 'network firewall is a physical firewall', the attribute of preventing outside dangers is notably more salient when associated with a physical firewall than with a network firewall. Other salient attributes of a physical firewall, such as its tangible and visible barrier, are not shared with a network firewall. Thus, while the firewall metaphor emphasises the function of danger prevention in network firewalls, it simultaneously downplays other significant attributes of network firewalls. This selective emphasis helps to divert attention away

[2] This semantic analysis excludes names like SEAL or PIG which, as abbreviations of technical terms, do not offer the same metaphorical potential.

Table 11.1 Attribute salience list for network firewall, physical firewall, and gatekeeper

Network firewall	*Physical firewall*	*Gatekeeper*
a. Monitors network traffic b. Controls network traffic c. Based on security rules d. Administrators define and update rules dynamically e. Prevents outside intrusions f. Blocks access to information g. Audits network communications h. Prevents information leaks i. Boundary is invisible to outsiders j. Cracking (even non-criminal) is considered hostile	a. Prevents the spread of fire b. Made of non-combustible material c. Static d. Visible and tangible	a. Human decision-maker b. Manages entry or access based on organisational policies c. Registers visitors' entry and exit d. Physically present

Source: By author

from other critical aspects of network firewalls, potentially skewing the understanding of their broader functionalities and implications.

Public library firewalls provide a clear example of this selective emphasis, as they have been used not only to prevent outside threats but also to block access to legitimate resources, such as LGBTQIA+-related content (Kaiser, 2000; Storts-Brinks, 2010). Such actions not only restrict access to educational and supportive materials but also risk marginalising vulnerable groups by reinforcing harmful biases. These practices reflect the control that librarians and network administrators routinely exercise behind firewalls as they dynamically determine filtering rules, block access to certain information, and audit network communications. The metaphor 'network firewall is a physical firewall', in contrast, amplifies the salience of external threat prevention, overshadowing discretionary and controversial roles. This 'salience imbalance' serves to narrow our perception of network firewalls, portraying them as passive protective tools, while minimising their potential for exclusion and censorship.

In the metaphor 'network firewall is a gatekeeper', attributes such as human decision-making and registering visitors' access are more salient than in the case of 'network firewall'. While network firewalls perform these functions in an automated and less visible manner, these attributes are highly prominent in the role of a gatekeeper. Here, salience imbalance draws attention to aspects of network firewalls that might otherwise be underemphasised, such as surveillance and administrators' discretionary judgement. By highlighting these less salient attributes of the network firewall through reference to the gatekeeper metaphor, understanding of the technology expands beyond the notion of mere danger prevention to include considerations of control and power.

These insights prompt a reevaluation of the traditional narrative about how the firewall metaphor gained popularity. Conventional views credit the metaphor's popularity to the similarities shared between network firewalls and physical firewalls (Anderson, 2020; Ingham & Forrest, 2002). The salience imbalance hypothesis suggests that more shared attributes do not necessarily make a metaphor more effective; rather, similarities and dissimilarities both contribute to our understanding of technology through the use of metaphor. Applying the salience imbalance hypothesis reveals that, in fact, network firewalls share more salient attributes with gatekeepers than with physical firewalls. With fewer shared salient attributes, the firewall metaphor directs attention towards the attribute of preventing external dangers, thereby emphasising protection and security while downplaying other aspects. In contrast, the gatekeeper metaphor brings attributes related to control, surveillance, and human agency to the forefront, highlighting the procedural and authoritative dimensions of network firewalls. By shifting the focus to unique attributes, each metaphor shapes our understanding of the technology in distinct ways.

This analysis also demonstrates how the firewall metaphor operates within broader securitisation trends in technology discourse. Securitisation studies suggest that security-focused narratives can legitimise restrictive measures while downplaying ethical concerns (Deibert & Rohozinski, 2010; Elbe, 2006; Van Rythoven, 2020). The analysis of the firewall metaphor illustrates how metaphors structure security discourse by framing the technology as protective, which in turn deflects attention from control, surveillance, and exclusion (Cramer, 2013; Kaiser, 2000; Stanton & Stam, 2006). In this way, technology metaphors are shown to be not merely ornamental or solely facilitative in helping the public understand new technologies; they shape security discourse and influence the public's perception of technologies and the companies behind them.

4 Cisco and Huawei

In the absence of comprehensive records, it is challenging to determine why DEC selected the firewall metaphor. Did the engineers seek to emphasise certain aspects of the technology, or was their selection an arbitrary decision? However, as the problems and consequences associated with firewall technology (including concerns about privacy, surveillance, and restricted access to information) garner increasing attention (Cramer, 2013), a more pressing question arises: are companies that sell firewall technologies communicating transparently about all of a firewall's features? Or, are they maintaining a perception of firewall technologies as harmless and benign?

To address these questions, I examined descriptions of firewalls on the official English websites of two industry-leading companies, Cisco (based in the United States) and Huawei (based in China). Both companies sell firewall products and appear dedicated to educating the public and consumers about firewalls. Cisco's (2024b) 'What Is a Firewall?' page, for example, outlines the evolution of firewall technology, from early proxy firewalls to the latest threat-focused NGFWs and virtual firewalls optimised for cloud services. In contrast, Huawei (2024) adopts a trendier approach, focusing their 'What Is an AI Firewall?' page on the integration of AI into their NGFW products, and skipping earlier developments.

Despite different temporal foci, both descriptions exhibit key similarities. First, both companies discuss a range of sophisticated and ever-evolving cybersecurity dangers while promoting their firewalls. Cisco's discourse is filled with terms such as 'modern threats', 'intrusion', 'risky', 'attacks', and 'suspicious', while Huawei, though it uses a narrower vocabulary, employs a timeline infographic illustrating the progression of security threats from 1990s viruses to its latest category, machine-to-machine attacks. These rhetorical strategies position each company's firewall products within a danger-prevention framework. Second, the descriptions consistently present the latest firewalls as intelligent systems capable of autonomous operations, employing terms such as 'intelligent', 'automation', 'awareness', 'algorithms', and 'learning' to refer to the systems themselves, thereby obscuring the significant human role in access decision-making. Third, and notably, both companies appear to avoid mentioning the controversies surrounding their involvement in more contentious uses of firewalls, such as auditing, access restrictions, national firewalls, and mass surveillance—issues for which they have faced media scrutiny (Clark & Chao, 2011; Hounsel et al., 2018).

To what extent do these media accusations reflect the actual deployment of firewalls? While Cisco and Huawei omit discussions of contentious uses, Kaspersky, a Russia-based cybersecurity company, better known for its antivirus software with a much smaller market share in firewalls, takes a slightly different approach in its 'What is a Firewall?' web page (Kaspersky, 2024). While still framing firewalls as tools for danger prevention, Kaspersky explicitly acknowledges their use for restriction purposes, starting with parental controls that limit children's access to explicit content, extending to workplace policies that restrict employees' access to social media, and culminating in more ethically questionable applications, such as China's Great Firewall, which has been described as a system that suppresses free speech by censoring dissenting voices and reinforces state control by excluding international platforms. This transparency contrasts with the selective narratives observed in Cisco and Huawei's descriptions, demonstrating the potential for more balanced discussions of firewall technologies.

This review of the integration of the firewall metaphor into practical discursive contexts reveals that, despite emerging societal and ethical concerns around firewall technology, the marketing departments of major firewall companies persist in using the firewall metaphor without critical assessment. Communications from Cisco and Huawei emphasise certain aspects of the metaphor, such as danger prevention, while downplaying others. This selective emphasis results in a narrowed public perception and understanding of the technology.

5 Repairing the Firewall Metaphor

The firewall metaphor is misleading. To centre neglected attributes of firewalls in our discourse, we need an alternative term, one that deepens our understanding of firewalls and offers new perspectives on their roles and implications in society. Firewalls are routinely deployed towards ethically questionable ends, which often reinforce existing power imbalances that are not indicated by the corporate promotional narratives. For example, national firewalls censor dissenting voices, shaping public discourse by restricting access to politically sensitive content (Li, 2009; Walton, 2001). Corporate firewalls monitor and regulate employees' internet access, granting employers significant control over digital visibility, while undermining individual privacy (Balozian et al., 2019; Stanton & Stam, 2006). Public library firewalls have historically restricted access to LGBTQIA+-related content, not only limiting access to crucial supportive resources but also reinforcing systemic marginalisation. By deciding what is accessible and what remains hidden, those who manage firewalls can wield disproportionate power over the flow of information, shaping both knowledge production and social hierarchies. Recognising this dynamic underscores the need for a metaphor that foregrounds both protection and restriction, rather than a metaphor that obscures the latter.

To address this need, I propose *access gatekeeper* as a new term to replace the firewall metaphor. Building upon the term 'gatekeeper' and incorporating 'access' to emphasise the crucial role of digital inclusion in contemporary society, *access gatekeeper* more accurately encapsulates the primary functions of these technologies: monitoring and controlling incoming and outgoing traffic. It draws attention to the critical, but often overlooked, human decision-makers who operate behind the scenes. There are always people—whether network creators, administrators, or end users—who, by setting and updating the filtering rules, determine what needs protection, whose interests are prioritised, who belongs within the system, and who poses a threat. While network firewalls are necessary to address evolving security threats, fairness in access is equally important. Access gatekeeper is a better metaphor than firewall because it reminds us of the conscious balance required between prevention and access, prompting those in power to exercise their authority with greater consideration of the ethical responsibilities and social consequences of this technology.

In proposing access gatekeeper as a replacement for firewall, I engage with the idea of metaphor repair (see Baljko, Chap. 2 in this volume) as a means of changing the salience or prominence of key attributes of the security technologies discussed in this chapter. Critical media and communication scholars have repeatedly called for new language to more aptly describe various technologies (Chown & Nascimento, 2023; Wyatt, 2021). While no metaphor is perfect—any chosen metaphor will emphasise certain features while downplaying others (Ortony, 1979, 1993)—renaming or repairing with care can shift perspectives and highlight neglected aspects of a technology. No metaphor is value-neutral; each represents a technological imaginary associated with specific values and attitudes, but also serves as a cultural space for negotiating social issues (Marvin, 1990). I therefore propose access gatekeeper as a new metaphor, one that enriches network security discourse and deepens our understanding by reflecting on the multifaceted nature of modern technologies.

6 Conclusion

This chapter has analysed the firewall metaphor within network security discourse. The firewall metaphor is often praised for articulating similarities between physical and network firewalls, particularly their shared role in preventing dangers. However, applying the theoretical lens of similarity theory (Tversky, 1977), I argue that the firewall metaphor does more than simply describe technology. By employing the salience imbalance hypothesis as an analytical tool (Ortony, 1979, 1993), the 'firewall' metaphor has been shown to emphasise similarities between physical and network firewalls while obscuring important attributes such as the power relations involved in filtering and monitoring functions. These obscured attributes are crucial for understanding the broader implications of these network security technologies. The analysis of communications from major firewall vendors shows that this metaphor is used in ways that limit critical discussion of the consequences of the use of these technologies.

Reflecting on the practice of renaming as a form of metaphor repair, I have advocated for replacing 'firewall' with *access gatekeeper*. This new term reframes the concept of network security not as a benign safeguard, but as a process of exclusion that has significant costs. I suggest that access gatekeeper more accurately encapsulates the primary functions of these technologies—monitoring and controlling network access—and highlights the responsibility held by those in authority to manage these technologies ethically. This renaming aims to act as a catalyst for further reflection and debate about the broader concept of network security, stimulating ongoing dialogue that goes beyond the simplistic representations commonly found in industry communications.

Acknowledgements I would like to thank the editors, Crystal Chokshi and Robin Mansell, for their invaluable guidance and support throughout this process. I am also grateful to Melanie Baljko, a contributor to this book, whose discussions on metaphor and technology have been particularly insightful and inspiring for this chapter.

References

Alneyadi, S., Sithirasenan, E., & Muthukkumarasamy, V. (2016). A survey on data leakage prevention systems. *Journal of Network and Computer Applications, 62*, 137–152. https://doi.org/10.1016/j.jnca.2016.01.008

Anderson, R. (2020). *Security engineering: A guide to building dependable distributed systems*. John Wiley & Sons.

Aristotle. (1991). *On rhetoric: A theory of civil discourse*. (G. A. Kennedy, Trans.). Oxford University Press.

Avolio, F. (1999). Firewalls and Internet security, the second hundred (Internet) years. *The Internet Protocol Journal, 2*(2), 24–32. https://ipj.dreamhosters.com/wp-content/uploads/issues/1999/ipj02-2.pdf

Balozian, P., Leidner, D., & Warkentin, M. (2019). Managers' and employees' differing responses to security approaches. *Journal of Computer Information Systems, 59*(3), 197–210. https://doi.org/10.1080/08874417.2017.1318687

Bendl, R., & Schmidt, A. (2010). From 'glass ceilings' to 'firewalls'—Different metaphors for describing discrimination. *Gender, Work & Organization, 17*(5), 612–634. https://doi.org/10.1111/j.1468-0432.2010.00520.x

Black, M. (1955). XII.—Metaphor. *Proceedings of the Aristotelian Society, 55*(1), 273–294. https://doi.org/10.1093/aristotelian/55.1.273

Black, M. (1977). More about metaphor. *Dialectica, 31*(3–4), 431–457. https://doi.org/10.1111/j.1746-8361.1977.tb01296.x

Black, M. (2019). *Models and metaphors: Studies in language and philosophy*. Cornell University Press. (Original work published 1962).

Buck, C., Olenberger, C., Schweizer, A., Völter, F., & Eymann, T. (2021). Never trust, always verify: A multivocal literature review on current knowledge and research gaps of zero-trust. *Computers & Security, 110*, 1–26. https://doi.org/10.1016/j.cose.2021.102436

Cheswick, W. R., Bellovin, S. M., & Rubin, A. D. (2003). *Firewalls and Internet security: Repelling the wily hacker* (2nd ed.). Addison-Wesley Professional.

Chown, E., & Nascimento, F. (2023). *Meaningful technologies: How digital metaphors change the way we think and live*. University of Michigan Press.

Cisco. (2024a). *Cisco secure firewall*. https://www.cisco.com/site/us/en/products/security/firewalls/index.html#tabs-35d568e0ff-item-194f491212-tab

Cisco. (2024b). *What is a firewall?* https://www.cisco.com/c/en/us/products/security/firewalls/what-is-a-firewall.html

Clark, D., & Chao, L. (2011, July 5). Cisco faces lawsuits, criticism over past China activities. *The Wall Street Journal.*. https://www.wsj.com/articles/SB10001424052702304569504576403701519852270

Cramer, B. W. (2013). The two Internet freedoms: Framing victimhood for political gain. *International Journal of Communication, 7*, 1261–1282. https://ijoc.org/index.php/ijoc/article/view/1624

Deibert, R. J., & Rohozinski, R. (2010). Risking security: Policies and paradoxes of cyberspace security. *International Political Sociology, 4*(1), 15–32. https://doi.org/10.1111/j.1749-5687.2009.00088.x

Elbe, S. (2006). Should HIV/AIDS be securitized? The ethical dilemmas of linking HIV/AIDS and security. *International Studies Quarterly, 50*(1), 119–144. https://doi.org/10.1111/j.1468-2478.2006.00395.x

Hounsel, A., Mittal, P., & Feamster, N. (2018). *Automatically generating a large, culture-specific blocklist for China*. 8th USENIX Workshop on Free and Open Communications on the Internet (FOCI 18). https://www.usenix.org/conference/foci18/presentation/hounsel

Huawei. (2024). What is an AI firewall? *Huawei Official Website*. https://info.support.huawei.com/info-finder/encyclopedia/en/AI+Firewall.html

Ingham, K., & Forrest, S. (2002). *A history and survey of network firewalls* [Technical report]. Computer Science Department, University of New Mexico. https://www.cs.unm.edu/~treport/tr/02-12/firewall.pdf

Kaiser, W. A. (2000). Use of internet filters in public schools: Double click on the Constitution. *Columbia Journal of Law and Social Problems, 34*(1), 49–78. https://heinonline.org/HOL/LandingPage?handle=hein.journals/collsp34&div=9&id=&page=

Kaspersky. (2024). *What is a firewall? Definition and explanation*. https://www.kaspersky.com/resource-center/definitions/firewall

Lakoff, G., & Johnson, M. (2008). *Metaphors we live by*. University of Chicago Press.

Li, Y. (2009). *我们的防火墙: 网络时代的表达与监管 [Our great firewall: Expression and governance in the era of the Internet]*. Guangxi Normal University Press.

Marvin, C. (1990). *When old technologies were new: Thinking about electric communication in the late nineteenth century*. Oxford University Press.

Ortony, A. (1979). Beyond literal similarity. *Psychological Review, 86*(3), 161–180. https://doi.org/10.1037/0033-295X.86.3.161

Ortony, A. (1993). The role of similarity in similes and metaphors. In A. Ortony (Ed.), *Metaphor and thought* (2nd ed., pp. 342–356). Cambridge University Press.

Patton, L. D., & Haynes, C. M. (2014). Using critical interpretive lenses to examine glass ceiling effects through qualitative research. *New Directions for Institutional Research, 2013*(159), 25–35. https://doi.org/10.1002/ir.20051

Ranum, M. J., & Avolio, F. (n.d.). *History of the FWTK firewall toolkit*. https://avolio.com/fwtk-history/

Readence, J. E., Baldwin, R. S., Martin, M. A., & O'Brien, D. G. (1984). Metaphorical interpretation: An investigation of the salience imbalance hypothesis. *Journal of Educational Psychology, 76*(4), 659–667. https://doi.org/10.1037/0022-0663.76.4.659

Rose, S., Borchert, O., Mitchell, S., & Connelly, S. (2020). *Zero trust architecture* [NIST Special Publication No. 800-207]. National Institute of Standards and Technology. https://doi.org/10.6028/NIST.SP.800-207

Sekuła, P., Ciaputa, E., Struzik, J., & Krzaklewska, E. (2022). Gendered excellence in physics. In F. Jenkins, B. Hoenig, S. M. Weber, & A. Wolffram (Eds.), *Inequalities and the paradigm of excellence in academia* (pp. 209–227). Routledge.

Stanton, J. M., & Stam, K. R. (2006). *The visible employee: Using workplace monitoring and surveillance to protect information assets—Without compromising employee privacy or trust*. CyberAge Books.

Storts-Brinks, K. (2010). Censorship online: One school librarian's journey to provide access to LGBT resources. *Knowledge Quest, 39*(*1*), 22–29. http://bit.ly/43kpONZ

Tversky, A. (1977). Features of similarity. *Psychological Review, 84*(4), 327–352. https://doi.org/10.1037/0033-295X.84.4.327

Van Rythoven, E. (2020). The securitization dilemma. *Journal of Global Security Studies, 5*(3), 478–493. https://doi.org/10.1093/jogss/ogz028

Walton, G. (2001). *China's golden shield: Corporations and the development of surveillance technology in the People's Republic of China*. International Centre for Human Rights and Democratic Development. https://publications.gc.ca/pub?id=9.696199&sl=0

Wyatt, S. (2021). Metaphors in critical Internet and digital media studies. *New Media & Society, 23*(2), 406–416. https://doi.org/10.1177/1461444820929324

CHAPTER 12

Altman's Golem*

~~ChatGPT~~

Nathaniel Laywine and Victoria Simon

1 Introduction

It is impossible to ignore the fervour that has followed the introduction of generative artificial intelligence (AI) technologies, especially large language models (LLMs). For instance, since its release in late 2022, ChatGPT has registered more than 180 million users (Duarte, 2024). In simple interfaces on web browsers or mobile apps, ChatGPT users enter a text-based query or command, known as a prompt, into a field on their screens. Prompts instantly generate text-based responses to complex questions. They provide information on various topics; offer creative writing assistance in producing jokes, lyrics, stories, or scripts; translate languages; and engage in interactive conversations.

N. Laywine (✉)
Department of Communication & Media Studies, York University, Toronto, ON, Canada
e-mail: njl@yorku.ca

V. Simon
School of Arts and Sciences, Felician University, Rutherford, NJ, USA
e-mail: simonv@felician.edu

C. Chokshi, R. Mansell (eds.), *The Need to Rename Tech*,
https://doi.org/10.1007/978-3-032-05155-4_12

Following ChatGPT's release, OpenAI partnered with Microsoft's search engine, Bing, to release the chatbot Sydney; Amazon released Lex; and Google released Bard, later renamed Gemini. These products share certain characteristics. As Lauren M. E. Goodlad (2023, p. 1) frames it,

> the world's largest tech companies are using the rhetoric of 'artificial intelligence' and even 'artificial general intelligence' (AGI), to market disembodied, virtual, and affectless statistical models, trained on vast datasets, to a public accustomed to associating such terms with fictional androids.

This anthropomorphic framing of AI harnesses the popular cultural imagination of science fiction. Despite the hype, chatbots such as ChatGPT and Gemini are not artificially 'intelligent' in a way that is usually associated with human notions of intelligence. They may seem uncannily alive to users, but they lack sentience, emotionality, and a theory of mind required to recognise the consciousness of their human interlocutors (Cuzzolin et al., 2020). All they can do is rely on probabilistic models to generate recombinations of words extracted from extensive corpora of training data.

The chatbot is a new technology, but the concept of a technological assemblage of inorganic material replicating human behaviour in the service of humans dates back to the Old Testament. In this chapter, we draw on folkloric tales of the mythical creature known as *the golem,* which we take from our shared Jewish cultural backgrounds and from scholarship in critical media studies. Relying on the figure of the golem, we establish a Jewish intellectual lineage beginning with folktales of the golem invoked by the Rabbi of Prague and reaching foundational cybernetic researchers such as Norbert Wiener and Sam Altman. The promise of golems, like that of chatbots, lies in their potential to perform assistive tasks. Yet this potential is accompanied by the prospect of peril when the golem's (or chatbot's) power and autonomy outstrip human control and lead to unintended consequences and harm.

Our chapter first explores folktales of the golem and then demonstrates how they inform technological developments from cybernetics and early computers to ChatGPT. We then discuss Altman's intentions to 'save the world', highlighting key features of ChatGPT's interface and its content generation. The final section situates our own research on ChatGPT, demonstrating this contemporary golem's inability to generate accurately content that exemplifies Jewish humour. We also discuss intersectional axes of identity provided by critiques of digital technologies from critical race, feminist, and queer perspectives. We suggest that this contemporary golem's limitations risk perpetuating stereotypes, disseminating mis/disinformation, and, potentially, contributing to cultural erasure. Finally, we rename ChatGPT as *Altman's Golem* to remind Sam Altman and others of the responsibility they bear in mitigating these risks.

2 Old World Golem Lore

Myths of the golem date back to the Talmud between 500 and 400 BCE (Cohen, 2016), although the classical golem archetype that is most widely known emerges from Ashkenazi (European) Jewish folklore. These versions describe the creature as a large, anthropomorphic being formulated from dust, clay, or mud and brought to life through ritual incantations to serve the needs of its creator—usually a wizened elder or community leader among Jews, such as a rabbi. Although golems were thought to resemble giant brutish men, they were not themselves human, since they could not engage in speech or rational thought. They lacked 'the breath of life' or the soul that links humanity to the divine (Goltz et al., 2020, p. 137). Golems, consequently, have no capacity to establish moral clarity between right and wrong or good and evil.

The most common golem tale is attributed to Rabbi Judah Loew ben Bezalel (known as Rabbi Loew or simply as the Rabbi of Prague), a sixteenth-century public figure and spiritual leader among Prague's Jewry who invoked a golem to protect the Jews from religious and cultural persecution. In many iterations of the tale, the Rabbi is said to have written the Hebrew word *emet* (meaning truth) on the golem's forehead to bring him to life so he could act as a soldier or bodyguard for vulnerable Jews. We might think of this as the first text-based prompt, the precursor to the blinking cursor at the bottom of Altman's ChatGPT interface. Whether it be a rabbi's sacred invocations or an OpenAI account holder's request for a recipe, human users engage in manipulations of a creature or a tool for their own gain.

In other versions of the story, the golem is invoked to perform menial tasks such as cleaning, building, or other domestic chores. Regardless of what the golem is called upon to do, the story always ends in disaster. The Rabbi can no longer control his creation, and the golem runs amok; the creature goes on an indiscriminate killing spree or grows so large that it tramples the very shtetl it was invoked to protect. The Rabbi is forced to deactivate the golem with a text-based prompt by removing a letter from the word *emet* to create the word *met,* which means dead or died. Ultimately, the golem's use value as a protector is outweighed by its limited cognitive abilities and propensity for destruction. In the following section, we discuss how cultural anxieties about technologies often reflect a similar attitude.

3 Golem Tech

The 'Sisyphean cycle of moral panics' (Orben, 2020) around new technologies, in particular, technologies of automation, often invokes stories similar to golem folklore. This is a recurrent social pattern when new technologies are introduced to the public and seen as a threat to prevailing norms and social values. For example, the archetype of the 'robot' as a precursor to AI is associated with human anxieties about dehumanisation. As Kathleen Richardson (2015) reminds us, the etymology of the word can be attributed to the Czech *robota* (in contrast to the Yiddish *goylem*), which translates to servitude or hardship. Ruha Benjamin (2019, p. 37) extends this attribution to social differences, in particular, racialisation, suggesting that automation always contains traces of indentured servitude, revealing "an agitation about human domination over other humans". This is signalled in the master/slave discourses used throughout the history of computing (Chun, 2013; Eglash, 2007; Everett, 2009; McKenzie, 2019; Richardson, 2015). Gendered social divisions interlock with these racial ontologies in popular culture. Humanoid robots tend to take on binary characteristics of hypermasculine white men when they are depicted as elite killing machines in films such as *Terminator* or *Robocop* (Wilcox, 2023). On the other hand, the feminised voices of virtual assistants such as Siri and Alexa respond pleasantly when asked to perform administrative and domestic tasks, much like their therapeutic foremother ELIZA when asked to perform emotional labour (Rhee, 2023).

Sandu Frunză (2023) notes that the golem exists in the modern literary imaginary. He cites the popularity of German sci-fi author Gustav Mernyk's 1915 novel, *The Golem*, written in another historical moment when automation proliferated with startling speed. The story inspired decades of literary criticism (see Gelbin, 2021; Idel, 1990; Nocks, 1998).

Harry Collins and Trevor Pinch have described assemblages of science, technology, and their applications as golemesque. A technology-as-golem "will follow orders, do your work, and protect you … But it is clumsy and dangerous. Without control a golem may destroy its masters with its *flailing vigour* [emphasis added]; it is a lumbering fool who knows neither his own strength nor the extent of his clumsiness and ignorance" (Collins & Pinch, 1998, pp. 1–2). Just as the Rabbi of Prague learned, the affordances of golems are outweighed by the risks of great harm.

The inability to predict or control the golem's 'flailing vigour' has led to ethical debates about golems as technology. Nachshon Goltz, John Zelznikow, and Tracey Dowdeswell (2020) interpret golem lore as a pre-cautionary tale that warns against assigning a concept of personhood to robots. Zvi Rappaport (2006) argues that Jewish lore treats the golem with 'equanimity' when compared to Mary Shelley's Frankenstein, which is treated as a moral and natural abomination. In a 2019 exhibition at The Barbican Art Centre in London, Emily D. Bilski (2019, paras. 1, 8) notes the similarity between reciting combinations of Hebrew letters that "constituted the 'coding' that could animate inanimate material, much as computer code 'creates' AI", arguing that in a Jewish mystical tradition, "creating a golem was understood as a means to grow closer to the Creator and to achieve spiritual perfection", a higher order operation than merely extending human labour.

Fruitful intersections of Jewish mysticism and cybernetics, such as Bilski's, are present in the works of Kabbalistic scholar, Gershom Scholem, and in the work of the 'father of cybernetics', Norbert Wiener, two Jewish intellectuals on either side of the (perhaps not-so-divisive) gap between faith and science.[1] The relationship between technological innovation and godliness was not lost on either of these scholars. In his penultimate book titled *Gods & Golems, Inc.*, Wiener (1966, p. 95) states, "The machine, as I have already said, is the modern counterpart of the Golem of the Rabbi of Prague". Throughout this work, he ruminates on the difference between the abilities of God, humans, and machines to (respectively) divinely create, biologically generate, and mechanically reproduce their progeny. Wiener reminds us, "In constructing machines with which he plays games, the inventor has arrogated to himself the function of a limited creator, whatever the nature of the game-playing device that he has

[1]We might also attribute some of Wiener's fatherly legacy to Mexican physician Arturo Rosenblueth and the American engineer Julian Bigelow for their co-authored work (1943), 'Behavior, Purpose, and Teleology'. For other Jewish contributions to the field, see also Hal Abelson, Manual Blum, Shafi Goldwasser, Leonard Kleinrock, John von Neumann, and Joseph Weizenbaum.

constructed" (Wiener, 1966, p. 17). As limited creators, people do not always maintain mastery over their creations; sometimes they must struggle for control. In Christian theology, Wiener notes, the devil is God's creation, yet one with whom God must engage in an ongoing moral and existential struggle. So, too, for the rabbi who invokes and must inevitably deactivate the golem. And let us not forget Nick Bostrom's (2003) oft-quoted parable of the 'paperclip maximizer', where superintelligent computing systems that are programmed with a singular task (i.e., to produce paper clips) may deplete the entire world of its resources and human populations. Each act of creation, innovation, or invention contains within it a potential for destruction.

In a 1965 address to the Weitzmann Institute in Rehovot, Israel, Gershom Scholem responded to the Institute's development of the first computer in Israel, which he called 'the Golem of Rehovot', noting the commonalities among the then-emergent technology and the golem, and the upgrade of the former to the latter. Both draw upon 'mystical' combinations of letters to receive their commands: the kabbalistic combination of 22 Hebrew letters for the golem and the binary digital code of 0 and 1 for the computer. Both rely on 'energy' to operate—the golem runs on divine energy from mystical invocations; while the computer runs on electricity. While the golem maintains a human shape, the computer has no such form, but both are composed of inorganic materials to complete their tasks. What the computer lacks in external beauty, it makes up for in its ability to "grow in stature and productivity" and to develop more sophisticated operational features through upgrades and technical optimisation that golems cannot achieve (Scholem, 1966, para. 14). Still, he notes that neither is capable of producing speech, which "to the Biblical mind is identical with reason and intelligence" and which is expressed through spontaneous conversation (Scholem, 1966, para. 6).

We counter by suggesting that plenty of conversation lacks reason and intelligence. Yet the Golem of Rehovot was indeed unable to perform the function of speech, and ChatGPT demonstrates a significant upgrade in abilities that allows it, uncannily, to approximate human reason and intelligence. As the CEO of OpenAI, Altman's enthusiasm for his creation borders on radical techno-optimism when he suggests that such developments might provide technological solutions to the many social harms that befall humanity, and might be deployed for altruistic and benevolent ends (Andreessen, 2023). We explore this below.

4 Altman's Golem

Following the lineage of Jewish technological innovation to the contemporary corporate milieu of Silicon Valley, we arrive at the work of Sam Altman. Altman has been the public face of OpenAI since it launched ChatGPT in November 2022. His popularity among employees at OpenAI and collaborators at Microsoft's Azure OpenAI services allowed him to stave off a coup from OpenAI's board members in late 2023 when he was fired and rehired within one tumultuous weekend. In a 2016 profile in *The New Yorker*, Altman—who at the time was president of the YC Group and the Y Combinator, working within the context of nascent transhumanist, extropian, singularitarian, cosmist, rationalist, effective altruist, and longtermist (TESCREAL) ideologues (Troy, 2023)—was described by Tad Friend (2016, para. 7) in the following way: "like everyone in Silicon Valley, Altman professes to want to save the world; unlike almost everyone there, he has a plan to do it". Like other TESCREAL-faithful contributors, 'saving the world' implies an unbridled optimism in technology's ability to solve the world's social, political, and environmental injustices, without attending to how Big Tech perpetuates them (Gebru & Torres, 2024).

It takes a certain level of hubris to believe in one's ability to save the world. This ambition defies Wiener's warning about the devilishness of technological invention and the cautionary tale of the shtetl in Prague. To invoke the golem is to play at being God and perhaps even to state that "I alone am the LORD; and only I can rescue you" (Isaiah 43:11 as cited in Oswalt, 1998). With such self-confidence comes inevitable blind spots, which we also see in Peter Thiel, Jeff Bezos, Mark Zuckerberg, Elon Musk, and the handful of other celebrity billionaires who control companies with immense global influence over the everyday lives of billions of people, and whom Ben Little and Alison Winch (2021) characterise in their book, *The New Patriarchs of Digital Capitalism*. The rabbis who invoked the folkloric golems of clay and mud cannot straightforwardly be compared to these billionaires in most senses, although they were patriarchs in their own contexts. They held outsized power and privilege afforded to them by their status. Like Altman, they had normative ambitions to save and protect the world. They also seemed to take for granted that their respective golems were or would be made in their likeness.

AI engineering as a profession is notably male, a bias that often goes unrecognised (Browne et al., 2024; Cave et al., 2023; Stinson & Vlaad, 2024). This gendered dynamic is intertwined with a broader presumption of objectivity that feminist scholars of technoscience have long critiqued. Altman's Golem perpetuates this dynamic, presenting itself as an ostensibly neutral and universal tool while being shaped by a predominantly male-dominated field. Donna Haraway (1988, p. 581) has called the pale, stale, maleness of science and technology a God Trick, and a "conquering gaze from nowhere ... [that reifies] scientific and technological, late-industrial militarized, racist and male-dominated societies". In other words, technologies such as Altman's Golem attempt to represent the full spectrum of humanity by proffering totalising expression that is arguably cultureless and inexpressive. Scholars note the consequences of presuming the racial or gender neutrality of technologies, including in search engines. Works by Black and racialised scholars are crucial in demonstrating the white, male hegemonic values that shape the basic functions of quotidian and inescapable technologies (Benjamin, 2019; Costanza-Chock, 2020; Lawrence, 2023; Noble, 2018). As Armond Towns (2022) notes, the media studies field predominantly frames the media's users—indeed, humanity—as white, Western, and male.

It is ironic then that Altman does not acknowledge the limited characteristics of his technology, given his apparent concerns about the safety of Jews and underrepresented minoritised communities. In the aforementioned *New Yorker* article, Friend (2016, para. 26) quotes billionaire Peter Thiel, a friend of Altman's, who noted that "Sam is not particularly religious, but he is culturally very Jewish—an optimist yet a survivalist, with a sense that things can always go deeply wrong, and that there's no single place in the world where you're deeply at home". Altman has expressed ambivalent and complex feelings about his relationship to Judaism and safety.[2] In December 2023, for example, he wrote on X (formerly Twitter): "for a long time i said that antisemitism, particularly on the american left, was not as bad as people claimed. i'd like to just state that i was totally wrong. i still don't understand it, really. or know what to do about it. but it is so fucked". He went on to post similar concerns about Islamophobia and hatred within the tech community the following month (Altman, 2024a, 2024b).

[2] As Jewish scholars, we feel the notion of safety and Jewishness is very troubled because of the genocide in Gaza. This ongoing humanitarian crisis is outside the scope of this chapter. We nevertheless are motivated, as Jews, by concerns for the safety of minortised communities, worldwide, including any victims of warfare or injustice. The normative ambitions of this chapter are to resist majoritarian impulses and to advocate for safety and equity for all.

Just as Rabbi Loew was deeply concerned about the vulnerability of the Jews of Prague and hoped to build a safer, easier life for his community, Altman's hope is to protect vulnerable populations around the world. For both Rabbi and tech bro, the power to protect derives from unique privileges that emerge from the ability to access and control their golems. If we understand the digital 'global village' as the global shtetl, the needs and capabilities of golem tech have been extended, overcoming in some ways the limitations of Rehovot in their ability to produce text and speech. But digital technologies, like golems, are not always what they seem.

5 Golems Run Amok

OpenAI's purported mission and vision are "to ensure that artificial general intelligence benefits all of humanity" (OpenAI, 2024, paras. 1–2). Yet risks abound in the 'flailing vigour' of Altman's Golem with its risks negatively impacting upon minoritised communities.

In spite of Altman's Golem's user-friendly interface design, it is far from foolproof. The free version displays a white background and features a grey text box at the bottom of the screen where users can type queries or commands. Above the input area is a scrollable chat window that displays the conversation history and provides context for ongoing discussions. Previous chats are titled, and there are archives on the left side of the screen in a collapsible sidebar. Some versions include options such as toolbars for features—for example, uploading files, switching between chat modes, or accessing settings. The design aims for simplicity, allowing for easy navigation and interaction.

Prompts immediately generate responses written in a friendly and conversational tone and are, ostensibly, thorough and detailed in nature. In reality, responses are not always factually correct or meaningful, despite often being plausible. There is a short warning underneath the textbox that reads 'ChatGPT can make mistakes. Check important info'. Written as an imperative, this responsibilises users to determine the veracity of content while letting the golem off the hook. ('*You* check the important info, user', it seems to say.) This can be challenging when the chatbot generates outputs with apparent certitude.

Errors arise from the model's reliance on patterns in data rather than verification or an ability to 'understand' or 'know' the world and are referred to as hallucinations. However, Michael Hicks, James Humphries, and Joe Slater (2024) characterise the golem's erroneous output using

Frankfurt's (2005) philosophical concept of 'bullshit', that is, an indifference to the truth of one's statements. Perhaps this can be understood as knowingly deceitful:

> if we view it as having intentions (for example, in virtue of how it is designed), then the fact that it is designed to give the impression of concern for truth qualifies it as attempting to mislead the audience about its aims, goals, or agenda. (Hicks et al., 2024, p. 38)

Whether we believe that Altman's Golem is programmed to be wilfully deceptive or only callously indifferent to its own impacts, this issue reveals a significant departure from Scholem's description of the Golem of Rehovot, which he characterised as being unable to speak. A chatbot, however, produces seamless text (and in some versions, an automated voice) that distinguishes it from early computers. What is consistent, however, between the golem and the chatbot is an inability to assess the difference between right and wrong in its output, either factually or morally. A number of scholars note the risks of such 'bullshit' to minoritised groups when false or derogatory content is generated and widely circulated (Abid et al., 2021; Ahmed et al., 2024; Bender et al., 2021; Crawford, 2021; Goodlad, 2023). This content caricatures and flattens the experiences, values, and worldviews of groups of people, thereby perpetuating mis/disinformation and risking the erasure of non-dominant worldviews.

We have experimented with Altman's Golem by prompting it to create outputs that reflect aspects of our Jewish identity. In each case, we observed its 'flailing vigour'. Its clumsy efforts to respond to our commands resulted in troubling consequences. For instance, we asked Altman's Golem to generate jokes in a quintessentially Jewish comedic style. This unique valence of comedy relies on a mix of self-deprecation and self-praise; dark or gallows humour; wordplay, irony, or sarcasm; and, crucially as we understand it, the humorous deployment of contextual knowledge of what it means to be Jewish (Laywine et al., 2024). The Golem resoundingly failed at this task by producing jokes that ranged from corny alliterations to well-worn offensive stereotypes about Jewish people, crafting jokes where setups and punchlines alike involved conniving businessmen or nagging and chronically anxious Jewish women. In almost every response, it defaulted to commonly used Yiddish words sometimes associated with the semi-integrated urban and suburban American Jewish experience—*schlep* and *oy vey*, along with a preponderance of references to food items such as deli fare, bagels, lox, gefilte fish, and matzah balls.

We concluded the following:

> ChatGPT's comedic styling (if we could call it that … and we don't need to) draws more on irreverence and absurdism than on any contextual, cultural knowledge that might lead to the successful landing of a punchline due to a shared sensibility and lexicon. For ChatGPT, words like "bagel" or "Oy vey" are punchlines without a setup. (Laywine et al., 2024, para. 10)

Elsewhere, we have argued that the golem cannot succeed in generating specifically Jewish *content* without the ability to generate specifically Jewish *context*, a crucial component of Jewish comedic sensibility and epistemology. Haraway's 'God Trick' has become something of a 'Goy Trick' that is decidedly non-Jewish.

There are implications beyond mere joke craft. As we argue, Altman's Golem is even less skilful at generating content (humorous or otherwise) that speaks to the experiences of those with intersectional identities (Simon et al., 2024). We prompted the golem to construct narratives—to 'tell us stories'—featuring characters with (our) intersectional identities along the lines of race, gender, sexuality, and/or ability. The results clearly indicated that key words or phrases functioned in the golem's algorithm to produce content in fixed categories that were determined by symbolic associations.

This creates several problems. First, Altman's Golem "treats intersectionality as an additive operation (i.e., rainbow + yarmulke = queer Jew), rather than an integral one, in which the components of an intersectional identity are changed dialectically in relation to one another" (Simon et al., 2024). Second, this reduces differences within identity categories and defaults to a hegemonic position. Altman's Golem associates identity markers without context or access to decision-making processes that exist in 'black box' algorithms. "In essence … [this creates] the patina of intersectionality, drawing on stereotypes of minoritized identity, rather than acknowledging that actual intersectional identity emerges from lived experience at the nexus of interlocking sites of oppression" (Simon et al., 2024, para. 5).

If the golem's output is intended to serve and protect all of humanity, it fails to deliver on its promise. By whittling complex dynamics of identity into denotative totems, this may threaten to reproduce stereotypes, disseminating mis/disinformation, and potentially contributing to cultural erasure. In short, Altman's Golem-generated content risks the dehumanisation of minoritised communities and, perhaps, of everyone. Once again, the golem tramples those whom it is meant to serve.

6 Conclusion

This account of specifically Jewish preoccupations with golems and ChatGPT serves as a reminder about what is at stake in failing to notice the absence of another's spirit, or their humanity. The capacity to recognise humanity underlies ethical concerns in strands of Jewish existential philosophy and politics (Buber, 1923/1958; Frankl, 1946/2015; Levinas, 1999). Neither ChatGPT nor the mythical golem is human, yet the invocations and applications of both to human tasks eerily approximate human labour and ingenuity. We wonder how the increasing prevalence of golem-generated content on mainstream platforms and in daily life might, in time, come to complicate or undermine our ability to recognise one another as human. For Martin Buber, it is through recognition of one another's humanity that we recognise ourselves and, indeed, a higher spiritual power: "Spirit is not in the I but, between I and Thou" (Buber, 1923/1958, p. 39). The failure to recognise another's spirit is a moral failure and risks causing great harm to them, as well as to oneself.

This failure is a form of dehumanisation that carries enormous existential risk, for "to control a people's culture is to control their tools of self-definition in relationship to others" (wa Thiongo as cited in Whaanga, 2020, p. 36). Altman's Golem calls attention to a pressing issue for minoritised populations: how will future generations perceive themselves if they follow hegemonic constructions of their identity that carry the risk of cultural erasure? Jews are not the only minoritised group that is impacted by the new forms of dehumanisation. The irony is not lost on us, however, that our cultural stories, including those codified as training data, have warned about such a threat for centuries. This chapter is written from the perspectives of its Jewish authors, and it is concerned with the decidedly goyish (i.e., non-Jewish) content that is generated by the golem about Jewish people. We present our analysis in the spirit of solidarity with other members of minoritised communities who may share similar concerns. It is in this spirit that we rename ChatGPT as what it is: *Altman's Golem*. We ask Sam Altman and those developing AI systems to consider our cautionary tale.

Acknowledgements With deep appreciation, the authors would like to thank Aram Sinnreich for his ongoing collaboration, kibbitzing, and friendship. We also thank Zach Pearl and Nora Rosenthal for their thoughtful feedback on this chapter at various stages.

References

Abid, A., Farooqui, M., & Zou, J. (2021). Persistent anti-Muslim bias in large language models. *Proceedings of the 2021 AAAI/ACM Conference on AI, Ethics, and Society*, pp. 298–306. https://doi.org/10.1145/3461702.3462624

Ahmed, S., Jaźwińska, K., Ahlawat, A., Winecoff, A., & Wang, M. (2024). Field-building and the epistemic culture of AI safety. *First Monday, 29*(4), 1–19. https://doi.org/10.5210/fm.v29i4.13626

Altman, S. [@sama]. (2023, December 7). *For a long time I said that antisemitism, particularly on the American left, was not as bad as people claimed* [Post]. X. https://x.com/sama/status/1732925866836210151?s=20

Altman, S. [@sama]. (2024a, January 4). *Muslim and Arab (especially Palestinian) colleagues in the tech community I've spoken with feel uncomfortable speaking about their recent experiences* [Post]. X. https://x.com/sama/status/1743080079515959364?lang=en

Altman, S. [@sama]. (2024b, January 4). *I am Jewish. I believe that antisemitism is a significant and growing problem in the world, and I see a* [Post]. X. https://x.com/sama/status/1743084034723627349?s=20

Andreessen, M. (2023, October 16). The techno-optimist manifesto. *Andreessen Horowitz*. https://a16z.com/the-techno-optimist-manifesto/

Bender, M., Gebru, T., McMillan-Major, A., & Mitchell, M. (2021). On the dangers of stochastic parrots: Can language models be too big? *Proceedings of the 2021 ACM Conference on Fairness, Accountability, and Transparency*, pp. 610–623. https://dl.acm.org/doi/pdf/10.1145/3442188.3445922

Benjamin, R. (2019). *Race after technology: Abolitionist tools for the new Jim code*. Polity Press.

Bilski, E. D. (2019). Meet the golem: The first 'artificial intelligence'. *The Barbican Centre.*. https://artsandculture.google.com/story/meet-the-golem-the-first-artificial-intelligence-barbican-centre/BAXhTNxULrWYKg?hl=en

Bostrom, N. (2003). *Ethical issues in advanced artificial intelligence*. https://nickbostrom.com/ethics/ai

Browne, J., Drage, E., & McInerney, K. (2024). Tech workers' perspectives on ethical issues in AI development: Foregrounding feminist approaches. *Big Data & Society, 11*(1), 1–11. https://doi.org/10.1177/20539517231221780

Buber, M. (1958). *I & thou* (R.G. Smith, Trans.). Scribner. (Original work published 1923)

Cave, S., Dihal, K., Drage, E., & Mackereth, K. (2023). Shuri in the sea of dudes: The cultural construction of the AI engineer. In J. Browne, S. Cave, E. Drage, & K. McInerney (Eds.), *Feminist AI: Critical perspectives on algorithms, data, and intelligent machines* (pp. 65–82). Oxford University Press.

Chun, W. H. K. (2013). *Programmed visions: Software and memory.* MIT Press.

Cohen, J. (2016). From the Golem-Talmud [Article in exhibition catalogue GOLEM]. *Jüdisches Museum Berlin..* www.jmberlin.de/en/node/4711

Collins, H. M., & Pinch, T. (1998). *The golem: What you should know about science* (2nd ed.). Cambridge University Press.

Costanza-Chock, S. (2020). *Design justice: Community-led practices to build the worlds we need.* MIT Press.

Crawford, K. (2021). *Atlas of AI: Power, politics, and the planetary costs of artificial intelligence.* Yale University Press.

Cuzzolin, F., Morelli, A., Cirstea, B., & Sahakian, B. J. (2020). Knowing me, knowing you: Theory of mind in AI. *Psychological Medicine, 50*(7), 1057–1061. https://www.cambridge.org/core/journals/psychological-medicine/article/knowing-me-knowing-you-theory-of-mind-in-ai/C935A66A018117BA5B1991071393655F

Duarte, F. (2024, December 3). Number of ChatGPT users (Mar 2024). *Exploding topics.* Retrieved December 5, 2024, from https://explodingtopics.com/blog/chatgpt-users

Eglash, R. (2007). Broken metaphor: The master-slave analogy in technical literature. *Technology and Culture, 48*(2), 360–369. https://doi.org/10.1353/tech.2007.0066

Everett, A. (2009). *Digital diaspora: A race for cyberspace.* SUNY Press.

Frankfurt, H. G. (2005). *On bullshit.* Princeton University Press.

Frankl, V. E. (2015). *Man's search for meaning* (New edition). Beacon Press. (Original work published 1946)

Friend, T. (2016, October 3). Sam Altman's manifest destiny: Is the head of Y Combinator fixing the world, or trying to take over Silicon Valley? *The New Yorker..* https://www.newyorker.com/magazine/2016/10/10/sam-altmans-manifest-destiny

Frunză, S. (2023). The golem and the artificial intelligence: A new opening towards storytelling. *Journal for the Study of Religions and Ideologies, 22*(66), 65–77. https://thenewjsri.ro/index.php/njsri/article/view/434

Gebru, T., & Torres, É. P. (2024). The TESCREAL bundle: Eugenics and the promise of utopia through artificial general intelligence. *First Monday, 29*(4), 1–42. https://doi.org/10.5210/fm.v29i4.13636

Gelbin, C. S. (2021). The golem: From enlightenment monster to artificial intelligence. *Bulletin of the German Historical Institute, 69*, 79–94. https://www.ghi-dc.org/fileadmin/publications/Bulletin/bu69/GHI69fall_05FEA-GelbinonGolem_Fpp.pdf

Goltz, N., Zeleznikow, J., & Dowdeswell, T. (2020). From the Tree of Knowledge and the Golem of Prague to kosher autonomous cars: The ethics of artificial intelligence through Jewish eyes. *The Oxford Journal of Law and Religion, 9*(1), 132–156. https://doi.org/10.1093/ojlr/rwaa015

Goodlad, L. M. E. (2023). Editor's introduction: Humanities in the loop. *Critical AI, 1*(1–2). https://doi.org/10.1215/2834703X-10734016

Haraway, D. (1988). Situated knowledges: The science question in feminism and the privilege of partial perspective. *Feminist Studies, 14*(3), 575–599. https://doi.org/10.2307/3178066

Hicks, M. T., Humphries, J., & Slater, J. (2024). ChatGPT is bullshit. *Ethics and Information Technology, 26*(38), 1–10. https://doi.org/10.1007/s10676-024-09775-5

Idel, M. (1990). *Golem: Jewish magical and mystical traditions on the artificial anthropoid.* SUNY Press.

Lawrence, C. D. (2023). *Hidden in White sight: How AI empowers and deepens systemic racism.* CRC Press.

Laywine, N., Simon, V., & Sinnreich, A. (2024). Laughing to keep from [user input undefined]: ChatGPT, Jewish humor, and cultural erasure. *First Monday, 29*(7), 1–10. https://doi.org/10.5210/fm.v29i7.13375

Levinas, E. (1999). *Alterity and transcendence.* Columbia University Press.

Little, B., & Winch, A. (2021). *The new patriarchs of digital capitalism: Celebrity tech founders and networks of power.* Routledge.

McKenzie, C. (2019, February 12). Master-slave terminology alternatives you can use right now. *The Server Side.* https://www.theserverside.com/opinion/Master-slave-terminology-alternatives-you-can-use-right-now

Noble, S. U. (2018). *Algorithms of oppression: How search engines reinforce racism.* NYU Press. https://doi.org/10.18574/9781479833641

Nocks, L. (1998). The Golem: Between the technological and the divine. *Journal of Social and Evolutionary Systems, 21*(3), 281–303. https://doi.org/10.1016/S1061-7361(98)80004-0

OpenAI. (2024). About. https://openai.com/about/

Orben, A. (2020). The Sisyphean cycle of technology panics. *Perspectives on Psychological Science, 15*(5), 1143–1157. https://doi.org/10.1177/1745691620919372

Oswalt, J. N. (1998). *The Book of Isaiah: Chapters 40–66.* Eerdmans.

Rappaport, Z. H. (2006). Robotics and artificial intelligence: Jewish ethical perspectives. In C. Nimsky & R. Fahlbusch (Eds.), *Medical technologies in neurosurgery* (pp. 9–12). Springer. https://doi.org/10.1007/978-3-211-33303-7_2

Rhee, J. (2023). From ELIZA to Alexa: Automated care labour and the otherwise of radical care. In J. Browne, S. Cave, E. Drage, & K. McInerney (Eds.), *Feminist AI: Critical perspectives on algorithms, data, and intelligent machines* (pp. 155–173). Oxford University Press. https://doi.org/10.1093/oso/9780192889898.003.0010

Richardson, K. (2015). *An Anthropology of robots and AI: Annihilation anxiety and machines*. Routledge.
Rosenblueth, A., Wiener, N., & Bigelow, J. (1943). Behavior, purpose and teleology. *Philosophy of Science, 10*(1), 18–24. https://doi.org/10.1086/286788
Scholem, G. (1966, January). The Golem of Prague & the Golem of Rehovoth. *Commentary*. https://www.commentary.org/articles/gershom-scholem/the-golem-of-prague-the-golem-of-rehovoth/
Simon, V., Laywine, N., & Sinnreich, A. (2024). *What's with all the tapestries? Intersectionality and the discursive vacuum of generative AI*. SSRN. https://papers.ssrn.com/sol3/papers.cfm?abstract_id=4960597
Stinson, C., & Vlaad, S. (2024). A feeling for the algorithm: Diversity, expertise, and artificial intelligence. *Big Data & Society, 11*(1), 1–13. https://doi.org/10.1177/20539517231224247
Towns, A. R. (2022). *On Black media philosophy*. University of California Press. https://doi.org/10.1525/9780520976016
Troy, D. (Host). (2023, Jun 14). Understanding TESCREAL with Dr. Timnit Gebru and Émile Torres. (Season 2, Episode 3) [Audio podcast episode]. In *Dave Troy Presents*. Podcast Co. https://podcasts.apple.com/ca/podcast/understanding-tescreal-with-dr-timnit-gebru-and/id1610914569?i=1000617036014
Whaanga, H. (2020). *AI: A new (r)evolution or the new colonizer for Indigenous peoples?* An Indigenous Protocol and Artificial Intelligence Position Paper. The Initiative for Indigenous Futures and the Canadian Institute for Advanced Research (CIFAR). https://researchcommons.waikato.ac.nz/server/api/core/bitstreams/bbc6e245-3b21-4642-b361-86e0f5831064/content
Wiener, N. (1966). *God & Golem, Inc.: A comment on certain points where cybernetics impinges on religion*. MIT Press.
Wilcox, L. (2023). No humans in the loop: Killer robots, race and AI. In J. Browne, S. Cave, E. Drage, & K. McInerney (Eds.), *Feminist AI: Critical perspectives on algorithms, data, and intelligent machines* (pp. 83–100). Oxford University Press.

CHAPTER 13

Servants of Capitalism*

~~Angel Investors~~

Gemma Milne

1 Introduction

'Angel investors' are the guardians of entrepreneurs who, by using their supernatural powers of unicorn-spotting, bestow monetary salvation and sage advice, saving startups from a descent into market oblivion. In an environment where founders feel the need to shepherd their ideas through the nine circles of technology transfer, hoping to be one of the chosen ones to cross the Valley of Death, angel investors provide divine intervention.

Their presentation as particularly helpful people who go above and beyond—contrasting with more transactional financing relationships such as bank loans, venture capital, or government grants—is part of angel investors' allure. Paul Graham (2009, para. 45), perhaps one of the most famous angel investors, summarises the angelic view in his influential blog post *How to be an Angel Investor*: "The most successful angel investors I know are all basically good people. Once they invest in a company, all they

G. Milne (✉)
Adam Smith Business School, University of Glasgow, Glasgow, Scotland
e-mail: gemma.milne@glasgow.ac.uk

C. Chokshi, R. Mansell (eds.), *The Need to Rename Tech*,
https://doi.org/10.1007/978-3-032-05155-4_13

want to do is help it". And, as the opening paragraph of the angel investor guide on startups.co.uk, a prominent entrepreneurship resource in the United Kingdom (UK), states, "they are considered the most flexible, compassionate and fervent investors in the ways they use their leverage, expertise and connections to help steer projects they believe in" (Lennox, 2023, para. 2). Angel investors can also be positioned as saviours of the economy more broadly, due to their specific intervention at the early stage of a business's life and their provision of catalysing support to make entrepreneurship succeed. Accordingly, in 2015, the UK Business Angels Association and the Centre for Entrepreneurs published a report titled *Nation of Angels: The Unsung Heroes of Britain's Economy* (Enterprise Research Centre, 2015).

These investors do provide more than just money at a challenging point in the startup journey, but are they 'angelic'? Surely we could call them, instead, 'early-stage investors', acknowledging the specific moment at which they take a risk on a business and provide venture financing. After all, on the face of it, what they do is quite simple: invest their money in startup companies at an early stage in the entrepreneurial process, sometimes also providing advice from previous business successes, in return for potentially large future financial returns. In the meantime, they receive beneficial tax breaks. Getting in early means getting a piece of a potentially prosperous pie; sharing expertise increases the chances of their investment being realised; and providing resources for projects that align politically or morally with a specific vision of the future means exercising material power that very few people possess. Arguably, such potential benefits make early-stage investing self-serving rather than angelic, and a sober renaming could reflect that reality.

But there is more to be disrupted in the powerful metaphorical work enacted by 'angel', a term that acts as an effective, convenient smokescreen for the system that angel investors both prop up and are propped up by. When angel investing, with its moral-good connotations, is portrayed as one of the most crucial steps in taking entrepreneurial ventures to market, we succumb to the very idea of capitalism not only as God, but also as the only way to do things in the world. Instead, we should point more directly to the role of the angel as depicted in religious texts: a servant of a higher power. A critical renaming can 'make the familiar strange' (Gunderson, 2020), in a bid to move from incremental to transformative social change. Instead of 'angel investor', why not 'servant of capitalism'?

Angel investors exist simply because of the flawed status quo capitalist process behind making ideas material, and if we are to believe there are other, better ways of bringing new technologies and science into the world, we must directly challenge and reckon with the lack of disenchantment that we, as subjects of modernity, ironically pride ourselves on. Seeing angel investors for what they are helps us to unveil the capitalism-upholding work that they do. And maybe, without our tacit acceptance, capitalism, and its system of servants, would crumble.

2 The Work of 'Angels'

Angels are spiritual figures who, on behalf of a divine being, provide counsel, guidance, protection, and rescue. They are associated predominantly with Christianity, Judaism, and Islam, acting in these traditions as messengers of God or as assigned guardians for humans. They are not to be worshipped in and of themselves; rather, they act as vessels for the will of the divine being. Not least of all, one of their functions is to remind the humans who seek their guidance to persist in their reverence for their God. In more New Age spiritual communities, angels are looked to for advice and healing relevant to life's modern ills; in these contexts, an openness to and awareness of angels is akin to channelling the energy required for individuals simply to operate in twenty-first-century society.

Outside explicitly religious and spiritual frameworks, the word 'angel', and associated imagery, is used across secular contexts and popular culture.[1] From describing someone who is caring, kind, and selfless to remembering deceased loved ones, particularly children, who are 'taken too soon', 'angel' circulates in public consciousness in myriad ways. We coo at the cute child chosen to be the angel in the nativity play; we sing along to countless songs praising angelic love interests; we refer to nurses and frontline workers as angels who dedicate their lives to those beyond themselves.

Connotations of 'angel' in modern everyday usage surround ideas of guardianship, goodness, and grace that transcend human and earthly ills. Calling someone an angel shelters them from condemnation, moral questioning, and doubt. It is this metaphorical work—this protection—that the word 'angel' gives to a person and the activity they undertake. It needs to be exhumed from the world of venture finance.

[1] For an incisive overview, see Pallister (2001).

3 What Angel Investors Do

'Angel investor' refers to individual investors in early-stage companies (Wetzel, 1983). They are often so-called 'high-net-worth individuals', sometimes with previous experience in successfully building startups, and they tend to make their investments between the 4Fs stage (family, friends, fools, and fans) and the venture capital (VC) stage (Drover et al., 2017; Freear et al., 1994). In other words, they have reasons beyond personal connections to invest, and they do so with their own monetary wealth (however that may have been acquired). In return for their investment, they receive a stake in the company. This means that if or when the company is, for example, bought by another company or floated on the stock market, the angel investor receives a portion of that (theoretically) much larger sum of money, which they take as profit for their early investment.

To understand why the term 'angel' is used for these kinds of investors at this stage of venture financing, it is necessary to unpack the status quo process (and its associated limiting imaginaries) of materialising ideas through entrepreneurship. This process is often referred to as 'lab to market', and it is the manifestation of a long history of neoliberal projects that constructed, promoted, and formally legalised the very phenomenon of science and technology commercialisation (Allen & O'Shea, 2014; Biddle, 2011; Irzık, 2007; Mirowski, 2011, 2012).

Nowadays, if someone has an idea they would like to make a reality, whether that be a drug to treat heart disease, a website for analysing financial data, or an Instagram-for-hamsters app for sharing photos of tiny furry friends, that person has several options. In societies dominated by market capitalism, however, one option stands out: find money to pay for the work needed to make the idea desirable enough for other people to pay for it in the future.

There are many steps in this process, including forming a company, protecting intellectual property, conducting technical tests, building effective teams, attracting media attention, designing business models, and so on. However, the key catalyst for this process—and what ultimately determines whether an idea 'makes it' to material reality—is money. Money pays for labour and resources, over a period of many years, with the goal of delivering that drug, financial analysis website, or Instagram-for-hamsters app to a global market of people who will pay to access it. Those people then provide the money needed to keep the whole enterprise going into the future.

Finding money to pay for something that does not yet exist, then, is the name of the game. And a game it truly is, filled with rules, teams, players, and talents. Typically, the people trying to bring ideas into the world (we usually call these people 'entrepreneurs') have no choice but to play.

So-called angel investors come in at a particular moment during this entrepreneurial process: between the 4Fs and the VCs, as noted earlier (Drover et al., 2017; Wetzel, 1987). This moment usually occurs when entrepreneurs have run out of people from whom to solicit favours, but before they have something justifiably 'sellable'. Perhaps the entrepreneur has not gathered enough efficacy evidence; perhaps the technology is not ready to be deployed to large swathes of people; perhaps the culture of the day is not quite set for something that will challenge societal norms. In short, this early stage, sometimes termed 'the Valley of Death', is a risky time in the entrepreneurial process. Because angel investors fly in to fill this gap, their money is seen as vital bridging capital (Al-Shaikh & Siddiqui, 2021; Frank et al., 1996; Lefebvre et al., 2022).

Angel investors, thus, are perceived to have a degree of blind faith in emerging businesses, and entrepreneurs highly value it. Startup founders, however, are not the only ones who praise angel investors for their faith. At the thirtieth anniversary celebration of the Enterprise Investment Scheme Association, a trade body set up to promote policies and initiatives that help private individuals invest in small companies (and realise a few tax breaks), British Member of Parliament Kanishka Narayan was invited to speak about the importance of angel investors to the UK innovation ecosystem. In a LinkedIn post reflecting on the event, he said, "Over the last decade, I saw angel investors in British tech repeatedly back innovators when there was little consensus or data ... A vibrant preseed [*sic*] and seed ecosystem is the foundation on which our vibrant tech and capital markets rely" (2024).

But angel investors are bestowed their title for reasons beyond providing ostensibly necessary resources. They are perceived to act against their own best interests for the benefit of society. To all appearances, angel investors take on huge personal risk in order to bet on projects that are interesting or important in theory, but may not work in practice (and thus may not provide them with a financial return). There is, arguably, an altruistic motivation behind their investments (Sullivan & Miller, 1996; Taylor, 2019).

4 Returning the Angel Investor to Earth

The fandom associated with entrepreneurship is well documented. The 'hero inventor' was particularly prevalent during the Industrial Revolution in Victorian Britain (MacLeod, 2010). Thomas Carlyle, in his 1840 lectures, described the Great Man as he who is put on earth to lead and shape the arc of history (Spector, 2016). Nowadays, we have the 'Silicon Valley visionary', 'technological elites', and the 'genius founder' (Daub, 2020; Livermore, 2020; Noble & Roberts, 2019). The aura of those who are seen to be bringing new, challenging-to-materialise things into the world continues to enchant new disciples through the ages.

Holding those with vast amounts of money in high esteem, especially when you are after said money for your projects, is also not new. Whether it is the artist's patron or the corporate philanthropist, approaching those with desired resources is all about fawning and reverence, despite conflicting or insincere motivations that may be at play (Giridharadas, 2018). When it comes to financial investors, people such as Warren Buffett are positioned by those who follow the markets as ultra-intelligent sages with some kind of higher insight (Hagstrom, 2024), who then enact that power by putting their (or rather, other people's) money where their mouth is.

The importance of the angel investor is made clear in startup media outlets, entrepreneurship training schemes, and investment how-to guides.[2] On the UK's Angel Investment Network blog, angel investors talk about their 'passion' for investing, "the joy of discovering and nurturing innovative ideas" and the "warm, fuzzy feelings" they get from "mentoring promising founders" (Hicks, 2024b, paras. 5, 7). The guardian and protector role is also reinforced through business media outlets, with such venues foregrounding how much the angel investor "care[s] deeply" for the companies they invest in and how they are looking to be "proud of an investment" (Nowshin, 2023, paras. 25, 22). Venture Studio Founders Fund emphasises the power of the angel investor in its guide to finding and working with angels: "Once you've brought in one 'super angel' (a particularly active or renowned angel), they can bring a lot of momentum through introductions to other angels, syndicates, or other VCs" (Founders Factory, 2023, para. 9). Entrepreneurs, when searching for advice on how to engage with angel investors, are encouraged to show

[2] I am based in the United Kingdom, hence, I include examples predominantly from UK sources.

"genuine interest" (Hicks, 2024a, para. 7) in the angels as individuals and to "start with passion and drive" (Kundzina, n.d., para. 3) to get the investors to believe in them and their ideas.

Additionally, there are various government schemes constructed to encourage angel investing, such as the UK's Seed Enterprise Investment Scheme (SEIS) and Enterprise Investment Scheme (EIS), both of which offer very generous tax breaks. Globally, there is a myriad of programmes to encourage women and people of colour into angel investing in a bid to support more diverse entrepreneurs with a more diverse investor pool (and, by extension, improve society as a whole). Examples include the UK's Angel Academe, an angel investing network with predominantly female members, which invests in female-founded startups; Black Angel Group, a collective of black angel investors, which is predominantly based in the United States; Pipeline Angels, also US-based, for female and gender non-conforming investors, which also invests specifically in diverse founders; and Epic Angels, a female-only angel investor network based in Asia Pacific. Such is the strength of the 'angel investor social importance' rhetoric that in March 2024, the UK government reversed an increased wealth threshold for angel investor accreditation after intense industry lobbying argued that it would negatively impact the ability of underrepresented groups to invest (Hornstein, 2024).

We can reasonably contest any and all of these assumptions about, and associations with, angel investors. One might assert, for example, that some investors do not have previous startup experience but, nevertheless, benefit from being associated with entrepreneurial success; that they do not 'just know' about good investment choices but rather have privileged access to business spaces with insider knowledge; that they do not 'call it early' with their investments but rather, by investing, bring these companies into being in a self-fulfilling prophecy; that they predominantly invest in their own networks, so they are not necessarily supporting the best businesses but just reinforcing existing inequalities; and that they are not simply 'giving back' but rather making deliberate financial management choices that come with beneficial tax breaks and potentially lucrative returns.

All of that is to say, angel investors are repeatedly positioned as having high social importance as well as characteristics and offerings to be revered; yet, arguably, they do not take on as much risk as is celebrated by their advocates. Not only that but they also stand to see huge financial benefits, and tend to keep their wealth circulating amongst the same privileged networks. Even more problematically, these individuals have disproportionate input into which products get made, which companies exist, who gets access to financial resources, and which forms of economic development happen in society. As such, the term 'angel investor' does an undue amount of positive discursive work. Fundamentally, angel investors are people who provide financing at a particular moment in time. They are merely early-stage investors, and that is one name by which we could very sensibly call them.

5 The Need to Remove Our Blinkers

The idea of 'making the familiar strange' (Gunderson, 2020) calls on sociologists to accept that the main barrier to sociological knowledge is the experience of the world as unchangeable. To overcome this, a process of 'social defamiliarization' is required to disrupt patterns of thinking (Gunderson, 2020). Taking something 'normal' and describing it in a way that unveils how abnormal it is can be a powerful force for change. An example might be 'money', an object that is often perceived as a simple fact of social existence as opposed to something socially constructed and, thus, changeable.

Exposing more people to the idea that capitalism is not a simple fact of society is, arguably, what is needed to bring about meaningful change. It has almost become clichéd to lean on Mark Fisher and Fredric Jameson's assertion that it is easier to imagine the end of the world than the end of capitalism (Fisher, 2012). With so much work still to be done in interrupting these kinds of social imaginaries, the adage speaks to the work that renaming, when done correctly, can do.

By renaming 'angel investors' as 'early-stage investors', we shift the focus away from the worship of and enchantment with the individuals themselves, but we do not interrogate our worship of and enchantment with the higher power they serve. With this sobering renaming, we might feel a sense of tech-criticism-gotcha, but we fail to puncture the façade of the system in which the very idea of an angel investor exists in the first place: that of growth-at-all-costs market capitalism.

To puncture, then, we must first go back to our 'lab-to-market' process—the very narrative that says that ideas can only be made real in the world by following a journey of proving their future financial worth to those with the power to bestow it—and reckon with how imprisoning a narrative it is. The lab-to-market process can be thought of as an example of what Charles Taylor (2007, p. 590) calls “closed world structures”: self-contained ideologies within cultures that function as “unchallenged axioms”. These closed world structures are shut off from outside critiques that could threaten their legitimacy, and they become self-fulfilling prophecies in the marketplace of ideas due to their structural ability to withstand counterarguments (Baker, 2020).

Angel investors exist because of the sustained power of the lab-to-market imaginary. But there *are* other ways to make things real in the world—other ownership structures, other motivating incentives, and other legal rulings. One only has to look to cooperatives, community ownership models, national investment organisations, and open-source movements as examples of alternatives that exist today, not to mention the multitudes of proposals for alternatives to capitalistic organisation and development (Cohen, 2017; Martell, 2023; Monticelli, 2022; Parker et al., 2013; Schiller-Merkens, 2024; Zanoni et al., 2017). The process in which the angel investor is ‘required’ is one option among many.

If we question the lab-to-market imaginary, then we can intervene in the power that the wealthy have in shaping our worlds. With different funding mechanisms and different approaches to ‘making real’ our ideas, the need for the rich to swoop in and provide the ‘bridge’ from one development stage to the next—and therefore control what does and does not safely cross the Valley of Death—dies.

6 Calling Angel Investors What They Are

We might tell ourselves that modernity has brought with it a shift to scientific rationality and deauthorisation of the magical, mystical, and religious, but there is much to be said about how the role of the sacred, of enchantment, and of magical thinking still operates today—albeit in different forms (Joas, 2021; Malešević, 2022; Schwarzkopf, 2020; Storm, 2017). In technocapitalist spaces, in particular, such enchantment is explicit in the eschatological enthusiasm of Silicon Valley entrepreneurs (Geiger, 2020); the religiosity on show in response to developments surrounding artificial intelligence (Epstein, 2024; Singler 2024); the programmers referring to themselves as ‘technopagans’ (Aupers, 2009); and Elon Musk’s ‘magicians of the Twenty-first Century’ (Crandall et al., 2021). It is not surprising that such a term as ‘angel investor’ is so readily used and unquestioned in modern entrepreneurship culture.

Indeed, the religious metaphor has purchase; these are powerful ideas that a vast number of people intuitively understand, regardless of how religious they are. Metaphors need shared cultural references in order to be put to work in social environments (Deignan, 2003), and we—in the West at least—have inherited a culture infused with Abrahamic religion. One only has to look at the prevalence of religious metaphors across politics and business (think 'company mission' or 'empire-building') to see how historical, yet established, metaphors turn into powerful ideas (Koller, 2009). Metaphors, especially those that inject religious ideas into culture, can ground "the otherwise ineffable in language" (Kimmel, 2004, p. 280).

But if the task is to reckon with ideas that are cognitively challenging to interrogate—as is the growth-at-all-costs market capitalism of Fisher's (2012) 'capitalist realism'—then we need effective tools to interrupt imaginations at scale. A religious metaphor, especially one that so immediately brings up moral-good connotations, is too readily accepted. We need something that surprises, that gives us pause, and that perhaps makes us recoil, in order to force our trains of thought to jump tracks.

A key tenet surrounding angels in Abrahamic religions is worth repeating: they are not to be worshipped. Rather, they act as vessels for the will of the divine being, including reminding those they encounter to continue in their reverence for their God. In short, angels serve a higher power, and they exist to keep that higher power at the forefront of mind in everyone they encounter.

Angel investors do serve a higher power—capitalism—but the word 'angel' typically does not call 'capitalism' to mind. In the light of this failure, let us conceptualise a new name that does the angels' work for them—something that connotes the work they do in serving their higher power and keeping that power front of mind for capitalist subjects one and all. I propose we rename angel investors as *servants of capitalism*.

7 Wait, Are You for Real?

Maybe renaming angel investors as *servants of capitalism* is just a bit of fun, bordering on flippant satire, in the face of a worthy project around renaming elements of technocapitalist society. Or maybe it is the sort of intervention required to help us see things for what they are—not just the angel investors themselves, but the system that they uphold and that upholds them in return.

The task of convincing enough people that there are other viable, less harmful ways of materialising innovations, and that we do not need angel investors for businesses to succeed, is hard. While there are alternatives aplenty in theory, examples in practice tend to be fragmented, smaller in scale, and hugely under-resourced. Such is the dominance of the lab-to-market process. Entrepreneurs are often trying to find the easiest, quickest, and safest processes for getting access to financial resources to build their businesses; it makes sense that they would follow the status quo in this regard. Examples such as commons-based social enterprises, platform cooperatives, and more recently, Distributed Autonomous Organisations (DAOs) are experimenting with post-capitalist entrepreneurship (Cohen, 2017), but they are by no means mainstream in either practice or popular discourse.

More attention needs to be given to alternative systems for making ideas real if we are to design, test, and improve those systems in practice and at scale. In order to stimulate that attention, it must be made clear that the current system is flawed and in need of something else to replace it. The task is that of uncovering taken-for-granted processes and shining a light on their deficiencies; one part of this current capitalist system, or perhaps a symptom of it, is the existence and the reverence of angel investors. This narrative needs to be countered.

Words have power. They have the power to move us, to seize us, to speak to our core emotional base, and to elicit a fitting reaction. ‘Servants of capitalism’ is funny, yes, but it is also jolting and, probably for some, offensive. It does forceful metaphorical work that confronts us with an alternate, less enchanting, and more arresting mirror of reality.

Acknowledgements Huge thanks go to Lawrence Yolland, Colin Mason, Fabian Muniesa, Vassilis Galanos, Arun Jacob, Niall MacKenzie, and Heather Parry for their comments and discussion—both challenging and encouraging! I would also like to thank the peer reviewers and the editors for the care and expertise they gifted to my work.

References

Allen, T. J., & O’Shea, R. P. (Eds.). (2014). *Building technology transfer within research universities: An entrepreneurial approach*. Cambridge University Press.

Al-Shaikh, M. E., & Siddiqui, K. A. (2021). Crossing the valley of death: Lessons for young entrepreneurs. *Entrepreneurship and Sustainability Issues, 9*(1), 644–662. https://doi.org/10.9770/jesi.2021.9.1(40)

Aupers, S. (2009). 'The force is great': Enchantment and magic in Silicon Valley. *Masaryk University Journal of Law and Technology, 3*(1), 153–173. https://journals.muni.cz/mujlt/article/view/2530/2094

Baker, B. D. (2020). Sin and the hacker ethic: The tragedy of techno-utopian ideology in cyberspace business cultures. *Journal of Religion and Business Ethics, 4*(1), 1–28. https://via.library.depaul.edu/jrbe/vol4/iss2/1

Biddle, J. (2011). Bringing the marketplace into science: On the neoliberal defense of the commercialization of scientific research. In M. Carrier & A. Nordmann (Eds.), *Science in the context of application* (pp. 245–269). Springer.

Cohen, B. (2017). *Post-capitalist entrepreneurship: Startups for the 99%.* Productivity Press.

Crandall, E. K., Brown, R. H., & McMahon, J. (2021). Magicians of the twenty-first century: Enchantment, domination, and the politics of work in Silicon Valley. *Theory & Event, 24*(3), 841–873. https://doi.org/10.1353/tae.2021.0045

Daub, A. (2020). *What tech calls thinking: An inquiry into the intellectual bedrock of Silicon Valley.* Farrar, Straus and Giroux.

Deignan, A. (2003). Metaphorical expressions and culture: An indirect link. *Metaphor and Symbol, 18*(4), 255–271. https://doi.org/10.1207/S15327868MS1804_3

Drover, W., Busenitz, L., Matusik, S., Townsend, D., Anglin, A., & Dushnitsky, G. (2017). A review and road map of entrepreneurial equity financing research: Venture capital, corporate venture capital, angel investment, crowdfunding, and accelerators. *Journal of Management, 43*(6), 1820–1853. https://doi.org/10.1177/0149206317690584

Enterprise Research Centre. (2015). *Nation of angels: The unsung heroes of Britain's economy.* Centre for Entrepreneurs & UK Business Angels Association. https://www.centreforentrepreneurs.org/research/report/nation-angels/r/recOv39kDh6eOnBN8

Epstein, G. (2024). *Tech agnostic: How technology became the world's most powerful religion, and why it desperately needs a reformation.* MIT Press.

Fisher, M. (2012). *Capitalist realism: Is there no alternative?* (1st ed.). Zero Books.

Founders Factory. (2023, April 18). *Angel investors: An honest guide to finding & working with individual investors.* https://foundersfactory.com/articles/angel-investing/

Frank, C., Sink, C., Mynatt, L., Rogers, R., & Rappazzo, A. (1996). Surviving the "valley of death": A comparative analysis. *The Journal of Technology Transfer, 21*(1–2), 61–69. https://doi.org/10.1007/BF02220308

Freear, J., Sohl, J. E., & Wetzel, W. E., Jr. (1994). Angels and non-angels: Are there differences? *Journal of Business Venturing, 9*(2), 109–123. https://doi.org/10.1016/0883-9026(94)90004-3

Geiger, S. (2020). Silicon Valley, disruption, and the end of uncertainty. *Journal of Cultural Economy, 13*(2), 169–184. https://doi.org/10.1080/17530350.2019.1684337

Giridharadas, A. (2018). *Winners take all: The elite charade of changing the world*. Knopf.

Graham, P. (2009, March). *How to be an angel investor*. https://www.paulgraham.com/angelinvesting.html

Gunderson, R. (2020). *Making the familiar strange: Sociology contra reification*. Routledge.

Hagstrom, R. G. (2024). *The Warren Buffett way* (30th anniversary ed.). John Wiley & Sons.

Hicks, T. (2024a, May 22). Dragon slayer: How to get funded faster with less time-wasting and pain. *Angel Investment Network Blog*. https://www.angelinvestmentnetwork.net/dragon-slayer-how-to-get-funded-faster-and-with-less-pain/

Hicks, T. (2024b, May 23). The motivations of angel investors: Insights and advice for startups. *Angel Investment Network Blog*. https://www.angelinvestmentnetwork.net/the-motivations-of-angel-investors-insights-and-advice-for-startups/

Hornstein, O. (2024, March 4). Chancellor to reverse 'short-sighted' angel investor policy. *UKTN*. https://www.uktech.news/news/government-and-policy/chancellor-reverse-angel-investor-policy-20240304

Irzık, G. (2007). Commercialization of science in a neoliberal world. In A. Buğra & K. Ağartan (Eds.), *Reading Karl Polanyi for the twenty-first century: Market economy as a political project* (pp. 135–153). Palgrave Macmillan US.

Joas, H. (2021). *The power of the sacred: An alternative to the narrative of disenchantment* (A. Skinner, Trans.). Oxford University Press.

Kimmel, M. (2004). Metaphor variation in cultural context: Perspectives from anthropology. *European Journal of English Studies, 8*(3), 275–294. https://doi.org/10.1080/1382557042000277395

Koller, V. (2009). Missions and empires: Religious and political metaphors in corporate discourse. In A. Musolff & J. Zinken (Eds.), *Metaphor and discourse* (pp. 116–134). Palgrave Macmillan UK.

Kundzina, K. (n.d.). *How to prepare a pitch for angel investors*. The Pitch. https://thepitch.uk/funding/prepare-pitch-angel-investors/

Lefebvre, V., Certhoux, G., & Radu-Lefebvre, M. (2022). Sustaining trust to cross the valley of death: A retrospective study of business angels' investment and reinvestment decisions. *Technovation, 109*. https://doi.org/10.1016/j.technovation.2020.102159

Lennox, S. (2023). *Angel investment: How to attract an angel investor explained*. Startups. https://startups.co.uk/funding/investors/angel-investment-explained/

Livermore, S. (2020). *Average Joe: Be the Silicon Valley tech genius*. Wiley.

MacLeod, C. (2010). *Heroes of invention*. Cambridge Books.

Malešević, S. (2022). Disenchantment, rationalisation and collective self-sacralisation [Review of the book *The power of the sacred: An alternative to the narrative of disenchantment*, by H. Joas]. *Journal of Political Power, 15*(2), 369–379. https://doi.org/10.1080/2158379X.2022.2055281

Martell, L. (2023). *Alternative societies: For a pluralist socialism*. Bristol University Press.

Mirowski, P. (2011). *Science-mart: Privatizing American science*. Harvard University Press.

Mirowski, P. (2012). The modern commercialization of science is a passel of Ponzi Schemes. *Social Epistemology, 26*(3–4), 285–310. https://doi.org/10.1080/02691728.2012.697210

Monticelli, L. (Ed.). (2022). *The future is now: An introduction to prefigurative politics*. Bristol University Press.

Narayan, K. (2024, September). Over the last decade, I saw angel investors in British tech repeatedly back innovators when there was little consensus or [Image attached] [Post]. LinkedIn. https://www.linkedin.com/posts/kanishka-narayan_over-the-last-decade-i-saw-angel-investors-activity-7243299876350963712-YSdr

Noble, S. U., & Roberts, S. T. (2019). Technological elites, the meritocracy, and postracial myths in Silicon Valley. In R. Mukherjee, S. Banet-Weiser, & H. Gray (Eds.), *Racism postrace* (pp. 113–130). Duke University Press.

Nowshin, S. (2023, April 21). *Angel investing 101: Everything you need to know*. Sifted. https://sifted.eu/articles/angel-investing-101

Pallister, K. A. C. (2001). *Entertaining angels unawares: The social construction of angelic imagery in millennium era culture*. [Doctoral dissertation, University of Alberta]. University of Alberta Libraries. https://doi.org/10.7939/r3-h9y3-2b74

Parker, M., Cheney, G., Fournier, V., & Land, C. (Eds.). (2013). *The Routledge companion to alternative organization*. Routledge.

Schiller-Merkens, S. (2024). Prefiguring an alternative economy: Understanding prefigurative organizing and its struggles. *Organization, 31*(3), 458–476. https://doi.org/10.1177/13505084221124189

Schwarzkopf, S. (2020). *The Routledge handbook of economic theology*. Routledge.

Singler, B. (2024). *Religion and artificial intelligence: An introduction*. Routledge.

Spector, B. A. (2016). Carlyle, Freud, and the Great Man Theory more fully considered. *Leadership, 12*(2), 250–260. https://doi.org/10.1177/1742715015571392

Storm, J. A. J. (2017). *The myth of disenchantment: Magic, modernity, and the birth of the human sciences*. University of Chicago Press.
Sullivan, M. K., & Miller, A. (1996). Segmenting the informal venture capital market: Economic, hedonistic, and altruistic investors. *Journal of Business Research, 36*(1), 25–35.
Taylor, C. (2007). *A secular age*. Harvard University Press.
Taylor, K. P. (2019). Angel investor-entrepreneur fit: The nexus of angel motivation and entrepreneur personality and passion. In A. Caputo & M. M. Pellegrini (Eds.), *The anatomy of entrepreneurial decisions: Past, present and future research directions* (pp. 197–210). Springer International Publishing.
Wetzel, W. E., Jr. (1983). *Angels and informal risk capital*. University of Illinois at Urbana-Champaign's Academy for Entrepreneurial Leadership Historical Research Reference in Entrepreneurship. https://ssrn.com/abstract=1505193
Wetzel, W. E., Jr. (1987). The informal venture capital market: Aspects of scale and market efficiency. *Journal of Business Venturing, 2*(4), 299–313. https://doi.org/10.1016/0883-9026(87)90023-1
Zanoni, P., Contu, A., Healy, S., & Mir, R. (2017). Post-capitalistic politics in the making: The imaginary and praxis of alternative economies. *Organization, 24*(5), 575–588. https://doi.org/10.1177/1350508417713219

PART V

~~Socialising~~

CHAPTER 14

Antiagora*

~~Facebook~~

Brooks DeCillia and Gabriela Perdomo

1 Introduction

In the summer of 2023, with unrelenting forest fires ravaging Canada's northern boreal forest, Delaney Poitras' already scary evacuation from her home in Fort Smith became even more harrowing when she could no longer turn to Facebook for reliable news and information. "There was no information being posted", the Northwest Territories resident told CBC News about the social media platform, adding, "We were basically left in the dark" (Heydari et al., 2023, para. 2). Meta Platforms, which owns Facebook, Instagram, and Threads, implemented a Canada-wide ban on all news content in the summer of 2023 in response to government attempts to make it pay for news reposted on its platforms. Accustomed to seeing and hearing live streams of official news conferences and evacuation updates on Facebook, Poitras said Meta's decision worsened her difficult situation (Evans, 2023).

B. DeCillia (✉) • G. Perdomo
School of Communication Studies, Mount Royal University,
Calgary, AB, Canada
e-mail: bdecillia@mtroyal.ca; gperdomo@mtroyal.ca

C. Chokshi, R. Mansell (eds.), *The Need to Rename Tech*,
https://doi.org/10.1007/978-3-032-05155-4_14

For Poitras and many northern—mostly Indigenous—people, Facebook has, until recently, played a crucial role in connecting communities with news and information during emergencies such as mandatory fire evacuations. "It's how we all keep in touch", stressed Poitras (Evans, 2023, para. 8). As crisis communication research has shown, people turn to social media during emergencies for insider information and to check in with family and friends. At the same time, they use traditional media more for educational purposes (Austin et al., 2012). Increasingly, however, people have become used to accessing those more traditional media channels through social media. In the Northwest Territories, the local news organisation Cabin Radio issued a communication about Meta's news blocks in July 2023: "We're annoyed, because here we are in the middle of a severe wildfire season, with a bunch of evacuations, and your ability to access our reporting is about to be restricted. It makes no sense and, frankly, it's dangerous" (Williams, 2023, para. 6). A month later, Canadian Prime Minister Justin Trudeau echoed that denunciation of Meta's news ban, accusing the platform of putting "profit ahead of people's safety" (Yousif, 2023b, para. 1). After a decade of disseminating news in Canada, Meta's decision to ban access to journalistic content marked the end of an era. It no longer fulfilled founder Mark Zuckerberg's vision of a personalised newspaper (Sengupta, 2013) or the "digital equivalent of a town square" (Zuckerberg, 2019, para. 1). As these analogies suggest, Facebook had long been touted as a globalised, virtual version of the agoras of ancient Greece (Frier, 2019).

Like the other contributors to this volume and many critical media scholars, we support the notion of proposing new language to describe and explain different technologies. New names might better capture their promises, limitations, and, importantly, harms. Our chapter seeks to map the trajectory of Facebook's town square metaphor and its successor, the private living room, to illustrate what they illuminate and obscure. In doing so, we want to reframe Facebook for what it *is* and what it *does*. To do this, we use events that unfolded in the summer of 2023 in Canada as a case study. We argue that Facebook's ban on news content was part of an existing trend at Meta towards decoupling from news—not just in Canada but globally—and that this has resulted in Meta's use of the 'living room' metaphor for Facebook in recent years. We contend that Facebook's metaphorical disguises have always obscured what Jaron Lanier (2006) conceptualises as the 'antigora'—or what we designate as the *antiagora*—the opposite of the ancient Greek agora.

In a foreboding essay from the first decade of this century, Lanier describes the fragmentation of the World Wide Web into siloed corners, or 'antigoras', explained as "privately owned digital meeting arena[s] made rich by unpaid or marginally paid labour provided by people who crowd its periphery" (Lanier, 2006, para. 20). Echoing Lanier, we contend that Facebook's town square metaphor, which we call the Facebook agora, has always been ill-suited to describe the social media platform. Indeed, we argue that even though, at times, the pretence of the vibrant agora seemed to manifest in the platform, with news, information, and personal tales flowing freely, Facebook never entirely recreated a single, shared square where the global citizenry could gather. There were always fragmented spaces, unequally calibrated voices, hidden hierarchies, and ulterior motives lurking in the platform's corners, sustained by algorithms, imbalances in internet access, language barriers, and vested interests. We are not alone in arguing that Facebook has failed to fulfil the promise of its town square metaphor (Lanier, 2006, 2017). Shoshana Zuboff, author of *The Age of Surveillance Capitalism* (2019), aptly describes Facebook as an agent of surveillance capitalism, information asymmetry, manipulation, and anti-democratic impulses. In short, its nature is more acutely encapsulated by Lanier's 'antigora'. Moreover, as Meta increasingly distances itself from news dissemination, we insist that Facebook's attempt to reimagine itself as a 'private living room' (Zuckerberg, 2019) remains an inadequate metaphor for the social media platform and its true effect on our social order and democratic life. First, however, we foreground our argument by discussing how we frame it theoretically.

2 Some Brief Notes on Theory

Surrounded by the Acropolis to the northwest, the hill of the Areopagus to the south, and Market Hill to the west, the agora of ancient Athens thrived as a public and discursive space. First appearing in the work of Homer, the agora—Greek for 'open place of assembly'—became the heart of the religious, judicial, social, and commercial operations of ancient Greece. As classical Greek society flourished, so did the agora, with almost every Greek city having a similar public space by 600 BCE. The agoras offered a focal point for free-born citizens to gather, trade, debate, and assemble for military campaigns. Great minds like Hippocrates, Socrates, Plato, and Aristotle proposed revolutionary ideas to students and citizens in the Athenian town square. Consequently, the agora of Athens, as the cynosure of ancient Greece's culture of philosophical and political debate that inspired the Roman Forum, is considered the birthplace of democracy and Western thought.

In 2019, Mark Zuckerberg declared that Facebook had become "the digital equivalent of a town square", akin to classical Greece's agora (para. 1). Zuckerberg's words carried significant weight for two reasons. First, the Facebook founder—with a net worth of billions of dollars—controls the company Meta with what one whistleblower has called an "iron grip" (Cunliffe, 2023, para. 14). Second, Facebook is not merely a tool for digital communication. It has indeed been a gathering space for multiple voices, where everyone could speak and be heard. As such, Zuckerberg's town square metaphor was shrewd: it powerfully romanticised and aggrandised the role of a website he initially created for male Harvard University students to rate the attractiveness of their female peers. In calling Facebook an agora, Zuckerberg invoked the ideals of ancient Greek democracy as well as the more contemporary connotations of the town square, which also represents, in Western thought, an extended symbolic space for public life and civic debate. Abraham Lincoln and Stephen Douglas famously elevated themselves on stumps in packed town squares and fairgrounds across the prairies of Illinois in the fall of 1858 to debate slavery for hours. A century later, in the shadow of the Lincoln Memorial in Washington, D.C., Martin Luther King Jr. famously proclaimed 'I have a dream' to the quarter million people assembled on the Mall. The significance of the public square in major historical events cannot be understated. From Tahir Square in Cairo and the Plaza de Tlatelolco in Mexico City to Beijing's Tiananmen Square and London's Trafalgar Square, the public square has long functioned as the focal point of dissent and protest, emblematic of individual liberty and a collective desire for freedom (Rosier, 2020).

Echoing the idea of the ancient agora, Jürgen Habermas (1962/1989, p. 176) imagined what he called "the deliberative public sphere", made up of "private people gathered together as a public and articulating the needs of society with the state". As a foundational theory in communication and media studies, the public sphere conceptualises how collective discussion creates public opinion, which, in turn, informs policy debates and "legitimate[s] authority in any functioning democracy" (Rutherford, 2000, p. 274). Despite receiving criticism, this description of the public sphere has reverberated throughout Western thought, and it underpins Zuckerberg's metaphor of Facebook as the modern era's digital public forum.

Originally called the *öffentlichkeit* by Habermas, the public sphere is imagined as an unrestricted realm of social life where it is possible to 'form' public opinion. The shared space includes individuals who, together, become a public capable of articulating the needs of society to the state (Habermas, 1962/1989). For communications and media scholars, the public sphere remains influential for its theorisation of an ideal form of speech, understood as the "unifying, consensus-building force of a discourse in which the participants overcome their at first subjectively based views in favour of a rationally motivated agreement" (Habermas, 1990, p. 315).

The Habermasian public sphere has been criticised for being atheoretical (Calhoun, 1992), ahistorical (Curran, 1991; Downie, 2004), impossible in an agonistic political system (Mouffe, 1999), quaint in a modern globalised age (Volkmer, 2014), and devoid of an understanding of historical and structural inequality (Fraser, 1990), for instance, by privileging "white vantage points" that neglect slavery and the "racial violence required to make this space possible" (Willems, 2023, p. 21). Nevertheless, Habermas' public sphere remains a North Star of sorts for those who envisage 'communicative power' as "transform[ing] political into 'rational' authority within the medium of this public sphere" (Habermas, 1964/1974, p. 53). It also continues to inform media and communication scholarship on the importance of public broadcasting and the news media. However flawed, Habermas' public sphere concept remains prominent in our understanding of the cultural and democratic importance of public spaces for discourse, contestation, meaning-making, and democratic legitimacy.

In his most recent reconsideration of the concept, Habermas (2023) evaluates the implications of the increasing digitisation of our public sphere for deliberative democratic politics. In his 2023 essay, he highlights how social media's empowering promise has yet to come to fruition, undermined as it is by platform algorithms that help create information bubbles and discursive echo chambers. Habermas contends that a public sphere shaped substantially by social media sabotages deliberative politics and democracy, and warns that social media has sidelined traditional media, eliminating the important informational role played by journalists in rational public discourse. As the coming pages argue, this concern became materially manifest as fires raged in northern Canada in the summer of 2023—the same summer Facebook turned off the news.

3 A Summer of Wildfires and News Blackouts

At the airport in the Northwest Territories' capital of Yellowknife, the lines grew excruciatingly long in late August 2023. Anxious residents and startled tourists were ordered to evacuate immediately as an out-of-control wildfire threatened to reach the town's boundaries within days. Close to 70 per cent of the Arctic city's 20,000 residents boarded planes and cars filled with their belongings to escape the moving inferno. The emergency was just one of dozens that marked a grim season of record-breaking wildfires in Canada. In total, 200,000 people in areas from British Columbia in the west to Nova Scotia and Quebec in the east would flee their homes to escape the rapidly moving fires.

This unabating fire season coincided with a seemingly unrelated event: that summer, Canada's federal government had introduced the Online News Act, or Bill C-18, which aimed to force digital technology companies such as Google and Meta to pay media outlets for news content that was posted, shared, or repurposed on their platforms. In response, Meta and Google announced their plans to block all access to Canadian news (Yousif, 2023b). While Google implemented the threat only partially, blocking selected news content and only in some areas, Meta's response was absolute. A company statement from 1 June read, "We intend to end the availability of news content in Canada permanently following the passage of *Bill C-18*" (Meta, 2023, para. 21). The ban was swiftly implemented, effectively blocking all Canadian and international news content on Facebook and Instagram, the company's two most popular social media platforms. No publication escaped the blanket ban; even student publications and satirical blogs were blocked. Meanwhile, more than 5000 fires raged in northern Canada, and thousands of people from remote communities faced evacuation alerts, sometimes on short notice and with conflicting information from different levels of government. Amidst the simultaneous crises, the lack of access to reliable information on Facebook and Instagram, where most people were used to accessing their news, sowed chaos and confusion as families and communities missed vital updates, including callouts for help, evacuation notices, and reports on local government actions. The federal government called the news blocks 'reckless' (Ljunggren, 2023) and 'inconceivable' (Tunney, 2023). For smaller, local news organisations that had built strong community connections through Facebook, watching their vital ties with their audiences wholly rupture was devastating as the lack of exposure for these organisations threatened to render them invisible. Indeed, an organisation monitoring access to news on Facebook determined that Meta's news ban triggered a 90 per cent drop in engagement with Canadian news outlets on the social media platform (Yousif, 2023a). As the fires burned, so did a question: was this the end of the Facebook agora?

4 Deconstructing Facebook's Town Square Metaphor

To answer this question, we return to ancient Greece's agora and to questions about inclusivity and supposedly enlivened debates. It is tempting to imagine the agora, as so many have, as a dynamic space where a cacophony of voices participate freely and actively in consequential democratic conversation. But the Greek agora was also a place of exclusion. Slaves were prohibited from discussing the concept of democracy at the agora, as were women. Even in Habermas's recounting of the emergence of the bourgeois public sphere in the eighteenth century, which arose in the coffee houses of Germany and Great Britain to challenge the *ancien régime*'s traditional spaces of deliberation of the court and government, women, lower-class men, and racialised people were excluded from this deliberative discourse. A constant critique of this theory legitimately stresses that Habermas' liberal concept of the public sphere ignores structural inequalities.

Zuckerberg, however, invoked the imagery of an idyllic agora to tout the significance of the Facebook feed. In hindsight, the metaphor was more telling than it initially appeared. Zuckerberg used it to sell his social media company as a place where citizens would gather to share information, learn from each other, debate, and deliberate, all in one space (Gartenberg, 2019). But the metaphor inevitably contained the same issues that the Greek agora and Habermas's public square did: Facebook's town square was also a locus of power imbalances and information asymmetry (Zuboff, 2019), where some voices travelled further than others, and not all citizens found themselves in the same space.

The company and Zuckerberg had material reasons to perpetuate the myth of a town square. The physical town square—usually surrounded by churches and cathedrals—symbolises the cynosure of free speech in liberal democracies. Suppressing free speech in these spaces sparks cries of censorship. By suggesting that Facebook was the digital equivalent of a town square, Zuckerberg could argue that the social media company deserved the same free speech protections as individuals in the town square and "shouldn't be the arbiter of truth of everything that people say online" (McCarthy, 2020, para. 3). It was a convenient argument to skirt responsibility. Despite the company's complex apparatus of content moderation, free speech protection absolved Meta from responsible communications practices, unlike news organisations with their ethical obligations to fairness and the truth (Napoli & Caplan, 2016). As the global COVID-19 pandemic has shown us, however, this logic has consequences. For instance, a study in the United Kingdom concluded that unregulated social media platforms such as Facebook were super spreaders of conspiracy theories about the virus, representing a real health risk (Allington et al., 2021). Both the pandemic and the wildfires in Canada made it plain that Meta's profit motive dictates its actions, and the company demonstrates little obligation to adhere to normative ideals that animate public spheres and their dedication to protecting the larger society from harm. We "must no longer treat Facebook", argues the artist Matthew Rosier (2020), "as a town square—a public space, but must instead recognize it for what it is—a company, which must be regulated to protect us from harm" (para. 15).

5 Before the News Bans

Meta's founder has hailed its platform's ability to disseminate news and information, promoting news produced by journalists for much of the last decade. The social media platform might not have intended to become a news-sharing hub from its inception; still, the 2010s marked an era of engagement with news organisations as the company realised that Facebook users organically turned to the platform for sharing news content (Darcy, 2023). During that time, Facebook boasted about propping up news organisations whose business models were crumbling (Levy, 2020). In 2013, Zuckerberg launched a fresh redesign of Facebook's main feed and hailed it as 'the best personalized newspaper' (Sengupta, 2013). Let us call this the heyday of the Facebook agora.

Legacy media organisations were happy to partake in the digital town square, hoping that reaching audiences there would increase traffic to their news sites. Meanwhile, independent news outlets emerged worldwide and found in Facebook an invaluable partner, one that helped them find, connect with, and grow loyal audiences. For journalists, Facebook's ostensible agora was *'the place to be'* (Ortutay, 2023). The platform offered a natural space for interactive, connected, and publicly engaged journalism

(Beckett, 2016). It was a lively digital space where people and communities could learn from and about each other. In the Western construction of journalism, however, sharing news content comes with great responsibility, and this was something Facebook was never willing to take on.

Lofty initiatives to support the news always coexisted awkwardly with Facebook's role in decimating advertising revenues for news publications, which only increased as people grew accustomed to scrolling for headlines on the platform and as traffic to news sites stalled. There was also the question of Meta's poor record of handling misinformation and disinformation, which was made especially visible after the 2016 American presidential election with the Cambridge Analytica scandal (Cadwalladr & Graham-Harrison, 2018). The revelation that political operatives had gained access to the private information of millions of Facebook users and then targeted them with a deluge of misinformation to sway their votes, all without their knowledge, showed the company's cynical weaponisation of the supposedly benign space of free and virtual gathering. It became evident, in brief, that the global town square was stealing its visitors' information for political and economic gain.

While Meta's news ban in Canada is reckless, it should not be surprising. In 2021, Meta faced a maelstrom of criticism when whistleblower Frances Haugen, a former Facebook data scientist, alleged that the social media platform was also fomenting genocide, failing to stop the spread of misinformation, and exposing teenage girls to a deluge of body-shaming content (Pelley, 2021). These revelations ruptured Facebook's metaphorical veil, reminding many that Meta is ultimately beholden to economic shareholders, not civic stakeholders. The company is sensitive to this criticism. In 2021, the social media company changed its corporate name from Facebook to Meta—Greek for 'beyond'—as part of a major rebrand in the wake of a rash of critical news stories based on internal leaked documents suggesting that it put profits over safety (Thomas, 2021). For a while at least, Meta tried to curb the spread of mis- and disinformation and hate speech on Facebook and Instagram. Yet, weeks before Donald Trump returned to the White House, the social media giant announced a major u-turn on fact-checking, scrapping independent scrutiny for so-called 'community notes', similar to Elon Musk's X platform. Critics condemned the move, calling it a "blatant attempt to cozy up to the incoming Trump administration—with harmful implications" (Booth, 2025, para. 12).

To be sure, Facebook's back end was never structurally built to become a town square. Facebook's billions of users have, in fact, never inhabited a common digital space. There is no shared point of contact where all voices co-exist because each user's algorithmically generated Facebook feed responds to their desires and, most importantly, their fears. This means no one in the supposed shared town square sees the same thing. As Zeynep Tufekci (2015, para. 5) has pointed out, Meta's own research confirmed that its systems help form information echo chambers, even as the company insisted that the newsfeed algorithm it controls is "some sort of independent force of nature or something that is merely responsive to you, without any other value embedded in its design". For years now, national governments and organisations have pointed out that Meta should be held responsible for its role in destroying newsrooms (by draining them of revenue and reaping profits from the sharing of news content it does not directly produce) and for muddying the news waters by allowing corrupt information to run freely (Constine, 2018). By 2018, the company faced controversy about whether it should be considered a 'publisher' rather than a platform (Levin, 2018). This move would have had significant implications, such as making the company's obligations to the truth more explicit. Facebook wanted none of it.

Indeed, in the face of efforts by several countries and jurisdictions such as Canada, Australia, and the European Union to introduce stricter regulations for technology giants to increase their accountability for disseminating information, Meta has hinted at wanting to break up with journalism altogether (Tinworth, 2022). The Canadian government's introduction of the Online News Act in 2023 only accelerated this. A significant move towards this decoupling from news was set in motion in 2019, when Zuckerberg said he was changing Facebook's signature newsfeed to work not as an open and public place of gathering—that is, no longer as an agora—but as a small and private sphere akin to a living room (Zuckerberg, 2019).

6 A Second Failed Metaphor

The thousands of people who fled their homes along highways of burning grasslands in northern Canada in 2023 learned in that terrifying moment what has now become crystal clear: Facebook's town square metaphor has run its course. So, what is left?

In 2018, the overhaul of the Facebook newsfeed sought to prioritise the circulation of personal posts, photos, and videos shared by individual users while limiting content from publishers. It was a first attempt at decoupling the platform from news content—and all the responsibilities that came with it. This distancing from the news is not particular to Meta alone. As an *Economist* editorial from 2024 noted, "the striking feature of the new social media is that they are no longer very social" (para. 1). The article calculated that only about three per cent of a typical Facebook newsfeed consists of actual news content.

In 2019, Zuckerberg explained that the Facebook newsfeed would provide a user experience more centred around the 'privacy' of intimate spaces, 'like a living room':

> People increasingly also want to connect privately in the digital equivalent of the living room. As I think about the future of the internet, I believe a privacy-focused communications platform will become even more important than today's open platforms. Privacy gives people the freedom to be themselves and connect more naturally, which is why we build social networks. (Zuckerberg, 2019, para. 2)

Zuckerberg's sweeping changes to Facebook shifted the platform from an expansive, public town square into a closed-in space where users communicate with smaller groups, and their content vanishes after short periods. The social media company positioned this as a reimagining of a communicative space and as a transition from broadcasting updates, photos, and videos to sharing with trusted groups in a private living room (Dwoskin, 2019).

Ari Ezra Waldman (2019, para. 4) challenges Zuckerberg's privacy argument as a self-serving "narrow definition of the concept [which works to] to distract us from the ways Facebook will likely continue to expand its invasion of our digital private lives for profit". For many critical scholars, it is no surprise that capitalist tools are used to perpetuate dominant capitalist norms and dictate the information produced (Bell, 1973). Manuel Castells (2009, p. 4) stresses that the communication process "decisively mediates how power relationships are constructed and challenged in every domain of social practice, including political practice".

As the town square metaphor did earlier, the living room metaphor obscures what Meta is—a private company beholden to its shareholders—and what it does: extracts its users' information for profit. Beyond this critical fact, what the company does also matters in terms of what turning its back on journalism does for civic life more broadly. In his critique of digital and social media, Habermas (2023, p. 44) raises concerns about the platformisation of political communication, arguing that these new forms of media diminish the "productive role of journalistic mediation and program design performed by the old media". Social media companies such as Meta, argues Habermas, diminish the gatekeeping function of journalists, making it easier to share low-quality information, including misinformation and disinformation, quickly and widely. Most troubling for Habermas, however, is how social media has diminished the quality of public deliberation because the platforms obscure "the distinction between 'public' and 'private,' and thus the inclusive meaning of the public sphere" (Habermas, 2023, p. 61), begging the question of whether there is a need for regulation to reclaim the public's autonomy in our deliberative democracy. The fact that Meta equated its digital space with a private living room, attempting to separate 'news content' from 'personal communications', contains some curious and powerful contradictions. In Zuckerberg's words, the allegedly more private Facebook prioritises the discovery of "new people, ideas and content, and giving people a voice" (2019, para. 4). Arguably, this is precisely what journalism does. Moreover, the pretence that living rooms are neutral, private, or inconsequential spaces runs counter to the truth. A living room can also be a powerful and political space, even a public sphere, as Philippe Gonzalez (2015) so keenly observed.

7 Conclusion

In strictly metaphorical terms, the seemingly benign concept of the living room starkly contrasts with the heyday of the Facebook-agora metaphor. In reality, both the agora and the living room belie the fact that Facebook has always functioned much more like Lanier's (2017, pp. 34–35) 'antigora':

> An antigora feels like an agora but is actually more like what Skinner would do with a panopticon. An antigora is usually controlled by a corporation in California or China. Those who enter are addressed as if they are conquering liberators. "Here is your zone of free speech. Share!" What actually happens is that those in the antigora are observed so well that information asymmetry arises. Those who stroll the antigora submit to surveillance, scrutiny, and manipulation; more lab rats than freedom fighters.

Behind the veil of these two metaphors lies the fact that Meta has always wanted the communicative and communal power of journalism, but with none of the responsibility that this carries. It wanted everyone but itself to do the work of weeding out corrupt and false information from the pool of legitimate news; it wanted all the content—and the eyeballs and the treasure trove of personal data that came with it—but refused to pay for the labour that went into producing it. Its relationship with journalism was never symbiotic, and it was never genuinely interested in pursuing democratic ideals. The relationship was always only parasitic, focused exclusively on what was financially beneficial for itself and its shareholders.

In its early days, Facebook's motto—'move fast and break things'—encapsulated its high-risk, high-reward ethos. *The Economist's* editorial (2024) argued that Meta's disruptive spirit persists as the company turned 20, remaining a magnet for criticism, including perpetual concerns about compromising users' privacy, spreading disinformation, undermining democracy, and failing to protect children from exploitation and abuse. Surely, it is time to reframe Facebook for what it *is* and what it *does*. Sally Wyatt (2021, para. 1) earlier made this argument: "I make a plea for critical scholars of the Internet and digital media to be simultaneously careful and imaginative in their own choice of metaphorical language". Like Wyatt, we urge scholars and the wider public to reject Meta's dubious suggested symbolism, for Meta's troubling metaphors—the town square as much as the living room—obscure the reality of its extractive mechanisms. Facebook is surely best characterised as an *antiagora*. Delaney Poitras knows that all too well. As she and thousands of others in Canada's north scrambled to flee the fires closing in on their communities, the life-saving information they needed was nowhere to be found. There was no town square or friendly living room to turn to.

References

Allington, D., Duffy, B., Wessely, S., Dhavan, N., & Rubin, J. (2021). Health-protective behaviour, social media usage and conspiracy belief during the COVID-19 public health emergency. *Psychological Medicine, 51*(10), 1763–1769. https://doi.org/10.1017/S003329172000224X

Austin, L., Liu, B. F., & Jin, Y. (2012). How audiences seek out crisis information: Exploring the social-mediated crisis communication model. *Journal of Applied Communication Research, 40*(2), 188–207. https://doi.org/10.1080/00909882.2012.654498

Beckett, C. (2016, October 13). Some examples of networked journalism. *Medium*. https://charliebeckett.medium.com/some-examples-of-networked-journalism-38d521ba221f

Bell, D. (1973). *The coming of post-industrial society: A venture in social forecasting*. Basic Books.

Booth, R. (2025, January 7). Ditching of Facebook factcheckers a 'major step back' for public discourse, critics say. *The Guardian.*. https://www.theguardian.com/technology/2025/jan/07/ditching-facebook-factcheckers-major-step-back-public-discourse

Cadwalladr, C., & Graham-Harrison, E. (2018, March 17). Revealed: 50 million Facebook profiles harvested for Cambridge Analytica in major data breach. *The Guardian.* https://www.theguardian.com/news/2018/mar/17/cambridge-analytica-facebook-influence-us-election

Calhoun, C. (1992). Introduction: Habermas and the public sphere. In C. Calhoun (Ed.), *Habermas and the public sphere* (pp. 1–48). MIT Press. https://calhoun.faculty.asu.edu/sites/default/files/publications/articles/habermas_and_the_public_sphere.pdf

Castells, M. (2009). *Communication power.* Oxford University Press.

Constine, J. (2018, February 3). How Facebook stole the news business. *Tech Crunch.* https://techcrunch.com/2018/02/03/facebooks-siren-call/

Cunliffe, R. (2023, July 1). Facebook whistleblower Frances Haugen: "I wouldn't wish Mark Zuckerberg's life on anyone". *The New Statesman.* https://www.newstatesman.com/the-weekend-interview/2023/07/facebook-whistleblower-frances-haugen-mark-zuckerberg-social-media

Curran, J. (1991). Rethinking the media as a public sphere. In P. Dahlgren & C. Sparks (Eds.), *Communication and citizenship: Journalism and the public sphere in the new media age* (pp. 27–57). Routledge.

Darcy, O. (2023, August 17). Publishers see dramatic drop in Facebook referral traffic as the social platform signals exit from news business. *CNN.*. https://www.cnn.com/2023/08/17/media/facebook-referral-traffic-reliable-sources/index.html

Downie, J. A. (2004). How useful to eighteenth-century English studies is the paradigm of the 'bourgeois public sphere'? *Literature Compass, 1*(1), 1–18. https://doi.org/10.1111/j.1741-4113.2004.00022.x

Dwoskin, E. (2019, March 6). From town square to living room: Zuckerberg announces sweeping changes to Facebook in new focus on privacy. *Financial Post.*. https://financialpost.com/technology/personal-tech/mark-zuckerberg-announces-sweeping-changes-to-facebook-in-new-focus-on-privacy-encryption

Evans, P. (2023, August 18). N.W.T. wildfire evacuees say Facebook's news ban 'dangerous' in emergency situation. *CBC News.* https://www.cbc.ca/news/business/nwt-wildfire-evacuation-meta-blocking-news-1.6939286

Fraser, N. (1990). Rethinking the public sphere: A contribution to the critique of actually existing democracy. *Social Text, 25*(*26*), 56–80.

Frier, S. (2019, March 7). Rebuild: Your Facebook is about to get more private, promises Zuckerberg. *The Sydney Morning Herald.* https://www.smh.com.au/business/companies/a-more-private-facebook-is-coming-promises-zuckerberg-20190307-p512ak.html

Gartenberg, C. (2019, March 8). What is Facebook? Just ask Mark Zuckerberg. *The Verge*. https://www.theverge.com/2019/3/8/18255269/facebook-mark-zuckerberg-definition-social-media-network-sharing-privacy

Gonzalez, P. (2015, May 19). My living room as a public sphere. An Iranian experiment. *Public Seminar*. https://publicseminar.org/2015/05/my-living-room-as-a-public-sphere/

Habermas, J. (1974). The public sphere: An encyclopedia article. (S. Lennox & F. Lennox, Trans.). *New German Critique*, *3*, 49–55. https://doi.org/10.2307/487737 (Original work published 1964)

Habermas, J. (1989). *The structural transformation of the public sphere: An inquiry into a category of bourgeois society* (T. Burger & F. Lawrence, Trans.). Polity. (Original work published 1962)

Habermas, J. (1990). *Moral consciousness and communicative action* (C. Lenhardt & S. Weber, Trans.). MIT Press.

Habermas, J. (2023). *A new structural transformation of the public sphere and deliberative politics* (C. Cronin, Trans.). Polity.

Heydari, A., Wong, W., Ritchey, J., & Concannon, K. (2023, September 25). Is the Canada, Meta news standoff coming to the US? *NPR*. https://www.npr.org/2023/09/25/1197954327/the-indicator-from-planet-money-canada-vs-meta-fight

Lanier, J. (2006, January 8). The gory antigora: Illusions of capitalism and computers. *Cato Unbound: A Journal of Debate*. https://www.cato-unbound.org/2006/01/08/jaron-lanier/gory-antigora-illusions-capitalism-computers/

Lanier, J. (2017). Why is the city square square? In A. Gill (Ed.), *The future of public space* (pp. 33–42). Metropolis Books.

Levin, S. (2018, July 3). Is Facebook a publisher? In public it says no, but in court it says yes. *The Guardian*. https://www.theguardian.com/technology/2018/jul/02/facebook-mark-zuckerberg-platform-publisher-lawsuit

Levy, S. (2020, March 30). Facebook could help journalism by making news easier to find. *WIRED*. https://www.wired.com/story/facebook-journalism-local-news-coronavirus/

Ljunggren, D. (2023, August 18). Canada demands Meta lift news ban to allow wildfire info sharing. *Reuters*. https://www.reuters.com/technology/canada-demands-meta-lift-ban-news-allow-fires-info-be-shared-2023-08-18/

McCarthy, T. (2020, May 28). Zuckerberg says Facebook won't be 'arbiters of truth' after Trump threat. *The Guardian*. https://www.theguardian.com/technology/2020/may/28/zuckerberg-facebook-police-online-speech-trump

Meta. (2023, June 1). *Changes to news availability on our platforms in Canada*. Meta. https://about.fb.com/news/2023/06/changes-to-news-availability-on-our-platforms-in-canada

Mouffe, C. (1999). Deliberative democracy or agonistic pluralism. *Social Research, 66*(33), 745–758. https://www.jstor.org/stable/40971349

Napoli, P. M., & Caplan, R. (2016). *When media companies insist they're not media companies and why it matters for communications policy.* SSRN. https://doi.org/10.2139/ssrn.2750148

Ortutay, B. (2023, May 8). Facebook fights for relevance as Gen Z turns away: 'I don't even remember the last time I logged in.' *Fortune*. https://fortune.com/2023/05/08/facebook-fights-for-relevance-gen-z-turns-away-old-people-mark-zuckerberg/

Pelley, S. (2021, October 4). Whistleblower: Facebook is misleading the public on progress against hate speech, violence, misinformation. *CBS News—60 Minutes*. https://www.cbsnews.com/news/facebook-whistleblower-frances-haugen-misinformation-public-60-minutes-2021-10-03/

Rosier, M. (2020, July 27). Empty squares. *Medium*. https://mattrosier.medium.com/empty-squares-719059d6464d

Rutherford, P. (2000). *Endless propaganda: The advertising of public goods.* University of Toronto Press.

Sengupta, S. (2013, March 7). Facebook shows off new home page design, including bigger pictures. *The New York Times*. https://www.nytimes.com/2013/03/08/technology/facebook-shows-off-redesign.html

The Economist. (2024, February 1). The end of the social network. *The Economist*. https://www.economist.com/leaders/2024/02/01/the-end-of-the-social-network

Thomas, D. (2021, October 28). Facebook changes its name to Meta in major rebrand. *BBC News*. https://www.bbc.com/news/technology-59083601

Tinworth, A. (2022, May 21). Facebook's long, slow breakup with journalism is underway. *OneMan&HisBlog*. https://onemanandhisblog.com/2022/07/facebooks-long-slow-breakup-with-journalism-is-underway/

Tufekci, Z. (2015, May 11). Facebook said its algorithms do help form echo chambers. And the tech press missed it. *Noema*. https://www.noemamag.com/facebook-said-its-algorithms-do-help-form-echo-chambers-and-the-tech-press-missed-it/

Tunney, C. (2023, August 21). Trudeau denounces Meta's news block as fires force evacuations. *CBC News*. https://www.cbc.ca/news/politics/trudeau-meta-wildfires-news-1.6942458

Volkmer, I. (2014). *The global public sphere: Public communication in the age of reflective interdependence.* Polity.

Waldman, A. E. (2019, March 11). Facebook's so-called pivot to privacy is a diversion. *Slate*. https://slate.com/technology/2019/03/facebook-privacy-pivot-zuckerberg-messaging-whatsapp-instagram-merging.html

Willems, W. (2023). The reproduction of canonical silences: Re-reading Habermas in the context of slavery and the slave trade. *Communication, Culture and Critique, 16*(1), 17–24. https://doi.org/10.1093/ccc/tcac047

Williams, O. (2023, July 28). How to follow our reporting when Facebook and Instagram block us. *Cabin Radio.* https://cabinradio.ca/138262/cabin-radio/how-to-follow-our-reporting-when-facebook-and-instagram-block-us/

Wyatt, S. (2021). Metaphors in critical Internet and digital media studies. *New Media & Society, 23*(2), 406–416. https://doi.org/10.1177/1461444820929324

Yousif, N. (2023a, December 19). Met's news ban in Canada remains as Online News Act goes into effect. *BBC News.* https://www.bbc.com/news/world-us-canada-67755133

Yousif, N. (2023b, August 21). Canada wildfires: Trudeau criticizes Facebook over news ban amid crisis. *BBC News.* https://www.bbc.com/news/world-us-canada-66573512

Zuboff, S. (2019). *The age of surveillance capitalism: The fight for a human future at the new frontier of power.* Profile Books.

Zuckerberg, M. (2019, March 6). A privacy-focused vision for social networking. *The New York Times.* https://www.nytimes.com/2019/03/06/technology/facebook-privacy-blog.html

CHAPTER 15

Parts & Labours*

~~Momfluencers and Momification~~

Evangeline Holtz-Schramek

1 Introduction

I would wager you either follow momfluencers or disdain them—or perhaps both, because of how seemingly insignificant they appear. According to Sara Petersen, a 'momfluencer' is "someone who has monetized her maternal identity on social media" (as cited in North, 2023, para. 6), which may take a form as described by Kate Knibbs (2023, para 2):

> Like many other moms, I have a favorite "momfluencer." She's a sunny neonatal nurse with four kids, enviable manicures, and a big, airy house. She convinced me to buy those Henleys (perfect for breastfeeding, she said, and she was right) as well as a whirring electric infant nail file (easier than clippers, she said, and she was right) and a weird headband I never wear. (Hey, no one's perfect.) She's now pregnant again, which has made me stop and wonder: Should *I* get pregnant again?

E. Holtz-Schramek (✉)
Communication Studies & Media Arts, McMaster University,
Hamilton, ON, Canada
e-mail: holtzsce@mcmaster.ca

C. Chokshi, R. Mansell (eds.), *The Need to Rename Tech*,
https://doi.org/10.1007/978-3-032-05155-4_15

Knibbs' description is illustrative of some of the dominant aesthetics of momfluencer culture, including "the luxury of space, smiling children, [and] having good taste and style" (Zhao & Bouvier, 2022, p. 10). Momfluencing began as an offshoot of the influencer economy—an economy driven by social media users' and creators' incorporation of brands, products, and corporate partnerships into their content through what Laurence Scott (2019) calls 'contractual enthusiasm', a visual cultural practice that depends upon the performance of ease and luxury. Momfluencing is no different. Momfluencers monetise by creating a seamless portrait of maternal success and by occluding realism, as advertising always has.

Since 2020, momfluencer culture has moved beyond seemingly benign product placements, such as those indicated in Knibbs' example. For instance, during the COVID-19 pandemic, momfluencer accounts were explicitly linked to QAnon conspiracy theories and anti-vaxx movements (Kelly, 2020; Loofbourow, 2020; Tiffany, 2020). In fact, The Centre for Countering Digital Hate found that 73 per cent of Facebook anti-vaccination content was linked to 12 individuals (as cited in Salam, 2021), many of whom infiltrated the platform's parenting groups through their status as momfluencers. Even more recently, the rise of the 'Tradwife' trend on social media platforms such as TikTok and Instagram suggests that feminist regressive politics are arising out of the religious alt-right in the United States (Ainley, 2024), politics that hold the abandonment of traditional gender roles accountable for what is perceived as widespread moral and socio-cultural failings. Notably, Tradwife accounts, while both topically and aesthetically aligned with the momfluencer economy, have been found primarily to target male audiences who engage with online "conspiracy theory content and fearmongering", as well as "extremist right-wing media figures ... such as Alex Jones" (Little, 2024, Methodology section, para. 11).

What is more, the aesthetics of a more benign momfluencer content (the kind that tries to sell Henley shirts) are being appropriated by a more malignant type (content that invokes QAnon dicta or preaches a return to a social order wherein women were relegated to the domestic sphere). Kaitlyn Tiffany notes how colour, for example, helps to conceal creators' sinister messages. One account she analyses includes copious "peach-tinted family photos and remodeled bedrooms" that give way to a text-based post that reads, "The deep state is evil and Satanic", scripted in "white letters on soft pink and teal" (Tiffany, 2020, para 7). Groups like the Proud Boys and QAnon have utilised the aesthetics of momfluencing—these 'white letters on soft pink and teal'—to advance racist and conspiracy-oriented content through organisations such as Moms for Liberty and the publics they reach (The Southern Poverty Law Center, 2021).

While writers and think tanks have begun to observe nefarious content within the online mothering and momfluencer sphere—what May Friedman (2013) calls the 'mamasphere'—they have yet to explain why this is happening. Why is it that the mamasphere is a hotbed for conspiracy theories and regressive politics, and why does this content continue to proliferate, seemingly unfettered? I will argue that a primary driver is language. In this chapter, I deconstruct the labels of 'momfluencer' and the analogous 'momification of the Internet' to advance a renaming of these terms that more accurately denotes what momfluencers and momification mean. To do so, I put forward *parts & labours*, a label that can offer more complexity, more nuance, and more faithful depiction of activities occurring in the online mothering realm.[1] Yes, many who mother online monetise their identities and, in so doing, present an unattainable picture of maternal femininity (this is the essence of the Instagram ethos under Web 2.0 platform capitalism). But these are not the only activities occurring in the mamasphere. It is not all dewy, airbrushed photoshoots attempting to sell botanical-infused sunscreen.

By re-envisaging the work that happens in these spaces as parts & labours, I gesture to the aforementioned problematic activities occurring in the mamasphere. I ask, what is happening just below the surface of what is commonly called momfluencing? Is it medical misinformation, white supremacy, or the evisceration of feminist footholds? Creators using digital platforms to spread malicious and uninformed content under the mantle of momfluencer aesthetics are using the 'parts', here the affordances of the platform technologies, to enact dubious 'labours', even more deceptive than the selling of untested products. But, while the dark arts of conspiracy theory dissemination and white supremacist and heteropatriarchal values are brought under the big tent of the work of 'momfluencers' and 'momification', concealing their mendacity through cursive fonts, so, too, are the honest, radical efforts of online parent creators and users denigrated. There is much online mothering work that seeks to make visible the discrete entities of feminist care work, the domestic, affective, and

[1] Sara Ruddick (1989, p. xii) explains mothering as "gender-free work" that "does not require a particular sexual commitment".

child-rearing practices that, by design under capitalism, go unseen and unpaid.

2 Cyberfeminist Dreams Versus Neoliberal Platform Capitalist Realities

Let us first engage in a genealogy of 'momfluencers' and 'momification' by understanding how these metaphors became entrenched and then inquiring as to what they actually *do*. What we now understand as momfluencers and the momification of the internet originated in the 1990s. When people who mother first began to linger in chatrooms nearly 40 years ago, truly radical things were taking place. There were, finally, novel venues in which to experience catharsis and community. In such spaces, the potential for consciousness-raising social change via community formation appeared unbounded. And such early adopters of cyberfeminist mothering were not mistaken in these beliefs: in chatrooms, questions were asked and answered, grievances were met with empathy, and support and relatability coursed through dial-up and ethernet cables and into people's psyches and hearts. This constituted what Zizi Papacharissi (2014, p. 16) calls an "affective public": a "public formation that is textually rendered into being through emotive expressions that spread virally through networked crowds". The affective public of nascent practitioners of online mothering (Papacharissi, 2014), thus began as a consortium of singular entities driven by shared feelings and experiences. They chatted, they posted, they shared. This blossoming occurred in conjunction with the rise of cyberfeminism, defined by María Fernández and Faith Wilding (2002, p. 22) as combining "a utopic vision of corrupting patriarchy with an unbounded enthusiasm for the new tools of technology".

This public became *so* consequential because mothering is *so* hard, and we had been alone in it for *so* long. The odd puff piece on a celebrity's parental journey, resplendent with *Homes & Gardens*-worthy loveseats and a styled hairdo, failed to land. Here were real people who could mirror back ordinary experiences: postpartum anxiety; often male-coded partners who did not pull their weight; the distilled overwhelm of a snowed-in day that demanded multiple crafts, relentless refereeing, as well as three meals and two snacks to design, plate, and de-crumb; not even to mention how to fit work in (how else were you going to buy those snacks?). Here was the technology that could transform a litany of individual stress points and unanswered calls for assistance into opportunities for catharsis as well as hope towards meaningful social and political change. Here the personal could become political on a sweeping transnational scale. Here was catharsis for the rest of us, those without nannies or psychotherapists, but, crucially, with internet access.

These were moms, and others who mother, sharing and exposing real life in non-networked and non-commodified spaces without full awareness of how their expressions might be co-opted. Then, something changed. Internet theorists argue that the rise of Web 2.0 social media platforms such as Facebook, Twitter, Instagram, and now TikTok is to blame for the shift from a democratic internet capable of forging communities to one in which every like, post, and link is made only in the service of self-branding and sales. In fact, according to Neetzan Zimmerman, the momification of the internet happened hand-in-hand with the affordances and tropes of Facebook: "Facebook was obviously always going to be co-opted by moms ... It's about gossip, baby photos, schmaltzy stuff—it's so mom already" (as cited in Dewey, 2016, para. 7). In her analysis of Zimmerman's neologism, Caitlin Dewey (2016, para. 7) cements the connection between the Web 2.0 platformisation of moms with advertising, writing that "marketers and advertisers adore mothers, the people responsible for the most household spending". Thus, Facebook moms became more visible to each other while also coalescing as a prominent demographic to advertisers, or what Tamara Shepard (2014) calls a gendered commodity audience. Here we see that, for both momfluencers and momification, neoliberal platform capitalism as executed via Web 2.0 tools presents the primary driver for the creation of these new terms.

3 So 'Mom'

We have established that the terms 'momfluencer' and 'momification' have been co-configured in step with platform capitalism, yet this does not explain the metaphorical dimensions at work through the addition of the prefix 'mom'. What does the additive adjectivisation of 'mom' *do* to the nouns of 'momification' and 'momfluencer'? Metaphor derives from the Latin words carry and over. Anne Carson (1998, p. 4) tells us that metaphors are dangerous because they are the "latches of being" insofar as they close the garden gate on an entity's meaning, encoding it as a certain kind of thing, a thing that cannot easily be disregarded, a thing whose original meaning has been carried over so far that only invisible traces remain on the palimpsest. Writers trade in metaphors yet remain aware of their implicit power. Almost a decade ago, I heard Zadie Smith speak at a live taping of Eleanor Wachtel's (2015) *Writers & Company* podcast. Her words elicited silent shock from her audience: "I don't care if something is like something else; I don't care anymore". She was talking specifically about similes, but perhaps she, too, was clocking the dangers of comparative mutation, of loss of origins, of authenticity.

Despite such concerns posed by prominent writers, human efforts to communicate involve metaphors, similes, comparisons, and analogies. Most of us do not share a lifetime of common experiences, and so we tell stories relying on strategies for meaning-making. One such strategy is to describe something in terms of its evoking something else. Masha Gessen (2023, para. 20) describes translating lines from Russian author Valeria Narbikova that equate to, "If there is something, then what's it like?" For Gessen, this is a profound statement regarding human communication. They understand Narbikova to mean that efforts to compare something to something else are "a plea for reference", "about making predictions", and motivated by a desire to understand (Gessen, 2023, para. 20).

So, what does the adjectivisation of the noun 'mom' tell us about this 'something' and 'what it's like?' For one answer, we can look to Gina Masullo Chen's (2013) investigation of mommy blogging. Pivotally, Chen (2013, p. 511) quotes blogger Liz Gumbinner on the topic of the term 'mommyblogger':

> I hate it hate it hate it. I hate the diminutive. I hate the cutesiness of it all. I hate the fact that before you've read a single post, it makes it beyond easy to dismiss a blog as being less clever/engaging/insightful/important as anyone else's.

Chen taps into something revelatory: the deployment of 'mom' or 'mommy' is language that minimises significance.

Chen's citing of the blogger's hatred of the cutesiness of mommyblogging can be understood to align with feminist critiques of cultural and internet spheres by Sianne Ngai and Crystal Abidin. Ngai (2005) cautions her readers to be wary of the 'cute' since it serves to conceal a thing's radical or theoretical potential. Analogously, Abidin's (2016, p. 16) discussion of "subversive frivolity" speaks to how female-coded internet spaces, practices, and actors, especially those of influencers, are often written off by wider society; instead, she instructs us to attend to the "under-visibilized and under-estimated generative power of an object or practice arising from its (populist) discursive framing as marginal, inconsequential, and unproductive", which enables its content creators to partake in "quietly subversive acts". Subversive frivolity—such as white letters on soft pink and teal—is integral to the propagation of conspiracy theories in the mamasphere.

To mom-ify something is, therefore, to dismiss and undermine the truth of what is actually happening in these spaces and amongst these digital actors. This performs a dual disservice: both to this group and its status within the broader socio-cultural sphere, and to the group's activities, which are sometimes, but often not, innocuous.

4 Virtual Mothering's White Feminist Expertise Complex

By way of an example, close your eyes if you are able and think of the word 'momfluencer'. Now make a "prediction" based on this term, as Gessen (2023, para. 20) reading Narbikova suggests acts of comparison in language can achieve. What appears in your mind's eye? Maybe you see something akin to Naomi Klein's (2023, p. 178) vision of "wavy-haired momfluencers turning child-rearing into a series of airy tableaux of sponsored organic content"? Regardless of what this figure might be posting about, or their age or social position, I wonder if they appear in your imagination as white? In fact, an overwhelming pattern found in studies of online mothering is the whiteness of it all. This finding is elucidated expertly by Jessie Daniels (2016, p. 55), who writes of the "ways in which constructing and protecting whiteness has been a core feature in the rise of the popular internet".

White supremacy in online mothering has continued unchecked and carries with it messaging long embedded within parenting culture, values consistent with the hegemony of 'patriarchal motherhood' (Rich, 1986): that there is a certain type of parent who is superior to another due to factors such as race, class as determined by a two-parent family that enables a female-coded partner to take on the majority of the mothering labours, ability, beauty, and educational privilege. Patriarchal motherhood serves heteropatriarchal capitalist ends: the female-coded partner is beautiful in accordance with heterosexual tenets of desire and respectability, does what she is told (by her male authorities), and cares for and nurtures the up-and-coming labour force without complaint. But where can she exert her own power within such a vortex? Of course, through her own white supremacy, which appears in the ways she engages online with women of colour, people with non-traditional family or gender dynamics, those who are lower class, or parents who are differently abled.

Since so much of parenting culture orbits around asking for and giving advice, the white momfluencer's surfeit of expertise (often deriving solely from her subject position) expands voluminously into Facebook group pages and Instagram and TikTok comment sections. Brooks DeCillia notes how advice can be understood as a humble brag that is correlated to the giver's positive perceptions of their own past decisions (personal communication, May 9, 2024). In terms of white supremacy and the provision of advice in the online mothering sphere, Svetlana Boym (2001, p. 8) writes that "modern nostalgia is a mourning for the impossibility of mythical return, for the loss of an enchanted world with clear borders and values". There is thus a claim to be made that white mothers within these online spaces conceive of them as prelapsarian locales, ones in which contemporary social justice and intersectional mores do not inhibit their self-perceived claims to superiority.

5 Estimating Complexity: Parts & Labours

At this stage, our observations are worth reiterating: dangerous things are happening in the mamasphere, and they are able to propagate without censorship due, in large part, to the ways we talk about these activities. Coding activities as 'so mom' or as 'momified', we minimise these actors and their practices. Further, many of us disparage advertising, especially the kind in which we see momfluencers engaged, yet we accept that this is just the stage of late capitalism we find ourselves in.[2] Thus, we have enabled an entire industry to bloom: one that trades in pastels, product promotion, and seemingly anodyne images of one's progeny, yet one undergirded by a lack of consideration for children's privacy, spiralling misinformation, and, at times, pernicious messaging.

There is still another damage to register. On an internet "underwritten by a male-centric ethic" (Megarry, 2020, p. 232), online mothering is

[2] One example of this type of advertising is "sharenting" (Blum-Ross & Livingstone, 2017, p. 110), wherein children's likenesses and identities are put on display to grow the parent's followers.

understood only as marketing, or as cultural production that is *less than*. But I do not buy this as the only story, and I am here to offer an alternative.

Momfluencers and momification, I argue, do not sufficiently register the heterogeneous activities occurring within the mamasphere. While the aforementioned egregious practices swirl in the foreground, there are also many who engage in acts of online mothering, using the internet's 'parts', for outcomes out of step with networked neoliberal capitalist aims, or those prescribed by external forces, like conspiracy zealots. And they do so to enact 'labours' that meet the needs of real parents: the need to be heard and witnessed, the need to ask questions without judgement and to receive empathetic responses.

Notwithstanding sequential gains for feminist movements overall, even in the democratic West, those who identify as women and are perceived as such continue to bear the brunt of parenting-related practices: the physical demands, the affective labour, and the 'mother load', which refers to parenting challenges in the United States, specifically, including skyrocketing child care costs, brief parental leave policies, high rates of preventable maternal mortality, and an 'uneven distribution of household chores' (The mother load, 2017). The COVID-19 pandemic made this imbalance painstakingly evident. *Parts & labours* gives credence to this continuing imbalance in that I argue that virtual mothering labours are indicative of the greater weights borne by female-coded and identifying parents within familial structures in the capitalist Western state. Caregivers must (at the very least) be psychically compensated through a renaming of their online activities, insofar as the terms 'momfluencer' and 'momification' fail to speak to the actual *work* (the labours) these actors perform, and how it impacts their actual *bodies* (their parts).

Parts & labours gestures towards the language of estimates and invoices in the trade industries. For instance, when a mechanic gives a customer an estimate, the estimate includes both the 'parts' (i.e., the physical components required to fix a problem), as well as the 'labour' (the time and effort necessary to fix the issue). I invoke this meaning to herald and applaud the work of many in the mamasphere who are posting in order to make evident their non-remunerated work. According to Angela Garbes (2022, p. 52), "if women around the world made minimum wage for all the unpaid hours of care work they performed in 2019, they would have earned $10.9 trillion. In America alone, they would have earned $1.5 trillion". We do not pay for this labour as a society due to the hegemonic control exerted by capitalism and colonialism. We must overturn this hegemony, and the subversion begins with language. Thus, while parts & labours connotes something typically coded as masculine, I redeploy these terms to refer to the practices that serve to make visible the profusion of activities undertaken by those who mother in the virtual realm, and especially those that call attention to systemic material critiques of feminist mothering under capitalism.

Many practitioners of online mothering are starting to resist its dogmatic cultural pressures, beginning to hack its platforms and affordances to forge insurgent critiques. Like the early proponents of mommy blogging during the rise of cyberfeminism, those who practice this radical parts & labours form of online mothering possess “a utopic vision of corrupting patriarchy with an unbounded enthusiasm for the new tools of technology” (Fernández & Wilding, 2002, p. 22). Their work begins from impulses like Petersen’s (2023, p. 225): “How would the hours of my day feel if I wasn’t consciously and subconsciously defining my motherhood against the motherhoods of so many strangers on social media?”. In the wake of a pandemic that disproportionately increased domestic and child-rearing labour for working mothers especially, which set them back decades in their career trajectories (Canadian Women’s Foundation, 2018; Taub, 2020), many who mother online have turned to social media with radical practices, those of the parts & labours varietals.

An entire sub-culture of humorous parenting videos on TikTok, for instance, is showing cracks in the airy-tableaux-of-sponsored-organic--content momfluencer veneer by creating content that both incorporates and resists staid tropes. Outwardly, such a video may appear to regurgitate unreflexive trends, but look or listen closer, and you will see such a creator’s entendre, a facial expression tied to a joke at their child, partner, or society’s expense that offers something authentic about how tired they really are of *all of this*, not only doing the work of mothering but also having to perform it online within the bounds of such narrow and pseudo-authoritative constructs. This creative work inhabits an internet now understood to be boring (Chayka, 2023), one in which more users are beginning to experience nostalgia for the early days of this technology and seeking to break the cycle of monetised surface-level performance.

6 Conclusion

Web 2.0 attempted to co-opt everything we once believed in regarding a do-it-yourself internet utopia by hypnotising us to sell chunks of ourselves to each other for a platform's gain. Not only this, but in the realm of online mothering, the metaphors invoked to explain this work have been denigrated, written off as enslaved to capitalism, and minimised in their importance. And yet, I admit that my own experiences as a new parent during a pandemic lockdown without family or friends nearby drove me to online mothering groups. While much of what I saw (and continue to see) in public momfluencer accounts smacks of white-goddess performance and misinformation run amok, in my private, closed Facebook groups I am heartened almost daily by people's vulnerability in describing their parenting challenges and, in turn, by the supportive replies they receive. Miranda July speaks to the rarity of online mothering groups in this regard: her protagonist goes through a traumatic birth experience, one that cannot be fully explained via medical research. She cannot access support from the hospital, and she has no friends who have experienced the same thing, and so turns to the internet to find community. July (2024, p. 95) writes of the other users/creators she encounters in a birth trauma space for survivors of Fetal-Maternal-Hemorrhage (FMT): "Most were posting just to say WTF. WTF just happened? … There was no actual dialogue, only solitary women putting their candle on the same altar".

The next time you see what appears to be just another dumb momfluencer TikTok, look again, as this work may be indicative of the parts & labours I promote. What is the voiceless scream emerging from this video? How might it actually *feel* to put one's candle on the same altar of maternal angst or catastrophe? How is a user/creator marshalling the affordances of the platform in question to hack these 'parts' for good, not just their own private gain? How are they attempting to make the endless 'labours' of mothering visible? Conversely, is there anything in the message that could cause harm? Is the creator attempting to sell more than just a product, such as an ideology or even a conspiracy?

Parts & labours is, thus, a call to reconsider online mothering activities occurring within the mamasphere. Just because a post might look 'so mom' in terms of the creator's identity, the topics invoked, or the styling, does not mean that it should be disregarded. It might be an arm of the deep-state conspiracy, or it might be evidence of that "modest comfort" (July, 2024, p. 275) parents seek online in the wake of a struggle for which they have no other support—it might be the only place they have to go. The full complement of these diverse online mothering labours necessitates a label that can break open these gates of meaning.

This project is, therefore, situated within the larger conceit of this book, namely that the metaphors we use to talk about a given technology influence how we understand it. Parts & labours is a call to reimagine language at the level of syntactic functionality—that is, what is the 'part', the word or phrase, and how is it being semantically wielded to achieve a 'labour' of understanding? And how, then, does this 'labour' continue to dampen, deaden, or coerce understanding across broader networks? By investigating the seemingly casual yet widespread adoption of the terms momfluencer and momification and advancing parts & labours in their place, this chapter emblematises the urgent need to deconstruct both the parts and the labours of language surrounding technology.

Acknowledgements With gratitude to Andrea Zeffiro, whose *Data Cultures* graduate course at McMaster University inspired this piece. Thank you to Kay Beckett, Brooks DeCillia, and Gabriela Perdomo for their early feedback, as well as to Crystal Chokshi and Robin Mansell for their unwavering commitment to this project. My work is made possible through the Social Sciences and Humanities Research Council of Canada.

References

Abidin, C. (2016). "Aren't these just young, rich women doing vain things online?": Influencer selfies as subversive frivolity. *Social Media + Society, 2*(2), 1–17. https://doi.org/10.1177/2056305116641342

Ainley, M. (2024, February 24). I lived the "trad wife" life for a week. This is what it taught me. *Vogue*. https://www.vogue.co.uk/article/trad-wife-trend

Blum-Ross, A., & Livingstone, S. (2017). "Sharenting," parent blogging, and the boundaries of the digital self. *Popular Communication, 15*(2), 110–125. https://doi.org/10.1080/15405702.2016.1223300

Boym, S. (2001). *The future of nostalgia*. Basic Books.

Canadian Women's Foundation. (2018). *The gender wage gap in Canada* [Fact sheet]. https://canadianwomen.org/wp-content/uploads/2018/08/Gender-Wage-Gap-Fact-Sheet_AUGUST-2018_FINAL1.pdf

Carson, A. (1998). *Autobiography of red*. McClelland & Stewart.

Chayka, K. (2023, October 9). Why the internet isn't fun anymore. *The New Yorker*. https://www.newyorker.com/culture/infinite-scroll/why-the-internet-isnt-fun-anymore

Chen, G. M. (2013). Don't call me that: A techno-feminist critique of the term *mommy blogger*. *Mass Communication and Society, 16*(4), 510–532. https://doi.org/10.1080/15205436.2012.737888

Daniels, J. (2016). The trouble with white feminism: Whiteness, digital feminism and the intersectional Internet. In S. U. Noble & B. Tynes (Eds.), *The intersectional internet: Race, sex and cultures online* (pp. 41–60). Peter Lang.

Dewey, C. (2016, January 21). The fastest growing 'news' site of 2015 was an obscure content farm for moms. *The Washington Post*. https://www.washingtonpost.com/news/the-intersect/wp/2015/07/16/how-moms-won-the-internet-and-what-that-means-for-the-rest-of-us/

Fernández, M., & Wilding, F. (2002). Situating cyberfeminisms. In M. Fernandez, F. Wilding, & M. M. Wright (Eds.), *Domain errors! Cyberfeminist practices* (pp. 17–28). Autonomedia. http://refugia.net/domainerrors/DE1a_situating.pdf

Friedman, M. (2013). *Mommyblogs and the changing face of motherhood*. University of Toronto Press.

Garbes, A. (2022). *Essential labor: Mothering as social change*. Harper.

Gessen, M. (2023, December 19). Comparison is the way we know the world. *n+1*. https://www.nplusonemag.com/online-only/online-only/comparison-is-the-way-we-know-the-world/

July, M. (2024). *All fours*. Riverhead Books.

Kelly, A. (2020, September 10). Mothers for QAnon. *The New York Times*. https://www.nytimes.com/2020/09/10/opinion/qanon-women-conspiracy.html

Klein, N. (2023). *Doppelganger: A trip into the mirror world*. Penguin Random House.

Knibbs, K. (2023, April 25). The case against momfluencers. *Wired*. https://www.wired.com/story/momfluencers-essay/

Little, O. (2024). Study: Tradwife influencers are quietly spreading far-right conspiracy theories. Media Matters for America. https://www.mediamatters.org/tiktok/study-tradwife-influencers-are-quietly-spreading-far-right-conspiracy-theories

Loofbourow, L. (2020, September 18). It makes perfect sense that QAnon took off with women this summer. *Slate*. https://slate.com/news-and-politics/2020/09/qanon-women-why.html

Megarry, J. (2020). *The limitations of social media feminism: No space of our own*. Palgrave Macmillan.

Ngai, S. (2005). The cuteness of the avant-garde. *Critical Inquiry, 31*(4), 811–847. https://doi.org/10.1086/444516

North, A. (2023). The expensive, unrealistic, and extremely white world of "momfluencers." *Vox*. https://www.vox.com/23690126/mothers-parenting-momfluenced-sara-petersen-tiktok-instagram

Papacharissi, Z. (2014). *Affective publics: Sentiment, technology, and politics.* Oxford University Press.

Petersen, S. (2023). *Momfluenced: Inside the maddening, picture-perfect world of mommy influencer culture.* Beacon Press.

Rich, A. (1986). *Of woman born: Motherhood as experience and institution.* W.W. Norton & Company.

Ruddick, S. (1989). *Maternal thinking: Toward a politics of peace.* Beacon Press Books.

Salam, E. (2021, July 17). Majority of COVID misinformation came from 12 people, report finds. *The Guardian.* https://www.theguardian.com/world/2021/jul/17/covid-misinformation-conspiracy-theories-ccdh-report

Scott, L. (2019, April 21). A history of the influencer, from Shakespeare to Instagram. *The New Yorker.*. https://www.newyorker.com/culture/annals-of-inquiry/a-history-of-the-influencer-from-shakespeare-to-instagram

Shepard, T. (2014). Gendering the commodity audience in social media. In C. Carter, L. Steiner, & L. McLaughlin (Eds.), *The Routledge companion to media & gender* (pp. 157–167). Routledge.

Taub, A. (2020). Pandemic will "take our women 10 years back" in the workplace. *The New York Times.*. https://www.nytimes.com/2020/09/26/world/covid-women-childcare-equality.html

The mother load. (2017, December 5). The Mother Load: America is failing mothers. Help us change that. *The Guardian.* https://www.theguardian.com/us-news/2017/dec/04/the-mother-load-guardian-editorial-help-us-donate

The Southern Poverty Law Center. (2021). *The year in hate & extremism 2021* [Report]. https://www.splcenter.org/20220309/year-hate-extremism-report-2021

Tiffany, K. (2020, August 18). The women making conspiracy theories beautiful. *The Atlantic.* https://www.theatlantic.com/technology/archive/2020/08/how-instagram-aesthetics-repackage-qanon/615364/

Wachtel, E. (Host). (2015, October 28). *CBC Writers & Company* [Radio broadcast/podcast episode]. CBC.

Zhao, W., & Bouvier, G. (2022). Where neoliberalism shapes Confucian notions of child rearing: Influencers, experts and discourses of intensive parenting on Chinese Weibo. *Discourse, Context & Media, 45*, 1–12. https://doi.org/10.1016/j.dcm.2021.100561

CHAPTER 16

Xtreme Streaming*

~~The Internet~~

Zach Pearl

1 Introduction

The following is a piece of fictocriticism: a feminist practice of writing that merges theory with fiction and elides subjective and objective voices intentionally to create moments of interruption and interference in the reading experience. The goal is not to confuse the reader but rather to necessitate a close and active reading that hinges on ambiguity and sustains multiple interpretations of the text. Fictocritical writing also often involves the mixing of genres and the treatment of text as a material in the form of cut/paste collage techniques and so-called 'citational writing'. Accordingly, the reader will find the form of the following piece moves suddenly between essay, poetry, academic reference, and quotational fragments, often without warning. The eighth and final section offers a detailed explanation of the philosophical motives behind this piece, and fictocritical writing, generally.

Z. Pearl (✉)
School of the Arts, Media, Performance & Design, York University, Toronto, ON, Canada
e-mail: zapearl@yorku.ca

C. Chokshi, R. Mansell (eds.), *The Need to Rename Tech*,
https://doi.org/10.1007/978-3-032-05155-4_16

> The most troubling phenomenon is certainly the river's very disappearance: the actual case of all this disturbance no longer exists, the water takes no course, the river's ribbon, that elementary form of all geographical perception, of which children, precisely, are so fond, shifts from a line to a plane, the accidents of space now have no context, there is no longer a hierarchy among the river, the road, the fields. (Barthes, 1957/2013, p. 63)

2 Slippage

As is generally true of a myth, this story contains elements of truth that will gradually disappear. Most of them will simply float away. Others may sink abruptly and remain eerily close, just out of reach. Either way, the most important one to wrest before it recedes is the hardest to grasp: *that one can always step into the stream but never out of it again.*

Benign in its premise, the stream—initially a wayward bit of current—moves insipidly, exponentially, from the source to the centre, subtly weaving, maybe gurgling at times, pushing through the craggy turn of the twenty-first century. Like a blossoming series of tubes, exponential swelling, the stream eventually emerged through cracks in the Californian desert before spreading, virtually like a virus, to every pond and projecting surface on the planet. And though, theoretically, a global network of tributaries seemed like a good thing at the time—a world where everyone gets that precious waterfront view—it turns out there are perpetual risks of catastrophic flooding, ecological contamination, and troll infestations under the many new bridges required to keep business-as-usual afloat.

Expansive by fast design, the stream regularly overflows its banks, breaking down the vistas, fragmenting all it embraces; first into inlets, then islands, and eventually sites of disaster tourism. One day, you look up from your backlit map to realise that the stream is going in every possible direction—making the world rather than emerging from it—and that you're just one little fish in an integrated circuit.[1]

I would venture to say you know very well the fishy sensation I speak of, regardless of geography, age, or occupation. It is perhaps a bold assumption, but who among us can say they are completely dry? Torrefied? How long could any of us realistically go without dipping a toe in that stream? We all squish with the same residue from the initial slip down its muddy banks, through the bramble of crosstalk, perhaps detouring

[1] This draws on Haraway (1985/2003).

through a rabbit hole or two before hitting the open water. *It's a short fall but a long way down.* And then you are swimming in all directions, never reaching the bottom or the border. You wake up dripping, and you go to bed damp. And even when the most well-meaning among us are done wringing the moisture from our fingertips, we wade right back in again. Only those in million-dollar bunkers or pre-contact island oases (ironically) avoid getting wet.

For the rest of us, the stream gets into everything. It is soaking through the floorboards and rotting the bedposts. Bits of the stream are forever trapped in our S-shaped ear canals and under our fingernails.

Still, I look myself over every morning for dry patches in a gesture of romantic futility. What mole, or knuckle, or follicle is virgin territory for the voices of other bodies to doggy paddle?

The stream is both a medium for monoliths and a collective message, singing its song of immanent contact between corporations and corpora, all the lubricated frictions that drive connection. Messages about the land are remixed and enunciated in real time, carried along by intricate parabolic geometry and invisible bodies of currency.

The cloud, the satellite, a (bit)torrent coursing from a server tree.

We live in a time of volatile, elemental media that transport bits of our bodies around in their mercurial compositions.[2] But perhaps the stream is the most persistent of them all because there is so much saturation, so much room to slide the signified under the skin … You might think you have left the water. You might towel off, redress, and drive far away. But its moist microbial agents cling silently to your pores and persist; all the beads of leftover signals and current radiate in lines of evaporating connections. They obscure your vision as you grip the wheel tighter, the haze reducing everything on the horizon to an amenable shoreline: *image, shape, surface, fluid.*

3 What Remains of Me That Is Not Already a Vector?

Have you tried having an honest conversation with yourself about the environment lately? It rarely goes well …

[2] This draws on Durham Peters (2015).

Looking in the black mirror, after a fresh shave:

We need to talk, buddy—about the squishy nature of things and the repercussions. The startling thinness of skin. The shapeshifting membranes that make life as we know it possible, yet toxic and 'terminal'. Openly closed systems and n-ary relations. How about the false opposition of angels and monsters? Both have multiple tongues. But only one gets to wear white? What about rapidly declining freshwater salmon despite mitigation? The background pandemic of bird flu? The fact that there are about 2.5 million microorganisms in that glass of tap water you've been drinking?[3]

The fish guts and the smartphone bits are contingent ontological objects constructing a particular reality that cannot be prised apart. You have just got to get through it. Luckily, the mind is wetware, able to move, exchanging small sections of space and inverting them, like a modular synthesiser made of grey Jell-O.[4] Being so immersed in-stream means moving your appendages around in a parallel, 'paralogical' circuitry.[5]

vessel—ventricle—vestige—vicar—vampire—venter—vacant—vehicle

The first technology was the bottle (or the bag), a 'container in general, a thing that [held] something else' to be utilised later. And 'the first cultural device was probably the recipient'.[6] So, in many respects, we are bottle beings: beings who took the form of the tool so essential to our Neolithic survival and applied it to each other, our gelatinous minds rearranging themselves into open-yet-closed containers for storage and transmission of seeds and soliloquies.

[3]This paragraph draws on Hayles (1999), Stuart (2021), and Vanhaecke et al. (2022).

[4]The term 'wetware' is most often attributed to British-Canadian artist Roy Ascott, who used it to describe the plasticity of the human brain as an instance of biotechnology. Ascott was a pioneer of the cybernetic art movement in the 1960s, working in early networked media like Telex, Videotex, and kinetic sculpture.

[5]Jean-François Lyotard (1984) uses the term 'paralogy' infrequently in his longform essay *The Postmodern Condition* to describe a 'countermove' in the context of his theory of language games for knowledge legitimisation. However, in his introduction to the book, Fredric Jameson (1984, p. xix) offers a clearer definition as "[a] search, not for consensus, but very precisely for 'instabilities,' as a practice of *paralogism*, in which the point is not to reach agreement but to undermine from within the very framework in which the previous [knowledge] had been conducted".

[6]The quotations are from Le Guin (1989, p. 166) and Fisher as cited in Le Guin (1989, p. 166).

The stream is another kind of container that requires us to be open *and* closed, absorbing it while we fail to grasp its bounds, to be both on its surface and within its depths as a vector recurrently becoming a vertex. And maybe this is why the stream vexes so … because its structure is too much like a looking glass for our own contradictions—a container staring us back in the face. In any case, the invaginated topography of streaming requires a radical shift in the way we talk about the mind-body interface, because the hyphen is a disappearing line and a moving target *at the same time*.

Personally, I prefer to picture a different arrangement altogether: the mind as a rich and chunky chowder with lots of celery, and dill, and constant stirring, able to swirl around and coalesce in myriad unique and creamy formations. Subsequently, the body is a hybrid of a diving bell and crockpot, securely holding the stewing chowder bits together while they somersault in miscegenating freefall, changing channels and navigating currents with nothing but a tempered sheet of glass separating imminent flux states.

Sounds kinda hot, right?

Of course, attached to the glass are equally borderline things, little barnacles, bacterium, and other brands of orgiastic opportunists that shift the narrative. (Or, more realistically, they are on the inside, too, but it is unpleasant to think about.) As fellow inhabitants of the stream, they distort the foreground as they clamp on and recast the borders of the craft, mutating the peripheries.

Still, there are no 'bad' actors here, in theory, only 'frequency, distribution, homogeneity, proximity'.[7] All things, organic and machinic, are equal constituents of the more-than-crockpot-sensing-and-swimming system, manifesting an intersection of hurtling desires that make up a cyborg's gazpacho in their paradoxical couplings. So, as I slipstream up and down the coastline of some ludicrous headline or unresolvable discourse, I play messenger and medium in an almost manic autopoietic two-step—the vessel that is also the destination.

[7] The quotation is from Latour (1996, p. 369).

4 To Feel the Stream as It Floods Your Shallow Boot

It rains here more now than it used to, well on
into the winter and into the 'spring', the melt
is never slow, always a stormy nervous erasure:
The ice giving way too quickly, deleterious.
Banks that overflow with the unforeseen.
Flooding as the norm and the anti-norm.
Streams of refuse and rhetoric, they intertwine.
Streaming as a pastime and a paradigm.

5 (Never) Alone, Again

I suppose that individuality is the material cost of mobility and 'perfect exchange'.[8] As we connect en masse, we recede as singular entities, swimming a perfect circle—the ouroboros freestyle. This implosive habit does have its upsides. There was a time when the stream was seen as a kind of beehive for autonomically solving Earth's problems: a whirlpool manoeuvre, where you could let yourself get swept up in a murmuring swarm of zoological emergence, accomplishing something otherwise impossible through unscrupulous, unanticipated collisions.

But the funny thing about swimming in-stream is the inevitable obliteration of vision. The blurriness below the surface makes it hard to differentiate between connection, proximity, and depth. The resolution is uneven, even when it comes to your besties.

Reaching out in the moving stream is like: 'Cool, bro. You do you while I do me (alone). Let's dance together (alone). We'll go shopping sometime (alone). See you at Jesse's wedding (alone, on my phone)'.

We are technically streaming together but in separate channels, whether ~~we~~ you like ~~it~~ me or not. Because it is viscous and vicious unless you are swimming on top, with dream liners and private servers.

By and large, the stream is the dirty 124-bpm club beat dragging you down and further in, infiltrating your subconscious need to _____ and then have a regretfully greasy taco at 2 am. It reverberates like a siren song, propelling you to the metaphysical dance floor to get slippery and loose until your heels fall off. And then it makes you regret every one of your

[8] See Haraway (2003).

bodily limitations by turning the lights on without warning and promptly shoving a beer-soaked coat into your empty hands.

6 Ideal Witness

I would like to imagine that someone saw this existential wave of over-saturation of extreme streaming coming from a distance. From a good ten city blocks, at least. I would like both of us to imagine that said imaginary individual had 30 to 60 seconds to prepare themselves for the deluge. And that somewhere between the cleaving sound of the levy breaking and seeing the white crest overtaking the shore (assuming they were on higher ground), there was an intersectional epiphany unfolding in record-breaking 'crisis time'.[9]

If only for a minute, I would like us to imagine that some myth-miscegenating cyber goddexx had the acuity to view the swelling stream, ever so briefly, as something more than an arrival or inevitability—rather as an evolution and a reckoning of vision. That they could briefly glimpse a possible future where the stream is a distributed '*natureculture*',[10] pervading every look, every glance, like a mesh or a screen of embodied relationality. A 'stream' that signifies more than the blue light of transmission.

I like to picture this star witness as a star, too: sharp, radiant, wide-eyed. A marine bio-techno-ecologist with an acute but not necessarily neurotic fascination with the origins of their coffee beans. Maybe they have precocious tendrils of hair, always smelling faintly of cedar, sea brine, and bergamot. And they would be diligently documenting the stages of parasitic mutualism by hand, notating the differentials between the organic and machinic in some charmingly antiquated timetable of how often I have underlined the word 'assemblage' or googled 'the singularity'.

That someone sincere and dedicated (and a bit strange) is important—to me—if for nothing more than the possibility of remembering the origin of the stream differently. Someone who can misremember the levies of time and techne as they were failing: the birth of organs without bodies and all manners of matter squeezing through the pixels of political consciousness, and then deliver those visions to us anew, on the smartphone screens that rest prominently next to our dinner plates.[11]

[9] See Hassan (2009).
[10] See Haraway (2016).
[11] See Deleuze and Guattari (1987).

Surely, there was a witness …
But, then again, only the event itself is sensible:[12]

Time passes. A lot of time passes. I'm waiting for it to stop, for it to gather itself into an image, of myself, of my life, of the world. I'm waiting for the movement to stop and reflect itself back to itself—reflection is the condition of action, isn't it? But it turns its face away, dissolves into a hundred tiny details on a cruelly indifferent time-line, dissolves me into a hundred tiny details, pure moving mass.[13]

7 Downspouts

The gutters are swelling with the anthropogenic backwash of the stream.

Plick, Plock. Pluck, Plonk.
nibi onje biimaadiiziiwin is not a metaphor.[14]

All the droplets half-full of hydrocarbons and forever chemicals are coming home to roost in our drinking water and our showerheads. The microplastics in my gut lining are dancing the samba of bioplasticity; they are also a part of the stream. In general, there is a mellifluous contingent of synthetic determinism lurching forward with panache and well-researched visual rhetoric designed to get behind your eyes. It is precisely why you are never alone these days, because you are a watery thing in the age of streaming. A philosophising sponge-thing with virtual limbs inundated by a heavy, steady flow of chatter. An articulated yet insufferably porous being, bound to absorb what immediately surrounds it—what haunts it.

Do you hear that? *Pluck, Plonk.*
Does porous a monster make? *Perhaps.*

If we resist the squishiness of our innately swampy ecology—being more than half made of water—it is a bit absurd, is it not? One might excuse some initial squeamishness on account of the harrowing scope of it all. The stratification of the stream proposes major challenges and exposes

[12] See Massumi (2002).
[13] The quotation is from McMahon (2002, p. 3).
[14] See Ansloos (2023).

us to all kinds of interstitial interfaces that only in retrospect show themselves as more than images or whispers: symbiotic temporary splices, waves (over)lapping at a violent speed. Streamers must reckon with the frailty of their own fleshy borders, for the materiality of streaming means the urgent making of kin:

> After the implosion of informatics and biologics, simulation is not derivative and inferior but primary and constitutive. "All life is an experiment." At the origins of things, life is constituted and connected by recursive, repeating streams of information … the circulatory systems that constitute kinship.[15]

The empty-headed boys all went down to the stream to kill frogs and talk dirty. Sometimes they would build a fort out of snapped branches and T-shirts and then talk about making a girl lick their tiny, hairless balls. And sometimes they would catch a fish and make the most unfortunate bystander make out with it for a full five seconds just to assert their primal dominance. These shadow plays of barbarism were of little interest to me. But I would nevertheless tag along, sometimes purely for the thrill of crossing boundaries and carelessly alternating between the mud and the mirth. There was a genderless boyishness about indulging in manipulating the land in simple ways—hand crafts—techniques that felt precarious yet affirming in their ludic joy, like twisting the head off a doll just to see what happens next.

> 'Beware, Barbie! Kids Find Torturing Fun'.
>
> 'Doll-beheading photos surface in tribute to Islamic State'.
>
> 'It [gets] hard to recall which form of masculinity is destroying civilization today'.
>
> 'Drill, Baby, Drill'—youtube.com/watch?v=DxsxXst5AZ0.
>
> '…quite high concentrations of these compounds in toys … in particular, teething toys'.
>
> '[T]he most concerning … is their persistence … their potential to bioaccumulate', Jobst said. 'It's not like you're exposed to this once and then it goes away'.[16]

[15] The quotation is from Haraway (1997/2012, p. 134).

[16] Titles of articles or quotations are from ABC News (2005), Sterman (2014), Houghton (2019, para. 15), Kutarna in Dangerfield (2023, para. 3, 16) and NowThis Earth (2023).

The stream was a layered environment, incorporating multiple thresholds: the road, the barbed wire fence, and the highway that separated our edge-of-nowhere suburbia from the 'wilderness'. And then, of course, there were the woods themselves; the treeline seemed to slope impossibly inward from every direction, like a tenebrous green silo. Once inside, you inevitably came upon a grey-brown stream bulging with all manner of debris. Coursing with reeds, snakes, prurient tadpoles, beer cans, telephone wire, and the occasional shotgun shell, all commingling in a mobius strip. Alternately beautiful and ugly, it turned upon itself like a cannibal. Red and white tumbled through black and blue incisors of invisible, crashing bodies. And then that stream and all its refuse were part of me.

8 Xtreme Streaming

I was wading into *The New York Times* on my way to Dublin for business.[17]

I was sitting in Toronto's Lester B. Pearson sorting windows and wireframes—treading water.

Left swipe, right swipe, left swipe, x-out. Pinch here, kick there. Float on a god's eye view of a grotto in Spain. Another Yemeni rebel base being drone bombed …

[Flight Status: Delayed / Retardée | ~~01:17~~ 16:30]

Huff.

No choice now really but to head downstream to the subreddits for a spell.

Niches in the bedrocks of an ecosystem are naturally dark and misinterpreted.

Niche species in a wave of dramatic climate change go underground for respite.

Yet, I PUSH THE PANE upward—to the next post, the next link, another border or shore. Forever descending in the stream while sitting perfectly still, in the kiddie pool of a new ecology taking its naturally invisible shape …

THE PATH OF TOTALITY

Dance, gawk or run in the dark, but don't look directly at the sun

[17] The following section makes use of excerpts from a special edition (Burcham et al., 2024) in the Sunday *New York Times* on travelling to somewhere different on the planet each week of the year.

NASA will be broadcasting from the Indianapolis Motor Speedway …

On the Canadian side of Niagara Falls, Cosmologists Without Borders …

PARIS, FRANCE

… [W]ell known monuments are being transformed into sports and entertainment venues.

GENEVA, SWITZERLAND

Satisfy your curiosity about quantum physics, and your cravings for chocolate … quantum karaoke, quantum air hockey, and miniature magnetic accelerators … Less mind-blowing but still satisfying to hungry scientists and laypeople alike …

earth.fm /

recordings /

echoes-in-the-alps /

Artist: Gianni Pavan /

Altopiano del Cansiglio, Italy

> 'Red Deer roaring and fighting on a cold, foggy evening … Notice the incredible natural reverberation'.[18]

SALAR DE UYUNI, BOLIVIA

Like all the best places, Salar de Uyuni, 12,000 feet high in the Andes, can be demanding … Demand for the 'white gold'—used in electric-car and smartphone batteries—is surging … The mining efforts could affect the area's beauty and ecosystem. Better go to the Salar soon.

MONTENEGRO

Others, like me, popped in and out.

The slate of talks for the days I was there was titled 'New Cities and Network States'. European tourists smoked cigars on the promenade while Zuzalu attendees bounded around making plans for excursions and exercise and shuttles to a private Grimes show later on.

MINGAN ARCHIPELAGO, QUEBEC

Sea-sculpted monoliths, puffins and indigenous heritage

… rise like fossilised works of art; kayak on the misty sea; and explore secluded beaches framed by marches and forests. Watching over the land are the people of the Innu First Nations [and NORAD].

WHITEHORSE, YUKON

[18] This section on Geneva draws from and quotes Pavan (n.d.).

… A WARM WELCOME IN A REMOTE CAPITAL

In the current 11-year solar cycle, magnetic activity in space will peak between January and October, potentially prompting more … ‘beer worth freezin’ for … far from the city, where you can stay in a cabin built to blend into the landscape …’

NIPIGON, ONTARIO

FOREST PRODUCTS AND PRIME FISHING … A SETTING OFF POINT

[NPR update]

ASIA Major (emergency)

A Philippine radio anchor was shot and killed while on a Facebook Live stream.[19]

BRISBANE, AUSTRALIA

… VERTIGINOUS VIEWS IN A CITY GEARING UP FOR ITS OLYMPIC MOMENT …

… a palm-lined pool … a celebration of queer arts and artists, and Vertigo … harnessed diners eat while dangling four stories above the ground. After dinner, they can abseil down the building.

BROWARD COUNTY, SOUTH FLORIDA

… LOOKING FOR A WELL-DESERVED GETAWAY? A 24-MILE SPAN OF GOLDEN BEACHES AWAITS YOU. …

> ‘Joaquin tried to duck into the women’s restroom, but the door was locked. … The bullet, along with parts of Joaquin’s hand bone, slammed into his temple, shattering his skull’.[20]

THIS OFFER WON’T LAST:

… WITH THE *TORONTO STAR* EPAPER, YOU CAN READ THE NEWS ONLINE IN ITS TRUE FORM …

$0.50 (Cdn) a week for your first year.

Cancel or pause anytime.

Privacy practices may vary.

[19] See The Associated Press (2023).

[20] The quotation is from Thompson (2024).

9 Exposition

The preceding is a work of fictocriticism, a subject I have written about and written within for many years (Pearl, 2019, 2020, 2022, 2023b).[21] Succinctly, fictocriticism is a feminist experimental writing practice that developed in the early 1980s in the Canadian arts and cultural criticism scene before migrating to Australian universities via the critical theory of Fredric Jameson, and then eventually to other Commonwealth nations as 'creative-critical writing' (Flavell, 2009; Pearl, 2023a). Fictocriticism, by design, has no exemplary form or necessary criteria, "[f]or the heterogeneity of fictocritical forms bears witness to the existence of fictocriticism as a necessarily performative mode, an always singular and entirely tactical response to a particular set of problems" (Gibbs, 2005, para. 3).

But having spoken with its progenitor, Jeanne Randolph, the base motive for fictocritical writing is clearly an ambition to subvert binarisms—of language, disciplines, politics, even ethics, and figuratively to mine the gaps between these polarities of interpretation. Writing fictocritically means collapsing distinctions between the validity of objective, academic writing and subjective or 'creative' writing to represent and explore the entangled nature of critique and subjectivity. By mixing registers, voices, and genres, fictocritical texts "make use of indeterminate forms" (Ulmer, 1994, p. 34) to elicit an associational rather than argumentative interpretation of their subject(s). The goal of such writing, as I have argued elsewhere (Pearl, 2019), is to haunt its own reading experience, introducing moments of doubt and incoherence that spur suspicion and critical insight (Kerr, 1995).

In the preceding piece, rather than explicitly argue for a name change of the internet to *xtreme streaming*, I offer a series of fragments that textually embody the infrastructure's immersive, multivocal, and sordid nature. I interchange essay, theory, memoir, poetry, citational writing, and copy/paste collage in a feminist literary gesture of 'fictioning' and 'worlding' (Burrows & O'Sullivan, 2019). Specifically, I employ the fragment as a tool and signet of glitch feminism, where 'positive irregularities' are injected "into these systems as errata, activating new architecture through [their] malfunctions" (Russell, 2020, p. 13). Glitch feminism, as first outlined by Legacy Russell (2020) in her manifesto on the term, insists on sociopolitical transformation through an intrinsically distributed concept

[21] This section returns to conventional in-text citation practice.

of identity in which the body *is* the practice of flux: navigating numerous screens; existing between worlds and communities; never offline but only away from the keyboard (AFK); scrolling from one mode of engagement to another. As Russell iterates in her manifesto and explores in depth in her book, *Black Meme* (2024), the inequitable, patriarchal social structures that govern the formation of one's identity in physical environments are now inextricably bound up with the shifting politics of the internet's viral media ecology. However ubiquitous in their circulation, images and videos of difference—Blackness, indigeneity, queerness, disability—are consistently instrumentalised in performative ways that mirror the systemic discrimination of these communities in real life. Relegated to the dispensable realm of 'poor images'—looping, low-resolution GIFs and hastily Photoshopped memes that no one must download, upload, or manage themselves—these representations often amount to pixel-based minstrelsy and the unabated two-way flow of heteropatriarchal technocracy between culture online and AFK (Russell, 2024).

Accordingly, the 'glitchy' shifts in genre and register throughout my piece are a fictocritical tactic to problematise the very notion of a unified, univocal perspective or an 'objective' and transparent text, opting instead for a textual aesthetic of poor imagery that forecloses both the possibility of a purely online or AFK persona and a coherent heteropatriarchal reading. Because there is no clear throughline, the fragments must be weighed and juggled like the very same windows and push notifications that constitute our contemporary reading and 'writing space' (Bolter, 2001).

In this way, fictocritical writing demands a highly reflexive reader who can embrace instances where "the role of the observer is appreciated and acknowledged rather than disguised" (Glanville, 2003, p. 1). By writing intentional moments of incoherence and interruption into the text, fictocritical writers interpolate and implicate their readers in feedback loops of 'creatively paranoid' (Moulthrop, 1991/2003) interpretation and employ "alienation as [a] method" (Burrows & O'Sullivan, 2019, p. 217). Such hyperactive reading arguably expands the figurative spaces in otherwise highly technical debates for articulating parallel storylines and alternative futures (Rosner, 2018). Accordingly, feminist notions of 'worlding' and worldbuilding, often owing to cyberfeminist and ecofeminist philosophical roots (Palmer & Hunter, 2018), remain a vital dimension of fictocritical writing insofar as fiction and storytelling can act as local and poetic refusals of colonialist and technocapitalist rhetoric.

If not already evident, this text emanates from an eco-techno-feminist standpoint that makes no categorical separation between fibre-optic cable networks and the networks of mycelia. This stance is heavily informed by theorists such as Donna Haraway, Karen Barad, Elisabeth Grosz, and Stacy Alaimo, who have argued for a 'feminist new materialism' that returns to a primarily materialist understanding of human and non-human relations (Grebowicz & Merrick, 2013). This standpoint is not so much in opposition but on the periphery of the technocratic worldview that technology is a means to control and contain so-called natural forces; the reality, of course, could not be further from such a binary. Likening the flood of digital interfaces and networked media to the most benign of waterways suddenly cresting their banks allows for thinking about technology as a series of 'swells' across history—the persistent threat of things that are largely felt yet unseen. As such, the intentional and uncomfortable juxtapositions that occur in the text above between the existential threats of climate change and telecommunication infrastructures are meant to illustrate what Mél Hogan (2018) has pointed out are recurring false divisions between self and environment. Perhaps counterintuitively, the argument of the text is that an ecology-based vocabulary of streams and streaming proves most capacious to describe the unfathomable scale and complexity of technological development amidst ecological collapse. Not only is the physical, natural environment increasingly overlaid and intertwined with our digital and virtual media, but the amount of physical infrastructure and capitalist resource extraction necessary to support the internet is a considerable threat to the future of a liveable planet: "Water is [always] cheaper than electricity" (Hogan, 2018, p. 638). This axiom is recurrently reflected in the text through the extended metaphor of the stream overflowing and mediating every experience—*xtreme streaming*—physical and virtual, figuratively eroding the linguistic borders between ecological and technological domains.

I realise that, in some ways, this is supplanting one metaphor for another—a stream for a web. However, I also believe we exist in a post-internet culture where even when I am not staring at a screen, the concept of life itself is heavily influenced and mediated by the internet's mere existence (McHugh, 2011). Thus, internet technology is so embedded in the constitution of physical and social spaces, so structural that it transcends the material/immaterial divide; the internet comprises both embodied and virtual realities, seeping into any adjacent surface or entity the same way a stream gradually infiltrates every nearby nook of available earth.

Perhaps the first step in a terminology revolution then is not to rename tech for the sake of clarity but for the sake of poetry, for the recognition that words, names in particular, are technologies in themselves, fluid and adaptive to suit the needs and motivations of whoever operates them. In *Our Own Metaphor* (2005, p. 288) by Mary Catherine Bateson, daughter of anthropologists Gregory Bateson and Margaret Mead, both of whom were instrumental in the development of second-order cybernetics and rethinking concepts of consciousness and subjectivity, she speaks fervently about the notion of cybernetics as the mapping of one form of complexity onto another. She argues that we, as complex beings, need the practice of poetry as a 'tool', a form of "knowledge about the world and about ourselves" to complete this internal-to-external mapping process, and that metaphor in particular allows us to conceive of ourselves as a set of amenable relationships able to make unlikely connections. In this vein, my fictocritical text is an extended metaphor for the phenomenology of networked environments that attempts to act as its own metaphor, rendering the lived user experience of the internet as a set of linguistic manifestations in flux—an ecological network of unstable words about the impact of twenty-first-century telecommunication infrastructure and how our spongy bodies are presently receiving it. In representing what is arguably the most significant technological development of the last century as a coursing body of textual fragments, I have attempted to graph and index the sensation of being *in* networked communication as an invented but no less natural or material force that reshapes the world around us as we bob and weave in its currents.

References

ABC News. (2005, December 20). Beware, Barbie! Kids find torturing fun. https://abcnews.go.com/International/story?id=1425715

Ansloos, J. (2023) *Nibi onje biimaadiiziiwin is not a metaphor: The relationship between suicide and water insecurity in First Nations in Ontario*. Yellowhead Institute. https://yellowheadinstitute.org/2023/05/03/suicide-and-water-insecurity

Barthes, R. (2013). *Mythologies* (R. Howard & J. Cape, Trans.). Hill and Wang. (Original work published 1957).

Bateson, M. C. (2005). *Our own metaphor: A personal account of a conference on the effects of conscious purpose on human adaptation*. Hampton Press.

Bolter, J. D. (2001). *Writing space: Computers, hypertext, and the remediation of print* (2nd ed.). Lawrence Erlbaum Associates.

Burcham, J., Haslin, A., Pra Doiztua, E., Smith, R., & Wright, S. (2024, January 10). 52 Places to go in 2024. *The New York Times*. https://www.nytimes.com/interactive/2024/travel/places-to-travel-destinations-2024.html

Burrows, D., & O'Sullivan, S. (2019). *Fictioning: The myth-functions of contemporary art and philosophy*. Edinburgh University Press.

Dangerfield, K. (2023, April 12). Canada banned these cancer-causing chemicals. But they're still found in kids toys. *Global News*. https://globalnews.ca/news/9614912/chlorinated-paraffins-canada-toys/

Deleuze, G., & Guattari, F. (1987). *A thousand plateaus: Capitalism and schizophrenia* (B. Massumi, Trans.). University of Minnesota Press.

Durham Peters, J. (2015). *The marvelous clouds: Toward a philosophy of elemental media*. University of Chicago Press.

Flavell, H. (2009). Who killed Jeanne Randolph? King, Muecke or 'fictocriticism'. *Outskirts, 20*. http://www.outskirts.arts.uwa.edu.au/volumes/volume-20/flavell

Gibbs, A. (2005). Fictocriticism, affect, mimesis: Engendering differences. *TEXT, 9*(1), 1–10. https://textjournal.scholasticahq.com/article/31879.pdf

Glanville, R. (2003). Second order cybernetics. In F. Parra-Luna (Ed.), *Systems science and cybernetics*. https://www.pangaro.com/glanville/Glanville-SECOND_ORDER_CYBERNETICS.pdf

Grebowicz, M., & Merrick, H. (2013). *Beyond the cyborg: Adventures with Donna Haraway*. Columbia University Press.

Haraway, D. (2003). A cyborg manifesto: Science, technology, and socialist-feminism in the late twentieth century. In N. Wardrip-Fruin & N. Monfort (Eds.), *The new media reader* (pp. 515–541). MIT Press. (Original work published 1985).

Haraway, D. (2012). *Modest_witness@second_millenium.femaleman©meets_oncomouse™* (2nd ed.). Routledge. (Original work published 1997).

Haraway, D. (2016). *Staying with the trouble: Making kin in the chthulucene*. Duke University Press.

Hassan, R. (2009). Crisis time: Networks, acceleration, and politics within late capitalism. *CTHEORY*, Resetting Theory Issue. https://journals.uvic.ca/index.php/ctheory/article/view/14767

Hayles, N. K. (1999). *How we became posthuman: Virtual bodies in cybernetics, literature, and informatics*. University of Chicago Press.

Hogan, M. (2018). Big data ecologies. *Ephemera: Theory & Politics in Organization, 18*(3), 631–657. https://ephemerajournal.org/sites/default/files/pdfs/contribution/18-3hogan.pdf

Houghton, J. (2019, December 17). ABC declares climate war on men, masculinity and logic. *SkyNews*. https://www.skynews.com.au/australia-news/abc-declares-climate-war-on-men-masculinity-and-logic/video/d4a7872a779a0c0b0fcef416573b0299

Jameson, F. (1984). Forward. In J.-F. Lyotard (Ed.), *The postmodern condition: A report on knowledge* (G. Bennington & B. Massumi, Trans.) (pp. vii–xix). Manchester University Press.

Kerr, H. (1995). Fictocriticism, the 'doubtful category' and 'the space between'. *Crossing lines: Formations of Australian culture: Proceedings of the 17th annual conference of the association for the study of Australian literature*, pp. 93–96. https://openjournals.library.sydney.edu.au/JASAL/article/view/9959

Latour, B. (1996). On actor-network theory. A few clarifications plus more than a few complications. *Soziale Welt, 47*(4), 369–381. https://www.jstor.org/stable/40878163

Le Guin, U. K. (1989). *Dancing at the edge of the world.* Grove Press.

Lyotard, J-F. (1984). *The postmodern condition: A report on knowledge* (G. Bennington & B. Massumi, Trans.). University of Minnesota Press.

Massumi, B. (2002). Introduction: Like a thought. In B. Massumi (Ed.), *A shock to thought: Expression after Deleuze and Guattari* (pp. xiii–xxxix). Routledge.

McHugh, G. (2011). *Post internet: Notes on the internet and art.* Link Editions.

McMahon, M. (2002). Beauty: Machinic repetition in the age of art. In B. Massumi (Ed.), *A shock to thought: Expression after Deleuze and Guattari* (pp. 3–8). Routledge.

Moulthrop, S. (1991). You say you want a revolution? Hypertext and the laws of media. In N. Montfort & N. Wardrip-Fruin (Eds.), *The new media reader* (pp. 691–704). MIT Press. (Original work published 1991).

NowThis Earth. (2023, November 2). *How petro-masculinity & the promotion of fossil fuels are connected* [Video]. YouTube. https://www.youtube.com/watch?v=DxsxXst5AZ0

Palmer, H., & Hunter, V. (2018). Worlding. In I. Van Der Tuin, R. Magli, and R. Cruz Santos (Eds.), *New materialism.* https://newmaterialism.eu/almanac/w/worlding.html

Pavan, G. (n.d.). *Echoes in the Alps* [Audio]. Earth.fm. https://earth.fm/recordings/echoes-in-the-alps

Pearl, Z. (2019). Ghost writing the self: Autofiction, fictocriticism, and social media. *English Studies in Canada (ESC), 45*(1&2), 161–188. https://doi.org/10.1353/esc.2019.0004

Pearl, Z. (2020, January 9). Break and enter: On the exhibition "Undomesticated." *Peripheral Review.* https://www.peripheralreview.com/break-and-enter-on-the-exhibitionundomesticated

Pearl, Z. (2022). Brandon is a network not a name: Fictocriticism & the cyberfeminist art of Shu Lea Cheang. *Open Library of Humanities, 8*(1). https://doi.org/10.16995/olh.6391

Pearl, Z. (2023a). Feminist digital ecology: Mimesis, fictocriticism, and altering technological space. *Configurations, 31*(3), 229–255. https://doi.org/10.1353/con.2023.a904489

Pearl, Z. (2023b). *Fictocritical cyberfeminism: A paralogical model for post-internet communication* [Doctoral dissertation, University of Waterloo]. UWSpace. https://uwspace.uwaterloo.ca/bitstream/handle/10012/19198/Pearl_Zachary.pdf

Rosner, D. K. (2018). *Critical fabulations: Reworking the methods and margins of design*. MIT Press.

Russell, L. (2020). *Glitch feminism: A manifesto*. Verso Books.

Russell, L. (2024). *Black meme: A history of the images that make us*. Verso Books.

Sterman, A. (2014, August 25). Doll-beheading photos surface in tribute to Islamic State. *The Times of Israel*. https://www.timesofisrael.com/doll-beheading-photos-surface-in-tribute-to-islamic-state/

Stuart, R. (2021, October 30). Will reviving B.C.'s declining salmon stocks require a rethink of hatcheries? *The Narwhal*. https://thenarwhal.ca/bc-salmon-hatcheries/

The Associated Press. (2023, November 5). A Philippine radio anchor was shot and killed while on a Facebook livestream. *National Public Radio*.. https://www.npr.org/2023/11/05/1210767916/a-philippine-radio-anchor-was-shot-and-killed-while-on-a-facebook-livestream

Thompson, J. (2024, January 29). To stop a shooter. *The Atlantic*. https://www.theatlantic.com/magazine/archive/2024/03/parkland-shooter-scot-peterson-coward-broward/677170

Ulmer, G. L. (1994). *Heuretics: The logic of invention*. Johns Hopkins University Press.

Vanhaecke, T., Bretin, O., Poirel, M., & Tap, J. (2022). Drinking water source and intake are associated with distinct gut microbiota signatures in US and UK populations. *The Journal of Nutrition, 152*(1), 171–182. https://doi.org/10.1093/jn/nxab312

CHAPTER 17

Conclusion

Crystal Chokshi and Robin Mansell

1 Introduction

Technologies are too often named in ways that downplay their social and political realities. Language is deployed to misrepresent what they *do*. What technologies *actually* do differs remarkably from the features their companies publicise, as the writers in this volume demonstrate. Actualities such as ableism, racism, extractivism, capitalism, and colonialism are not advertised by words such as 'angel investor', as Gemma Milne points out in Chap. 13. Nor are they signalled by 'the internet' until it is reframed, as done by Zach Pearl in Chap. 16, through mixing voices and genres in a narrative to elicit new readings of the associations we have with what is renamed as 'xtreme streaming'.

Sometimes the designers of technologies find cover in words that represent the very opposite of their embedded values and functionalities.

C. Chokshi (✉)
School of Communication Studies, Mount Royal University,
Calgary, AB, Canada
e-mail: cchokshi@mtroyal.ca

R. Mansell
Department of Media and Communications, London School of Economics and Political Science, London, UK
e-mail: r.e.mansell@lse.ac.uk

C. Chokshi, R. Mansell (eds.), *The Need to Rename Tech*,
https://doi.org/10.1007/978-3-032-05155-4_17

Other times, concealer words are applied to products by nodding to socially acceptable qualities—for instance, smartness, influence, and care. The linguistic strategies are many, but the duplicitous outcome is the same.

When we are duped by this use of language, we are made tractable, and that tractability has serious consequences. Without visibility into technology inputs and aftermaths, informed choices cannot be made about the technologies we use. Nor can we understand the impact of their incursions into our lives. As educators, for example, both of us have been encouraged to use learning management systems (LMS). Kate Maddalena's critical account and renaming of these systems in Chap. 3 makes us pause to consider why the use of LMS can lead to egregious outcomes that university administrators rarely, if ever, are willing to acknowledge. In our interactions with technologies, "for most people, most of the time … our interactions with … the screen involve calling up information without understanding the values built into [it]" (Mansell, 2012, pp. 97–98). To facilitate the detection of these values, the contributors in this collection use language to name technologies in ways that disrupt, inform, and illuminate.

2 Language and Allyship

Calling for such language is one way of doing the work of allyship. In many instances, technologies wager, above all, the interests of the most marginalised. Under the guise of knowing, optimising, predicting, saving, and socialising, corporately-sponsored technologies are systematically oppressive. This is well documented in a literature on digitalisation and the harms associated with commercial datafication, which is replete with accounts of asymmetrical customer and citizen relationships with Big Tech (Couldry & Mejias, 2019; Nieborg et al., 2024; van Dijck et al., 2018; Zuboff, 2019).

Deploying new names is a way of evoking new metaphors. These can serve as a step towards anti-ableist, anti-racist, anti-extractivist, anti-capitalist, and anti-colonialist technology development and practice. With this volume, as editors, we aimed to displace hegemonic language by disrupting prevailing myths about technology that all too easily come to be perceived as reality or 'fact'. When digital technologies are pushed to market by Big Tech and are naturalised, myths about them operate to distort what they actually *do* (Barthes, 1957; Mansell & Steinmueller, 2022). Our contributors consistently challenge hegemonic language that works to gain the consent of populations (Gramsci, 1971), recognising that apparent consent helps to ensure that Big Tech-designed technologies are hard to challenge.

Advertising texts and images promoting the benefits and efficiency gains claimed for new digital services and applications employ the discursive power of language to conceal and convey a 'common sense' that seems resistant to questioning (Gramsci, 1971). The prevailing common sense is witnessed in the promotion of advances in the infrastructure of communication, developments in artificial intelligence (AI) across sectors from health to education, in the creative arts, and in venture capital investment communities. For example, in renaming 'angel investors' as 'servants of capitalism', Gemma Milne in Chap. 13 shows us just how invested investors are in a vision of a technocapitalist society in which the preferences of Big Tech are prioritised and maintained through the use of images, stories, legends, and invocations of emotions.

When the prevailing common sense or social imaginary becomes deeply embedded in the way "people imagine their social existence" (Taylor, 2002, p. 106), the ways technology is implicated in discriminating against and subjugating subordinate groups are rendered invisible except to those who disproportionately bear the consequences and who are less well-resourced to fight back. Yet, when individuals and groups do become aware of injustice, they can engage in struggles to reshape technology designs and uses. One way to achieve this is through encounters with a surprising shift in the language and metaphors used to depict our engagements with technology. This can then encourage disruptive practice in a "dynamic interactive process" in multiple situations (Stalnaker, 1999, p. 96).

We can think of new terms as warning labels that encourage a heightened awareness of the need for an "insurrection of subjugated knowledge" (Foucault, 1972/1980, p. 81). For example, just as the label on a carton of cigarettes spells out harms concealed inside, so, too, do the new terms in this collection call attention to invisible technological risks. This important contribution helps to share knowledge that is otherwise often acquired privately and painfully. Rashmi Dyal-Chand (2021, p. 194) draws attention, for instance, to how autocorrect technology, which appears in applications for word processing, emailing, and texting, overwrites the names of people from non-dominant communities: "Aziza is changed to Alicia. Ayaan is changed to Susan. DaShawn and Fatima are underlined with red squiggly lines and offered [with] the respective suggestions 'Dash away' and 'Fat imagination' or 'Fathomable' to replace them". This kind of exclusion is often experienced with no one else present—while we type a text, perhaps—and we are made to bear the burden alone. Harms related to technologies that people encounter privately are all too common, such as Jewish stereotypes presented online, as described by Nathaniel Laywine and Victoria Simon in Chap. 12, or the failure of a large-scale open AI database, LAION 5B, to generate an image of a person of colour when prompted with the word 'girl', as Eryk Salvaggio shows us in Chap. 10. New names work to signal these and other harms; they create the potential for more informed choices about how, when, and under what conditions to engage with or resist technology.

Technologies such as social media and security software, sold to us as keeping us safe online, are essential infrastructures in an increasing number of people's lives. Their designs and operations in Big Tech's interests make it crucial to call out their misleading promises (Plantin et al., 2018). The risks and harms associated with our growing dependence on these technologies are made visible, for example, by Brooks DeCillia and Gabriela Perdomo in Chap. 14. They document Meta's withdrawal of local news from its Facebook platform in Canada at a time of crisis. This prompts the authors to reposition Facebook's 'town-square' metaphor as the 'antiagora'. Anran Wang renames network security 'firewalls' as 'access gatekeepers' in Chap. 11 to emphasise how prevailing security practices perform in ways that deny people equality of access to the communicative infrastructure. The absence of participatory input into the imposition of 'smart city' technologies on urban populations is signalled in Chap. 6 by Jess Reia and Luã Cruz's renaming of these initiatives as a form of 'technosolutionist urbanism' that neglects the needs of creatives and environmental protection, and denies people access to data justice.

Resistance to prevailing metaphors is essential. We are being surrounded by AI-enabled large language models that operate as 'predictive technologies'. In Chap. 8, Olivier Driessens renames these as 'automated predeterminations', illustrating how data processing techniques produce probabilistic outcomes that do not simply anticipate possible futures; they pre-empt certain futures without a possibility of questioning which futures are favoured or disfavoured and why, unless this is called to our attention.

3 Operatives ~~Users~~

The dominant way of naming those who engage with technology is as 'users'. This naming conveys nothing about individual and collective resistance in the face of a technology industry that typically casts its customers and publics as powerless. It does so by creating products with undisclosed logics and, as our contributors argue, naming practices that misrepresent what these products do. Some argue that "nobody can swim against" hegemonic namings when they have become embedded in policy and practice, for instance, the misleading naming of 'AI' (Floridi & Nobre, 2024, p. 10). Many scholars, however, turn to renaming as a means to subvert anthropomorphic language and the myths that deny people a sense of agency in their dealings with technology (Chokshi, 2023; Frau-Meigs, 2024; Natale & Ballatore, 2020).

In this collection, we are interested in more than language. We engage in a process of rethinking agency by revealing how the development and uses of technology are coupled with abuses of people's fundamental human rights (Mansell et al., 2025). We argue that people are entitled to know how technologies work—that we have the right to understand, upfront, what the business model is, and what data is gathered. We need to be able to assess when digital services and applications operate against our interests or violate public values. The technology industry pursues a less-is-more promotional approach: saying less about how a thing functions in the interest of deflecting attention from the risks and harms that its use entails.

What this volume offers in contrast is an 'analytics of power' (Deacon, 2002). Instead of accepting the views of Big Tech executives, we offer our readers the opportunity to understand that even small individual resistances through renaming can awaken new practices and strategies for resisting hegemonic impositions of digital technology. We do so in the belief that this can "motivate people to act, to imagine alternative political arrangements, and to contribute to long-term collective action" (Crooks & Currie, 2021, p. 201).

Consenting to the status quo, whether because we are forced to do so by an authoritative state or by a public or private organisation that employs us, we seem to have little choice beyond 'using' digital products. As dependence on these products escalates, we invite you, the reader of this book, to think of yourself not as a 'user' but instead as an *operative*. This naming invokes the potential for resistance to being conceptualised exclusively in terms of our value to Big Tech. As operatives, we are better positioned to put new plans for the design and use of technology into action.

Practices of resistance to the power of Big Tech—individually and collectively—are being documented across the Global North and Global

South. This collection adds to that growing catalogue. In Chap. 15, Evangeline Holtz-Schramek unpacks the online 'momfluencer' label to lay bare the feminist care work that endures in some momfluencer communities, despite the misinformation and perpetuation of white supremacy that takes place in others. Indigenous communities and municipalities are establishing their own norms and guidelines for governing information resources, often taking up commons-based practices that privilege human rights over commerce and profit. Gordon A. Gow's account of the history of naming the infrastructural resource—the radio frequency spectrum—signals in Chap. 5 how cultural values, in this case of the Māori people, are entangled in asymmetrical power relations with government and industry and in ongoing struggles over the management of this vital resource for communication.

Many initiatives of this kind are small-scale, but they underpin alternatives to the values of Big Tech, and they demonstrate the success of agonistic practices (Carroll et al., 2019; Mansell et al., 2025; Mejias & Couldry, 2024; Powell, 2021; Tierra Comun Network, 2023). This is visible in this collection in Chap. 9 in Gillian Russell and Frédérik Lesage's practice of disrupting promotional hype about digital technology. They introduce us to 'fabulation', an exercise in alternative storytelling about technologies. They illustrate how fabulation enables people to imagine technologies differently and so to reshape collective imaginaries about how they could be developed to align with democratic values and to empower people to challenge the status quo.

4 Doing Better Things with Words: Symbolic Renaming and Acting Operatively

Collectively, and inspired by others deploying a similar strategy, the writers in this collection argue for adopting new language as an important way to act *operatively*. As editors, we write from Canada and the United Kingdom, where we witness acts of renaming as a means of enacting values that depart from hegemonic uses of language. In both countries, schools, streets, and public buildings with troubling names—names tied to the residential school system or the slave trade, for instance—are under scrutiny. For example, Ryerson University was renamed Toronto Metropolitan University in 2022 in a move to distance the university from Egerton Ryerson, the university's former namesake, who was "one of the primary architects of [Canada's] residential school system" (CBC News, 2022, para. 3). In London, England, 'Black Boy Lane' has become 'La Rose Lane', paying homage to black poet, publisher, and activist, John La Rose (Agbonlahor & O'Neill, 2023). The ten-storey residential tower, Cecil Rhodes House, has become Park View House, shedding its tie to British imperialism and apartheid (Weaver, 2021).

Just as a Canadian school named after John A. MacDonald, Canada's first prime minister and residential school champion, is to be renamed after years of controversy to acknowledge condemnation of violence against Indigenous peoples, so the renaming of 'generative AI' as 'digital settler colonialism' is a condemnation of settler logics that pervade writing about the internet and AI, as Harriett Jernigan argues in Chap. 7. For those of us who encounter technologies in sleekly designed stores, on splashy billboards, and with the privilege of whiteness, renaming helps to prompt reflection on our own complicity with harm-marking symbols. It increases the likelihood that those in dominant groups will become sensitised to the need for changes in how our technologies are developed and deployed.

Unlike removing a nameplate on a building, our work envisages a different endgame. The success of our renaming initiative does not depend on whether companies such as OpenAI replace 'ChatGPT' with 'Altman's Golem', as proposed by Nathaniel Laywine and Victoria Simon in Chap. 12. Instead, a bottom-up adoption of new language within communities and areas of practice where operatives have conversations in homes, classrooms, and boardrooms is a way of signalling a different orientation towards technologies, ourselves, and others—it is a way in which discursive practice can bring emancipatory relations into being. We see this in Chap. 2, where Melanie Baljko renames 'assistive technology' as 'ableist technology' to encourage incorporation of disability and design justice principles in future computing curricula. By renaming software applications supporting healthcare as 'healthcAIre', Arun Jacob and Christina Boyles make a discursive move in Chap. 4 that calls attention to the intrusive body surveillance accompanying clinical informatics applications that embody images and untransparent large data sets.

The work renaming seeks to achieve is never easy. It is notoriously fraught. Cognisant of the fact that language brings things into being, some of our writers were hesitant to coin new terms. We respected their hesitation; it implies a desire to be careful precisely because language is so powerful. In the absence of small steps such as this, however, the chances of resistance to the hegemonic imaginary of technology, its ideology, and its practices are slim. This is so because the inequities of the established order "cannot be solved within it" (Fraser, 2022, p. 132). As such, this book strives to do better, not perfect, things with language. We are certain we have not got it entirely right. But rather than resign ourselves to language that upholds technological systems and practices that do not serve us, let us, together, at least try to seek—and speak—repair.

References

Agbonlahor, W., & O'Neill, A. (2023, January 23). Black Boy Lane in Tottenham renamed over racial connotations. *BBC*. https://www.bbc.com/news/uk-england-london-64376243

Barthes, R. (1957). *Mythologies* (A. Lavers, Trans.). Noonday Press.

Carroll, S. R., Rodriguez-Lonebear, D., & Martinez, A. (2019). Indigenous data governance: Strategies from the United States' Native Nations. *Data Science Journal, 18*(31), 1–15. https://doi.org/10.5334/dsj-2019-031

CBC News. (2022, April 26). Toronto university changes name amid controversy over Canadian educator's legacy. *CBC*. https://www.cbc.ca/news/canada/toronto/ryerson-toronto-metropolitan-university-1.6431360

Chokshi, C. N. (2023). *Doing things with words: The new consequences of writing in the age of AI* [Doctoral dissertation, University of Calgary]. PRISM Institutional Repository. https://prism.ucalgary.ca/items/9c087a63-42e0-4959-87c1-b39ca6db278e

Couldry, N., & Mejias, U. A. (2019). Data colonialism: Rethinking Big Data's relation to the contemporary subject. *Television & New Media, 20*(4), 336–349. https://doi.org/10.1177/1527476418796632

Crooks, R., & Currie, M. (2021). Numbers will not save us: Agonistic data practices. *The Information Society, 37*(4), 201–213. https://doi.org/10.1080/01972243.2021.1920081

Deacon, R. (2002). An analytics of power relations: Foucault on the history of discipline. *History of the Human Sciences, 15*(1), 89–117. https://doi.org/10.1177/0952695102015001074

Dyal-Chand, R. (2021). Autocorrecting for whiteness. *Boston University Law Review, 101*(1), 191–286. https://www.bu.edu/bulawreview/files/2021/03/DYAL-CHAND.pdf

Floridi, L., & Nobre, A. C. (2024). Anthropomorphising machines and computerising minds: The crosswiring of languages between artificial intelligence and brain & cognitive sciences. *Mind and Machines, 34*(Art. 5), 1–9. https://link.springer.com/article/10.1007/s11023-024-09670-4

Foucault, M. (1972/1980). Two lectures. In C. Gordon (Ed.), *Power/knowledge: Selected interviews & other writings 1972–1977* (pp. 78–108). Pantheon Books.
Fraser, N. (2022). *Cannibal capitalism: How our system is devouring democracy, care, and the planet – and what we can do about it.* Verso.
Frau-Meigs, D. (2024). *IA et EMI: Le retour de l'interpretation.* Intervention at Seminar IAN Lettres-Philosphie. https://www.pedagogie.ac-aix-marseille.fr/jcms/c_11208530/fr/-ia-et-emi-le-retour-de-l-interpretation
Gramsci, A. (1971). *Selections from the prison notebooks of Antonio Gramsci* (Q. Hoare & G. Howell Smith, Eds.). Lawrence and Wishart.
Mansell, R. (2012). *Imagining the internet: Communication, innovation, and governance.* Oxford University Press.
Mansell, R., & Steinmueller, W. E. (2022). Denaturalizing digital platforms: Is mass individualization here to stay? *International Journal of Communication, 16*(2022), 461–481. https://ijoc.org/index.php/ijoc/article/view/13093
Mansell, R., Durach, F., Kettemann, M., Lenoir, T., Procter, R., Tripathi, G., & Tucker, E. (2025). *Information ecosystems and troubled democracy: The state of knowledge on news media, AI and data governance.* NORDICOM.
Mejias, U. A., & Couldry, N. (2024). *Data grab: The new colonialism of Big Tech (and how to fight back).* WH Allen.
Natale, S., & Ballatore, A. (2020). Imagining the thinking machine: Technological myths and the rise of artificial intelligence. *Convergence: The International Journal of Research into New Media Technologies, 26*(1), 3–18. https://doi.org/10.1177/1354856517715164
Nieborg, D., Poell, T., Caplan, R., & van Dijck, J. (2024). Locating and theorising platform power. *Internet Policy Review, 13*(2), 1–17. https://policyreview.info/articles/analysis/introduction-special-issue-locating-and-theorising-platform-power
Plantin, J.-C., Lagoze, C., Edwards, P. N., & Sandvig, C. (2018). Infrastructure studies meet platform studies in the age of Google and Facebook. *New Media & Society, 20*(1), 293–310. https://journals.sagepub.com/doi/abs/10.1177/1461444816661553
Powell, A. (2021). *Undoing optimization: Civic action in smart cities.* Yale University Press.
Stalnaker, R. C. (1999). *Context and content: Essays on intentionality in speech and thought.* Oxford University Press.
Taylor, C. (2002). Modern social imaginaries. *Public Culture, 14*(1), 91–124. https://muse.jhu.edu/article/26276/pdf
Tierra Comun Network (Ed.). (2023). *Resisting data colonialism: A practical intervention.* Institute of Network Cultures, Amsterdam University Press.
van Dijck, J., de Waal, M., & Poell, T. (2018). *The platform society: Public values in a connective world.* Oxford University Press.

Weaver, M. (2021, March 18). Goodbye Cecil Rhodes: House renamed to lose link to British empire builder in Africa. *The Guardian*. https://www.theguardian.com/uk-news/2021/mar/18/goodbye-cecil-rhodes-house-renamed-to-lose-link-to-british-empire-builder-in-africa

Zuboff, S. (2019). *The age of surveillance capitalism: The fight for a human future at the new frontier of power*. Profile Books.

Index[1]

[1] Note: Page numbers followed by 'n' refer to notes.

C. Chokshi, R. Mansell (eds.), *The Need to Rename Tech*,
https://doi.org/10.1007/978-3-032-05155-4

www.ingramcontent.com/pod-product-compliance
Ingram Content Group UK Ltd.
Pitfield, Milton Keynes, MK11 3LW, UK
UKHW020937180926
475692UK00004B/80
9783032051547